GW00645187

HAWKER
Typhoon

HAWKER
Typhoon
THE COMBAT HISTORY

Richard Townshend Bickers

Airlife
England

Copyright © 1999 Richard Townshend Bickers

First published in the UK in 1999
by Airlife Publishing Ltd

British Library Cataloguing-in-Publication Data
A catalogue record for this book
is available from the British Library

ISBN 1 85310 908 8

Typeset by Rowland Phototypesetting Ltd, Bury St Edmunds, Suffolk.
Printed in England by The Bath Press Ltd., Bath.

Airlife Publishing Ltd

101 Longden Road, Shrewsbury, SY3 9EB, England
Telephone: 01743 235651 Fax: 01743 232944 E-mail: airlife@airlifebooks.com

Acknowledgements

My thanks go to all the pilots and ground crew who so kindly sent me their reminiscences of flying or servicing Typhoons; and of being under enemy air attack when RAF airfields in France, Belgium and Holland were strafed or bombed during the campaign that followed the Allied forces' landings in Normandy. I am also grateful to everyone who lent me photographs.

I am especially indebted to Ronnie Sheward, who ended the war in command of No 266 Squadron and won the Distinguished Flying Cross. He has not only given me most interesting accounts of many operations on Typhoons but also introduced me to others who flew them. To Peter Brett, another who rose to command his squadron, No 183, goes my gratitude for a detailed account of his career as a 'Tiffie' pilot.

Thanks also to the always helpful and courteous staff at the Royal Air Force Museum, the Public Record Office and the Royal Aeronautical Society.

Foreword

The Typhoon had a short life of only three years and eight months on war service, but during that time the damage it did to the enemy as a formidable ground-attack fighter was outstanding. As an interception fighter it also shot down a creditable number of enemy aircraft.

Typhoons would have scored even more successes against both ground and air targets if so many had not been destroyed or damaged by RAF and USAAF fighter pilots whose aircraft recognition was not good enough to distinguish them from the Focke-Wulf 190.

For most people, 1939–1945 fighter aeroplanes are, understandably, epitomised by the Spitfire and Hurricane. The Typhoon, versatile though it also was, has not received the attention it deserves. I hope that this account of its qualities will help to redress its comparative neglect in the history of the Second World War.

The abbreviations for officers' ranks are those that were current before, during and for many years after the war.

BELOW: Typhoon prototype P5212. (Philip Jarrett)

Contents

Chapter 1
Leading Particulars

Of the squadrons that flew Typhoons, some were of ancient lineage in the annals of the Royal Air Force and, *ipso facto*, the Royal Flying Corps; others were newcomers to the embattled skies over Britain and Continental Europe. In numerical order they were Numbers 1, 3, 4, 56, 137, 164, 168, 174, 175, 181, 182, 183, 184, 186, 193, 195, 197, 198, 245, 247, 257, 263, 266 (Rhodesia), 268, 438 RCAF, 439 RCAF, 440 RCAF, 485 RNZAF, 486 RNZAF and 609 (West Riding), formed in 1936, of the Auxiliary Air Force, which was embodied in the RAF on the outbreak of war. The first six of the above had fought in the First World War; No 80 had been disbanded in the inter-war years but was reformed in March 1937 from a flight of No 17 Squadron. The rest came into being between 1941 and 1943.

The visual impact of this redoubtable aeroplane was arresting. Burly and pugnacious-looking, it gave the impression that it could both hit phenomenally hard and sustain a lot of damage without being brought down. As a close-support fighter and fighter-bomber it was unsurpassed by any other single-seater in the world during its comparatively short

BELOW: Typhoon IB of A & AEE September 1942. Note gas-detector black paint diamond on white band forward of tail unit. (Bruce Robertson)

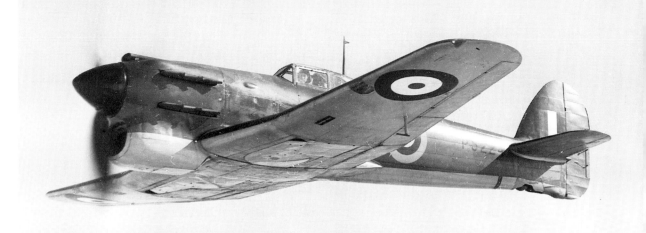

ABOVE: P5224 Hawker Tornado second prototype, October 1941, with radiator brought forward Typhoon-fashion. (Bruce Robertson)

career. It flew its first operational sorties on 30 May 1942, its last on the day the war ended, and by six months later all the Typhoon squadrons had been disbanded.

Its size was awesome in comparison with other contemporary fighters. A tall man standing beside a Spitfire could lay his hand on top of the cockpit canopy. To enter the cockpit all anyone but a very short pilot had to do was put one foot on the wing, mount and put the other foot on the seat. The Typhoon's cockpit was nine feet above the ground. Even someone over six feet tall had to put hand and foot into two niches covered by spring-loaded flaps and haul himself up to the door, which opened like a car's. These doors were disliked because they often came open in flight.

A pilot's first flight in any operational type is bound to entail some anxiety. The Typhoon was definitely not one to reassure a novice. Flying Officer (F/O) Peter Brett, who ended the war as a flight lieutenant (F/L), acting squadron leader (S/L), joined 183 Squadron in July 1943 with more than sixty hours on Hurricanes in his logbook. For the next two days he studied *Pilot's Notes* for the type and underwent written and oral examinations. He also spent as much time as possible 'climbing all over the Typhoon

and watching the take-offs and landings'. Of his early impressions, he says: 'The first thing I noticed was the noise! The Typhoon had an engine which was more than twice as powerful as a Hurricane's (which he had been flying) and this drove an enormous propeller fourteen feet in diameter. To hear a formation of four taking off together was really an ear-shattering experience.'

Of his first solo, he recalls: 'The size of the aircraft was daunting. Sitting in the cockpit, the first impression was of space. There was ample room for me to sit upright without having the seat on the lowest setting and my shoulders were at least six inches away from each side. The instrument panel seemed to be further away (than in a Hurricane) and the consoles each side of my knees gave a further impression of space. Looking forward, with the aircraft sitting on the ground with the tail down, all one could see was this enormously long nose stretching away for some six or seven feet in front. It gave somewhat the impression of driving a steam locomotive from the footplate. Taxying was impossible in a straight line and one had to swing a long way from side to side in order to be able to see what was ahead. Even on take-off it was not possible to see very far ahead, since it was inadvisable to raise the tail too far on the take-off run. With the aircraft in full flying attitude the clearance under the propeller was less than six inches, therefore we were advised to take off in a tail-down attitude, especially from grass airfields.'

Typhoons pulled strongly to the right, which meant applying left rudder when roaring down the runway before getting airborne.

Starting the engine could be a procedure that, once mastered, was no more difficult than for any other aircraft. An inexperienced pilot's early attempts, however, were often abortive. The Koffman starter had been designed for the Spitfire's and Hurricane's Merlin engines and was barely powerful enough for the Sabre.

The starting drill demanded care. First, the engine had to be primed, which varied according to whether it was cold, or warm after recent use. This done, the pilot pushed a starter-button that fired a Koffman cartridge. The engine usually started to spin a fraction of a second later. The cartridge injected gas under high pressure into one cylinder, whose piston put the crankshaft in motion. A man, sometimes two, always stood by with a fire extinguisher, no matter how experienced the pilot was, because if the engine did not start at the first attempt there was a danger of fire in the air intake. A failed start caused gas to leak into the cockpit. If, after three tries, the engine did not start, the crew turned the propeller manually to pump the gas out. The whole performance was then repeated.

Peter Brett recalls: 'It was a favourite trick of the engineering staff when teaching a new pilot how to start the engine, to have the pilot standing on the wing leaning into the cockpit. The starter would then slightly over-prime the cylinders and the unfortunate pilot would find

BELOW: Typhoon IB with black and white stripes intended to avoid confusion with FW190. (Bruce Robertson)

ABOVE: Typhoon IB second prototype, virtually the prototype production IB Typhoon. (Bruce Robertson)

himself knee deep in flames.' But they swept past in a second or two without scorching the astonished novice. He goes on: 'For the first time I had to open up the engine to zero boost which gave over 3000rpm. The vibration and noise were terrific.'

At the end of the runway, he completed his pre-take-off checks, the mnemonic for which was TMPFFSR. *Trim*: elevator neutral, rudder fully port. *Mixture*: rich. *Propeller*: fully fine pitch. *Fuel*: check contents and select tanks which are more than half full, pressurising off, drop tank cock off. *Flaps*: ten to fifteen degrees down, valve shut. *Supercharger*: moderate. *Radiator*: flap open. Raising the flaps too quickly caused it to sink; to avoid losing height the flaps had to be raised bit by bit.

He found himself at 5000ft astonishingly soon and when he put the nose down to descend to 1000ft before making a circuit of the airfield, the speed built up to nearly 400mph so quickly that he had to throttle back and go into fine pitch, waiting for the speed to fall to 250mph before joining the circuit for a practice landing.

Doing the obligatory spin could be a startling event. *Pilot's Notes* devoted an entire page to the subject. Among its gems were: 'Spins must be started between 15,000 and 25,000ft. Recovery must be started after not more than one turn. Use of the engine may help to recover

from spins to the left. At 25,000ft and above cases have occurred when the spin becomes flat. Recovery from a flat spin is difficult and up to 10,000ft may be lost during recovery. Until proficient, pilots should only practise spins to the left.'

Of his first spinning practice, Brett says 'knowing that pilots tend to understate things', he climbed to 22,500ft and tried a couple of straight stalls. He closed the throttle and eased back on the stick to keep the nose up. Airspeed dropped rapidly and the aircraft began to wallow. 'At the same time the rate of climb indicator started to move rapidly down below the zero and the altimeter began to unwind. As the speed dropped below 90mph there was a shuddering and suddenly the starboard wing dropped violently, rolling the aircraft to past the vertical. Shoving the stick forward and opening the throttle resulted in a couple of seconds of most uncomfortable negative G and then I was heading down, the airspeed was building up and the controls began to feel live again. Remembering the *Pilot's Notes* once again I let the speed build up to 250mph and then pulled out of the dive. I had lost 3000ft in the stall and recovery so climbed back up again before trying again.'

Then came the practice stall. 'This time as the shuddering began to warn of the stall I hauled right back on the stick and shoved on full left rudder. I wasn't going to take the chance of going into a right-hand spin. This time the left wing dropped. In effect the aircraft flipped over upside down, the nose fell towards the ground but the aircraft continued to rotate very fast and in less than two seconds I was in a full left-hand spin. I took the appropriate action, stick forward full opposite rudder and stood ready to open up the throttle. Nothing seemed to happen for about a turn and a half and then the nose pitched down, the rotation stopped and I was heading vertically earthwards. I had no idea what direction I was heading in as I pulled out of the dive, since the manoeuvres were so violent that I was thrown from side to side in

the cockpit. I was very glad that I had tightened my straps to an uncomfortable degree before starting. As I regained level flight I saw that this time I had lost over 7000ft. From that moment I decided that not only would I never intentionally spin a Typhoon again, but I would take damn good care not to get into a position where I was liable to stall without knowing all about it.'

What emerges from this is that the pilot showed great competence and, as the aircraft did recover after creating such anxiety, it was not a rogue, it was a bit of a handful – and so is a racehorse; a characteristic that is not unusual among fighter pilots, either.

ABOVE: Typhoon JP853 of 486 Sqdn. (Philip Jarrett)

Chapter 2

The Evolution of
Ground-Attack Fighters

At the start of the Great War of 1914–1918, now known as the First World War, aeroplanes were used mainly for visual and photographic reconnaissance and artillery observation – signalling to gun batteries the fall of their shells in relation to the target. Some occasionally carried a 20lb bomb or two in the cockpit, to drop by hand. Few were armed with a gun.

In Britain, some pilots tried ways of mounting guns, but without official encouragement. In America, Colonel Isaac Newton had invented the Lewis gun and fitted it to a Wright biplane. The Army was not interested, so he set up a factory in Belgium to manufacture it. In Germany, Franz Schneider of Luft-Verkehrs Gesellschaft (LVG) was seeking a means of synchronising a forward-firing machine-gun with the propeller's revolutions, so that bullets would pass between its blades. In France, Robert Morane and Raymond Saulnier, designers and builders of the Morane Saulnier aeroplanes, were making similar experiments with a French gun lent by its makers, Hotchkiss.

With a pusher type it was, of course, possible to fit a machine-gun in the nose. On 5 October 1914, a mechanic in *l'Aviation Militaire*, Louis Quénault, sitting beside his pilot, Sergeant Joseph Franz, in a Voisin, scored the first victory in the history of aerial warfare when he shot down an Aviatik with his Hotchkiss.

BELOW: Typhoon IBs of 56 Sqdn 1942. (Bruce Robertson)

ABOVE: Typhoon IB of No 56 Squadron. (Bruce Robertson)

This prompted Lieutenant-General Sir David Henderson, the Royal Flying Corps's first Commander (not Trenchard, as is generally assumed) to prophesy: 'This is the beginning of a fight which will ultimately end in great battles in the air, in which hundreds and possibly thousands of men may be engaged at heights from 10,000 to 20,000ft.'

It was in this sphere that progress was indeed made quickly, while close-support ground-attack lagged far behind in being developed.

Britain declared war on Germany on 4 August 1914. The Royal Flying Corps (RFC) flew its first operational sorties from bases in France on 19 August. Three days later, Lieutenant Louis Strange of No 5 Squadron, who had been permitted to fit a Lewis gun to his Henry Farman F20, took off to intercept an enemy aircraft but failed because of the extra weight: his aeroplane would not climb higher than 2000ft. By early 1915 many British, French and German pilots carried rifles or armed their aircraft with machine-guns; but they used them only to fire at the enemy in the air, not at ground targets.

A year later the RFC did begin to strafe trenches and columns of infantry marching on roads behind the lines. The Imperial German Military Aviation Service pilots, however, refrained because they were reluctant to fly over the British and French trenches, let alone behind them. This apparent timidity was actually discretion. The prevailing wind blew from west to east, which meant that if a German aircraft ventured as far as the opposing lines it would have to fly into a headwind, which would reduce its speed and give the defenders an advantage.

The pulverising effect of the RFC's attacks on the enemy's trenches was described by a German officer in 1916: 'The infantry had no training in defence against very low-flying aeroplanes. Moreover, they had no confidence in their ability to shoot these machines down if they were determined to press home their attacks. As a result they were seized by a fear amounting to panic; a fear that was fostered by the incessant activity and hostility of enemy aeroplanes.' (*The First Great Air War*, by the present author, Hodder & Stoughton 1988)

The diary of a German prisoner-of-war reads: 'During the day one hardly dares to be seen in the trench owing to the English aeroplanes. They fly so low that it is a wonder they do not pull one out of the trench. Nothing is to be seen of our heroic German airmen. One can hardly calculate how much additional loss of life and strain on the nerves this costs us.' (*The First Great Air War*, by the present author, Hodder & Stoughton 1988)

The performance of the British fighters at that time was superior to the German, hence their effect on the enemy's morale in air combat was as dire as the terror they struck in what the Germans called 'ground hogs'. The Royal Flying Corps began to lose the advantage in May 1916 with the introduction of the new Fokker EI, which dominated the skies for several months, but it did not deter ground attack. By 1918 the RFC – which, combined with the Royal Naval Air Service (RNAS), became the RAF on 1 April that year – was not only machine-gunning the enemy but also dropping fragmentation bombs on them.

Strafing always carried a high risk, because the RFC pilots had to return to their aerodromes in the teeth of a headwind. Enemy machines awaiting them over, or a short distance beyond, their own front had the benefit of a tail wind as they made head-on interceptions. The French *Aviation Militaire* did not take to strafing the German front line, support trenches, rest areas or road traffic with the same zest as the RFC.

It is significant that Manfred von Richthofen, 'The Red Baron', who, with 80 victories, shot down more enemy aircraft (all RFC) than any other pilot of any nationality, was not a ground attack exponent. It is equally noticeable that the second highest scorer, a Frenchman, René Fonck, who shot down 75, also disdained strafing. Edward 'Mick' Mannock, the RFC's most successful air fighter, with a score of 73, had no great reputation for shooting at ground targets either.

One of the war's most highly decorated pilots who did look on ground attack as equal in importance to successful air combat was William A. 'Billy' Bishop, a Canadian in the RFC who shot down 72 German aeroplanes. He did not neglect opportunities to destroy both aircraft and men on airfields and in trenches or gun posts. One spring day in 1917 when he was on contact patrol he spotted British infantry in attack being mown down by machine-gunners, which filled him with insatiable hatred for the Germans. Soon after, he again saw British troops being cut to

BELOW: 609 Sqdn Typhoon IA with Squadron Leader's pennant painted below cockpit hood late 1942. Note reduced white roundel on fuselage. (Bruce Robertson)

ribbons and forced to halt an attack. In a corner of an enemy trench were two machine-gun teams. Bishop dived and blasted them. The British resumed their advance. On 2 June 1917 he won the Victoria Cross (VC) for taking off at dawn to strafe a German fighter airfield, where he shot down five aircraft as they were taking off and destroyed or damaged many others parked outside their hangars.

Surprisingly, it was the Germans who built the first purpose-designed ground attack aeroplanes, the true predecessors of the Typhoon. All were two-seaters with armoured bellies and all appeared in 1917. The first was the AEG C IV, which could carry a 200lb bomb load and was armed with two machine-guns – a Spandau for the pilot and a Parabellum for the observer. The C IV equipped two *Staffeln* of a newly introduced type, the *Schlachtstaffel* or battle squadron, *Schlasta* for short. The others were the Hannover CL IIIa, which was similarly armed; the Junkers Ju JI, whose pilot had two Spandaus and his observer a Parabellum; and the Halberstadt CL II with one Spandau and one Parabellum plus a manoeuvrability that enabled it to evade ground fire.

Although the RFC did not fly any aircraft specifically designed for the close support of ground troops, it eventually recognised the necessity for this kind of operation. The first appearance of tanks in battle was not the only innovation in the Battle of Cambrai on 20 November 1917. They were supported by Sopwith Camels and de Havilland DH5s in the rôles of fighter-bombers. In the final battles of the war, the bombing and machine-gunning of the enemy both in and behind the lines provided vital support for infantry and armour. At the same period, in the Battle of Nablus, in Palestine (an area now part of Jordan), Bristol Fighters and SE5As did tremendous slaughter against the Turks and brought an end to the campaign in the Middle East.

When, twenty-seven years later, the Typhoon became famous as a formidable ground-attack single-seater, it happened fortuitously rather than by original intent.

Chapter 3

The Typhoon's Origin and Development

H. G. Hawker Engineering Co Ltd, formed in 1920 as a successor to the old firm of Sopwith, had soon become world-famous for its excellent fighters. The first of these was the Woodcock, which began production in May 1925. It was not surprising therefore that, after supplying the Service with this and a succession of other outstanding fighter aeroplanes, this aircraft constructor was successful in obtaining the contract for the Typhoon.

The Hawker Typhoon, however, came close to being aborted before its last-minute birth as a distinguished destroyer of the enemy in the air and on the ground. Its survival to play a prominent part in the RAF's battle order was, as the Duke of Wellington said about the Battle of Waterloo, 'the nearest run thing you ever saw in your life'. This aircraft was intended to succeed the Hawker Hurricane as an interceptor fighter, which had itself been innovative: not only because it was the RAF's first monoplane fighter and its first to exceed 300mph, but also because it was Britain's first to have a monocoque fuselage and, later, stressed steel wings as well. Hawker's duralumin tube and steel type of construction, which was one of the features that the two fighters were to have in common, was also unique to the manufacturer: so a lot was expected of the Typhoon. The Hurricane was sweet to handle, but its bulky successor turned out to be a maverick; hence the reluctance, at one stage, to proceed with its development.

The Typhoon's history began in 1937 with Air Ministry Specification F18/37, which put emphasis on the required cannon armament. Sidney Camm, Hawker's Chief Designer, had already discussed the requirement for two new fighters with the Air Ministry. On 15 January 1938 Appendix B was added to the specification, setting out the Operational Requirement in detail, and sent to all ten companies on the Air Ministry's Approved List of aircraft manufacturers. The specification called for the production of two new interceptor fighters designed to be powered by the 2000hp 24-cylinder engines that were being developed. Among the qualities demanded were a speed of at least 400mph at 20,000ft, a minimum of fifty per cent greater weight of fire than the Hurricane or Supermarine Spitfire and suitability to operate from grass airfields. Six 20mm cannon were envisaged, but until reliable guns of that calibre became available twelve Browning machine-guns would take their place.

Whatever engine was chosen, it would be at least sixty per cent heavier than the Hurricane's (and later, Spitfire's) Merlin. Sidney Camm had to come to terms with the fact that both these new aircraft would therefore compare with his sleek Fury and Demon fighters, and equally graceful Hart light bomber, like a cruiser-weight boxer with a ballet dancer. (In the 1930 annual Air Defence Exercise, the Hart was actually faster than the Siskin fighters that tried to intercept it.)

The Hawker R Type new fighter, later named Tornado, was to have the 24-cylinder X-configuration Rolls-Royce Vulture engine, which comprised four Rolls-Royce Peregrine engine blocks with a single crankshaft. It was also mounted in the Avro Manchester twin-engine bomber, whose subsequent ill repute was owed to this engine's inability to deliver its designed power and to its abundant failures.

The N-type new fighter, destined to be named Typhoon, which was also being built by Hawker, would have the Napier Sabre 24-

cylinder H-configuration sleeve-valve engine with two shafts. Each of this engine's upper and lower light alloy blocks had twelve opposed cylinders with two inlet and three exhaust ports and four-port sleeves. The power unit also comprised a two-speed supercharger, four-stroke updraught carburettor and Koffman starter. In case the Sabre failed to meet requirements, the Typhoon was designed also to be able to mount the Vulture.

The anhedral inner wing and dihedral outer wing panels gave both the Typhoon and the Tornado a slightly gull-winged look. There were fuel tanks in the leading edges and guns were housed outboard of the inward-retracting landing gear.

The Air Ministry placed an order for four prototypes, two with the Sabre engine and two with the Vulture.

By the end of 1939, three months after the declaration of war, Hawker had been given an Instruction To Proceed (ITP) which ordered 1000 Typhoons.

Initially, the Vulture engine behaved better than it had in the Manchester and the first Tornado prototype (P5219) was the first of the two new fighters to fly – on 6 October 1939. This had been built in the Hawker experimental shop at Kingston-on-Thames and was taken by road to the grass airfield at Langley, near Staines in Middlesex, where a final assembly plant was being set up. Philip Lucas, a flight lieutenant in the R.A.F. Reserve, who was soon to be appointed Chief Test Pilot, took it up for its maiden flight, which presented new problems: a high drag rise at speeds near 400mph, and compressibility. The latter was a phenomenon that would become familiar with the first generation of supersonic aircraft. The lessons learned from the Tornado were directly relevant to designing the Typhoon.

By March the next year the Vulture engine was developing 2010 horsepower. The production schedule laid down in July 1939 had catered for delivery of the first aeroplane by July 1940 and of the 500th by September 1941. The complex Sabre engine was causing delays to the Typhoon and the respective dates had to be put back to October 1940 and January

1942. The first prototype (P5212) did not make its maiden flight until 24 February 1940. In consequence, the Tornado was regarded as the more promising aircraft. Production of both new fighters was further retarded during the Battle of Britain – officially deemed to have begun on 10 July 1940 – when priority was given to the manufacture of Hurricanes. The Minister of Aircraft Production ordered manufacture to be concentrated also on Spitfires, and three bomber types: Blenheim, Wellington and Whitley. All this meant a nine-month setback in the constructing and prototype testing rate of Tornados and Typhoons.

The first production plan, pre-dating the decision to discontinue the Vulture engine, had envisaged the building of 500 Tornados and 250 Typhoons; the type of the remaining 250 was to be decided when the two engines came into series production. This, of course, was now thwarted. Hawker, already fully stretched by the demand for more Hurricanes, therefore sub-contracted Tornado production to A.V. Roe's Manchester factory and Typhoon production to the Gloster Aircraft Co at Hucclecote, near Gloucester. Both of these companies were members of the Hawker Siddeley Group.

The second Tornado prototype (P5224) was not flown until 5 December 1940 and the first production one (R7936) made its maiden flight on 29 August 1941. Only two more prototype Tornados were built before this aeroplane was cancelled because Rolls-Royce ceased making the Vulture engine.

The Typhoon profited further from lessons learned while testing the stillborn Tornado. The least of its grave imperfections was that the oil cooling was inefficient, so the air inlet for this purpose had to be redesigned and repositioned before manufacture, based on the final prototype, began. The next change was to move the radiator scoop from its original position in line with the wings, as in the Hurricane, to beneath the wings in the 'beard' position. Not only was the Sabre engine very heavy, but also the radiator and oil cooler had to be placed in the nose. In order for the aeroplane's centre of gravity to be correctly

ABOVE: Typhoon JR128 of 183 Sqdn being flown by Merrick Hyman. (Philip Jarrett)

positioned, the whole assembly had to be shifted seven inches astern. In consequence, the bearers, structural parts and upper nose panels had involved changes.

On 23 February 1940 the first prototype (P5212) was ready to be flown. Testing an aircraft before its maiden flight is a tentative business, beginning with ground runs. Philip Lucas made several that day, ending with a simulated take-off. He found that even with full left rudder at 70mph on the ground, the Typhoon pulled to the right. Next day he took it into the air for twenty minutes and, at 8000ft, did some stalls with flaps and wheels up and with them down. Coming in to land with full flap it descended more rapidly than expected, so he had to keep the forward speed higher than he had intended. He stringently criticised

the vibration, which made it difficult to read the instruments at maximum revolutions, and the engine noise, which was fifty per cent higher than the Tornado's and double that of the Hurricane. To reduce this nuisance, rubber grommets were fitted to the seat mountings and the instrument panel mountings were tightened. The engine manufacturer attributed the high level of noise to the exhaust pipes; and the vibration to the attachment of the engine to the main spar without any form of damping.

Lucas was making the next test flight on 1 February when a panel on the side of the nose came off and he forced-landed. He made eight flights during March and found that the noise was a trifle less. The highest speed to which he took it was 376mph and altitude 20,400ft. There was considerable oil loss, fuel flow was irregular and consumption greater than bench running had suggested it would be. On 4 April the aircraft flew again, with a fuel pump that had a slower drive, and showed an improvement.

The great expectations of the Typhoon were further considerably blighted by the dismal fact that the engine was cleared for only twenty-five hours' running between major overhauls. Even this miserly quota proved optimistic, for it was soon found that many engines did not achieve even as little as that. P5212's engine had now run for this length of time, of which only ten hours were in flight, so it had to be stripped and minutely examined.

The replacement engine fitted was mounted on thick rubber pads in front and ball-and-socket trunnions at the back. Flying with it for the first time on 7 May, Lucas found that engine and airframe vibration was a trifle less. His next sortie, on 9 May, nearly ended abruptly in one of the life-threatening accidents that make test pilots unattractive policy-holders to life assurance companies. At 10,500ft and 270mph, he felt a sudden lurch and violent agitation of the controls as P5212 swung hard to port. Striving for straight flight, he heard a loud and sustained noise behind his seat, which he correctly supposed was caused by a structural failure. He would have been fully justified in baling out, but instead he risked staying in the aircraft and attempting a landing. An instrument called a vibrograph had been fitted where the radio normally was, so he could not let the people on the ground know what was going on. He made a dicey landing and the bad news was that the vertical tube at the rear of the port-side longeron and the diagonal compression strut between the joint of the longeron and the top of the frame of the main fuselage had broken. This caused the monocoque fuselage to buckle along the port side as far as the wing trailing edge. Reinforcing the longeron joint cured that trouble but more was in store: on 7 July, when the aeroplane next flew, the new engine stopped and another forced landing ensued. The award of the George Medal to Lucas for his bravery on 9 May 1940 was gazetted in September.

In the following month the aircraft was given not only yet another engine but also an enlarged and thicker fin that had been tried out on the Tornado. This improved directional stability, but Philip Lucas still wanted better directional control at low speeds at which the rudder's effectiveness was reduced by the airflow aft of the new fin. In response to his request, a bigger rudder and trim tab were fitted. No design measure could be effective, however, in reducing the aircraft's powerful swing to the right, which was created by the high torque and engine speeds and the huge propeller. Applying hard left rudder was the only way to ensure straight take-offs and landings.

The fourth engine had six exhaust stubs on each side replacing the original three long,

BELOW: Arming a 266 Sqdn Typhoon. (Philip Jarrett)

ABOVE: 266 Sqdn Typhoon and foam used to extinguish engine fire. (Philip Jarrett)

BELOW: 266 Sqdn Typhoons in a hangar. (Philip Jarrett)

tapered exhaust pipes on both sides. This was intended to eliminate the entry of carbon monoxide into the cockpit, as the first fatalities from carbon monoxide poisoning were attributed to exhaust fumes entering under the cockpit doors. This modification did not achieve the desired result, so the stub exhausts were slightly lengthened. The change was found to reduce speed by 14mph, so short stubs were readopted and extractor louvres introduced. Carbon monoxide also insinuated itself past the engine bulkhead when engine heat affected the sealant on the bulkhead between cockpit and engine. The order for pilots to turn on the oxygen supply before starting the engine was the only sure safeguard.

The Air Ministry, alarmed by the Typhoon's vicious characteristics and many vicissitudes, sought an end to the dilemma about whether to persevere with the aircraft. Accordingly, the help of the Aircraft and Armament Experimental Establishment (A&AEE) – then, as now, at R.A.F. Boscombe Down – was invoked. Flight Lieutenant S. Wroath, who had many hours in the Hurricane and Spitfire and was on excellent terms with Lucas, was detached (in the RAF, personnel are not attached) to Langley. At the same time, Dr G. Hislop, the technical representative in charge of the Typhoon project at the Air Ministry, also moved there. Fortunately, the engine gave no serious trouble during Sammy Wroath's test flights, but he found its vibrations excessive and the pilot's field of view inadequate.

Until the victorious outcome of the Battle of Britain the RAF had been on the defensive. Now it was eagerly on the offensive, for which the Typhoon gave promise of being ideal. The most persuasive argument in favour of not abandoning it was its high speed and its manoeuvrability at such speed, which was now Fighter Command's top priority. In consequence of Wroath's and Hislop's favourable reports, the Typhoon lived on.

Progress accelerated: on 3 May 1941 the second prototype, P5212, which was armed with four 20mm Hispano Mk I cannon, made its first flight; and twenty-four days later R7576, the first production Typhoon, took to the air. The first thirty of the latter temporarily carried twelve .303-in Browning machine-guns, as not enough cannon were yet available, but none of them flew on operations. Three more test pilots joined the team at Langley: Hubert Broad, Kenneth Seth-Smith and Bill Humble.

The inadequacy of the 180-degree view forward from the cockpit was acknowledged and the first attempt to improve it so that the pilot could look astern was to fit quarterlights of Perspex panels. However, the near-fatal calamity experienced with the first prototype prompted design modification to the fuselage behind the pilot. Cockpit doors of a new pattern, a bigger rudder trim tab with a cord on the trailing edge and a better method of oil-cooling were also introduced.

Test flights yielded satisfactory performances. A climb to 20,000ft took 7.1 minutes; in level flight at 20,400ft the maximum true air speed (TAS) was 402mph; the aeroplane rolled fifty degrees per second at 310mph and 10,000ft. The interval between major inspections of the engine was now fifty hours.

Before the Typhoon entered squadron service and during its operational career, it suffered many vicissitudes and benefited from numerous modifications. Not least of its pilots' discomfitures was misidentification by Spitfire and Hurricane squadrons and anti-aircraft gunners. As late as 1 June 1942, by which time Typhoons had been in the battle line for nine months, Spitfires shot down two of 56 Squadron, killing one of the pilots. On 30 July and 19 August the same infamous error was made by other squadrons; the pilot of the first survived, the second's was killed. As will be seen, even in the last months of the war the gung-ho (and self-described 'hell-raising') fighter 'jocks' of the USAAF were apt to shoot at anything that moved in the sky; sometimes with accuracy.

In 1943 a sliding bubble canopy that obviated the doors was fitted to many Mk IBs and all Mk IIBs. In the same year the radio mast was replaced by a whip antenna. The addition of fairings around the gun barrels increased maximum speed by 8mph. Major inspection of the engines was now extended to 100-hour intervals.

ABOVE: 266 Sqdn Typhoon ZH-Z in foreground, 263 Sqdn Typhoon HE-S in background. (Philip Jarrett)

The next rôle for the Typhoon was as fighter-bomber. In 1942 it had been approved for carrying a 500lb bomb under each wing. In March the next year, while trials by Hawker with two 1000lb bombs were being done by Bill Humble, a company test pilot, the release mechanism for the starboard bomb did not operate. With his aircraft and its load weighing 13,248lb, the greatest yet, the situation was delicate; but he landed safely at 130mph. Tests included a bombing dive at 548mph and releasing the load immediately before pulling out.

In December 1942, two forty-five-gallon drop tanks were first tried out. They increased the aircraft's range from about 600 nautical miles at 5000ft to 1090nm. Two drop tanks and a rocket on the outboard side of each could be carried, usually on standing patrols and armed reconnaissance.

This was followed by tests with three-inch 60lb rockets. These were carried out by the Aircraft and Armament Experimental Establishment and at various other RAF stations. Clearance was obtained in May 1943 for a load of eight such missiles.

The Air Staff had hoped to have the new fighter in squadron service by July 1940, but delivery could not begin until August 1941, when R7576 went first to the Royal Aircraft Establishment (RAE). R7577 went to the Aircraft and Armament Experimental Establishment, R7578 to Napier, and R7579 to the Central Flying School (CFS). R7580 was delivered to the Air Fighting Development Unit (AFDU), thence to No 56 Squadron and finally to No 59 Operational Training Unit (OTU), where it spun into the ground on 13 June 1943. R5781 also went to AFDU before eventually going on to 609 (West Riding) Squadron. The first to be delivered direct to a fighting unit was R7582, which joined 56 Squadron on 26 September 1941.

BELOW: 266 Sqdn Typhoons in foreground, 263 Sqdn's in background. (Philip Jarrett)

Chapter 4

The Typhoon Enters Squadron Service

No 56 Squadron, the first to have the dubious privilege of becoming familiar with the latest addition to Fighter Command's Battle Order, was based at Duxford. Air Ministry chose a squadron at this station because it was a grass airfield: for among the Typhoon's already perceived defects were the brakes, and grass would slow its landing run more than a hard, smooth-surfaced runway. In addition to the engine and brakes, many unpleasant surprises awaited the squadrons for which it was destined. The next one to receive a Typhoon was 266 (Rhodesia) Squadron in February 1941 and 609 Squadron got theirs two months later. All three had been flying Spitfires.

The Typhoons with which the first three squadrons were initially equipped were the Mk IA type. These were soon superceded by the Mk IB before any of the newly converted squadrons resumed operations. The difference between these two marks was that the former had twelve .303-in Browning machine-guns (six in each wing) and the latter four 20mm Hispano cannons (two in each wing).

This super-high-speed fighter had been eagerly looked forward to since the arrival of the Focke-Wulf 190 on the scene earlier that year. Capable of 408mph and armed with two 13mm machine-guns and either four 20mm cannon or two 20mm and two 30mm, it was superior in speed and armament not only to the Mk V Spitfire but also to every other Allied

BELOW: Typhoon FB IB JR128 HF-L of 183 Sqdn. (Philip Jarrett)

fighter. It was also smaller than they were and therefore very difficult to hit. The fighter-bomber variant carried an 1100lb bomb. The FW190 was thus at an advantage against Fighter Command in air fighting and in hit-and-run low-level bombing.

No 56 Squadron was commanded by Squadron Leader P. Prosser Hanks DFC (later a group captain with the DSO). He began the process of converting his squadron from Spitfire VBs to the 'Tiffie' and in December 1941 handed over to S/L Hugh 'Cocky' Dundas DFC. By the end of the war Dundas was a group captain with also a DSO and bar, and eleven victories. In his post-war civilian career Dundas was awarded the CBE and later knighted. The squadron's jubilation at being the first to receive the Allies' fastest machine soon gave way to dismay and some trepidation when it turned out to be a prolific killer of those who flew it.

Development of the Napier engine had been so hasty that it was suffering from faults which should have been detected and cured before it was allowed to go into series production. Hence its leaving the factory in a state that often proved fatal.

The first fault the squadron detected was the poor starting. The next thing was that when the engine was running, the oil temperature often became dangerously high and and so did the temperature in the cockpit; pilots felt as though they were being roasted. The cause of the fatal accidents was difficult to determine, but eventually traced to three defects. One was seepage of carbon monoxide into the cockpit, owing to the deterioration of the engine bulkhead seals. Pilots rendered unconscious crashed and were usually killed. The consequence was compulsory switching-on of oxygen immediately on entering the cockpit.

Another defect was that the engine was apt to stop for no immediately obvious reason and cause a fatal crash. Investigation revealed that wear on the valve sleeves often caused a jam that blew up the cylinder: this gave the pilot less than a minute to take life-saving action by baling out or ditching. Ditching was unhealthy – the enormous air scoop took in a vast amount of water in a very short time: consequently, the aeroplane either tipped on to its nose and slithered below the surface, or became waterlogged and went down like an express lift. However, one outstanding and popular pilot, Eric Haabjoern, the Norwegian member of 56 Squadron who flew on the first Typhoon operation and ended the war as a wing commander, survived three Typhoon ditchings in the English Channel. Ironically he was killed on a mere ferrying flight after the war. A crash landing on the ground, however, was fairly innocuous thanks to the Typhoon's great strength.

The ultimate flaw, discovered when wreckage was examined after killer accidents, was that the tail unit was prone to break off in flight. This appalling defect was bravely investigated by Philip Lucas and Gloster's Chief Test Pilot, Jerry Sayer.

The cause turned out to be a manifestation already mentioned – compressibility. Until now this had been unheard of by anyone except scientists and advanced aeronautical engineers. This heavy, powerful aeroplane reached that state quickly. Aircraft react to its effect in various ways, according to the shape of their wings. On the Typhoon, the effect was to force its nose down beyond the vertical. This a pilot could not rectify until he had reduced speed. The conclusion was that the pilots had simultaneously throttled right back and brought the nose up by using the trimming gear; thus, when the speed dropped enough for the controls to act normally, the nose, under full trim, rose so violently that it imposed a breaking strain on the tail unit. It was also found that at high speeds elevator flutter often made the tail section break at the rear fuselage transport joint. This was partly cured by riveting twenty fish plates around the fuselage. All these defects resulted in the death of at least twenty-six pilots.

A salutary example of the inaccuracies and pseudo-dramatic events that are established in the annals of warfare, not least in air fighting legend, was revealed when the wreckage of a Typhoon was excavated fifty years after it crashed. It was identified as serial number R7592, delivered to No 56 Squadron on 26 October 1941, whose pilot was killed when it dived into the ground, out of control, on 1 November 1941 – the first Typhoon fatality. P/O J. F. Deck was flying it. An autopsy revealed that he had been overcome by carbon monoxide. The accident occurred forty miles from RAF Duxford, where the squadron was based. The biography of W/C Robert Stanford Tuck, DSO, DFC and two bars, recently appointed Leader of the Duxford Wing, states that the aircraft went in about a mile from the airfield, watched by Tuck among others. The story goes that Tuck had been about to take it up on a test flight but was called to the telephone, so detailed James Deck to replace him. He had already had a narrow escape from death when, one evening, he was prompted to leave a pub for no explicable reason – just a premonition of disaster. Shortly after, an enemy bomb fell on it and killed the friends with whom he had been having a drink. He had also survived a mid-air collision in 1938. A third narrow squeak would have made dramatic reading indeed. In late October 1941 Tuck and five other pilots had been sent to the USA to tell pilots of the USAAF what it was like to fly fighters in combat.

The most disappointing of all the Typhoon's undesirable features was the performance in speed and rate of climb at heights over 18,000ft. Fast though it was, it attained 50mph less than the Air Ministry had wanted.

The defect that Dundas criticised after his maiden flight was that the rear view was inadequate. The sloping cover astern of the cockpit in the IA was solid, instead of being transparent as on the Hurricane and Spitfire. Armour plating behind the pilot's head further obscured the rear view. There was a conference at Duxford in February 1942 to discuss Dundas's report and other matters. Sidney Camm was present. His comment on the poor rear view was, 'The aeroplane's so fast, you don't have to see behind you'. This testy remark, hardly in the best of taste from someone who would never have to face the enemy, did not amuse. The necessary modifications were quickly made: the metal was soon replaced by Perspex and the armour plating was repositioned

Meanwhile the fast and difficult to hit FW190

and the Messerschmitt 109 were making low-level fighter-bomber raids on the south coast of England against civilian and military targets at random. Spitfires could not catch them, so on 29 May 1942 one flight of 56 Squadron was detached to Tangmere and the other to Manston. Daily patrols brought no contact with the enemy, but on 1 June two (R7678 flown by P/O R. H. Duego and R8199 flown by Sgt K. M. Stuart-Turner) were shot down by Spitfires whose pilots mistook them for FW190s. Stuart-Turner was killed and Duego badly wounded. This mistake in identification would recur often, because the silhouette and head-on views of the FW190 and Typhoon were much alike, despite the fact that the latter was so much bigger. Nos 266 and 609 Squadrons were suffering the same molestation and casualties on the frequent fighter sweeps over northern France in which the Typhoon squadrons were operating with Spitfires.

To obviate these tragic misidentifications, which became more frequent when the United States Army Air Force appeared in the sky, conspicuous markings that should be easily recognised were tried. First, the nose forward of the wings was painted white. From 19 November 1942 black stripes were painted under the wings. From 5 December 1942 alternate black and white stripes were painted under the wings from the wing root to the inboard end of the aileron, the rest of the wing was grey and the spinner forward of the airscrew sky blue. From 21 January 1943 the whole spinner was sky blue. From 1 August 1943 the yellow day-fighter band was painted on the wing from the outboard side of the inward gun to the wingtip, centrally placed on the wing leading edge. Finally, with effect from 7 February 1944 the Typhoon reverted to the normal day-fighter finish. Such measures could be effective only if all the squadrons of every allied air force flying every current type of fighter were not only informed but also their Commanding Officers and Intelligence Officers ensured that every pilot and every anti-aircraft gunner was also informed. This is a counsel of perfection that has never been achieved in an air war and doubtless never will be.

The three Typhoon squadrons constituted a

Wing, led by W/C Denys Gillam DFC (later group captain, DSO and two bars, DFC and two bars AFC). How to make the best use of them was a dilemma for Fighter Command, as the aircraft's poor performance above 18,500ft of course ruled it out for the rôle of high cover; and it was not suitable for giving close escort. Dundas proposed that when Spitfires crossed the Channel on sweeps, usually escorting six to a dozen Blenheim bombers to tempt the enemy up to fight, the Typhoon Wing could be well employed in covering the whole formation while it withdrew, by making a fast sweep around its rear. This was agreed at Fighter Command Headquarters; but although the

scheme was tried several times, Dundas wrote that they 'never succeded in getting to grips with the enemy'. He added, 'We did, however, on several occasions get to grips with Spitfires.' All three squadrons suffered casualties from 'friendly fire'.

It was not until the Dieppe raid on 19 August 1942 that Typhoons had the first chance to prove their worth. The raid went disastrously wrong because a breach of security unwittingly betrayed the date and place at which it would be made. The seaborne landing was met with such heavy fire that the Army had sixty-eight per cent casualties. The Navy suffered many losses of ships and lives. The RAF destroyed

BELOW: 609 Sqdn Typhoon IBs with markings to facilitate recognition and avoid confusion with FW190. (Bruce Robertson)

ABOVE: Typhoon IB MN189 186 Sqdn in 1944. Previously in 440 RCAF Sqdn, when 186 was renumbered it returned to 440. (Bruce Robertson)

twenty-five bombers and damaged sixteen, shot down twenty-three fighters and damaged sixteen. It lost eighteen bombers and eighty-eight fighters and seventy-one pilots were killed or missing. The whole Typhoon Wing, under Denys Gillam's leadership, took part and was given the task of sweeping round to the north and east of the battle to intercept approaching enemy aircraft.

When they spotted some bombers below, Gillam ordered 56 Squadron to stay at the present altitude. They covered him and Nos 266 and 609 Squadrons, which he led down to engage the enemy. Dundas's squadron kept being dived on by German fighters (a welcome change from being set upon by Spitfires), but these pulled away when the Typhoons turned on them. The other two squadrons fared better and scored the first Typhoon victories. F/O R. N. L. Dawson of 266 Squadron who shot down a Do217 was presently shot down by a Spitfire.

The 266 Squadron Operations Record Book describes the events as follows:

The Wing took off from West Malling at 1400, 609 Squadron leading with Nos 266 and 56 giving top cover. They flew to Le Tréport, the two high squadrons at 16,000ft, where they saw three Dornier 217s escorted by FW190s. W/C Gillam ordered Yellow Section of 266 Squadron (F/L R. H. L. Dawson, flying R7815 and P/O W. S. Smythyman in R7813) and White 1, P/O M.

Munro in R7822, to attack. Smythyman saw a Dornier crash, which Dawson claimed to have shot down. Smythyman claimed one probable Do217. F/L A. C. Johnson (R7819) dived at 10 Fw190s, claimed a probable and was shot at by a Spitfire. Another Spitfire shot Smythyman down. The Wing landed at 1505.

The next recognition of the Typhoon's potentially most useful employment came when Dundas was told to study the best ways in which his squadron could engage in offensive ground attack and low-level air-to-air operations. Holland was the enemy-occupied country nearest to Matlaske, one of Coltishall's

BELOW: King George VI inspecting Typhoon armament, May 1944. ACM Sir Trafford Leigh-Mallory behind him, squadron commander to King's right. (Bruce Robertson)

two satellite airfields, to which 56 had moved on 25 August 1942. He decided to start with the Dutch coast and off-shore islands. Having learned from the Intelligence Section at No 12 Group Headquarters where the best potential targets and flak positions were, and hoping also to come across shipping that he could attack, he took off with Lieutenant Eric Haabjoern, F/O Wally Coombes and Sergeant Cluderay on an exploratory flight. (Haabjoern was later a flight commander and ultimately rose to the command of a fighter Wing).

As usual, they flew in the finger-four formation that Dundas had learned when flying Spitfires in the Tangmere Wing, led by Douglas Bader, and used for the rest of the war.

Appropriately, it was on 5 November, Guy Fawkes' Day, that he set off on this first operation of a new kind that the whole squadron hoped would see some fireworks that would singe Jerry. They crossed the North Sea at 100ft – below enemy radar coverage – and under low cloud, with occasional squalls that thrashed the sea into tall waves. Sudden engine failure would mean death to any pilot: they were much too low to bale out and an aircraft ditching in such turbulent water would sink in seconds.

Heading for Walcheren Island, they emerged from a squall to see vessels a mile ahead. One, on Dundas's line of flight, was a flak ship. It instantly opened fire. Flying at 270mph, he replied with his cannons and saw strikes on the target. Racing past astern of her, he heard an explosion behind and the Typhoon turned involuntarily to the left. Now he had to exert great effort to hold it straight and managed gradually to turn right-about. He was at last able to see, in his mirror, the damage done: a shell had blown a vast hole in the rudder and tail fin. 'I knew that if I eased off on the rudder

for an instant the aircraft would flick over and I would have about three seconds to live before crashing into the sea.' But he got back to Coltishall, which was a trifle closer than Matlaske.

On 6 November 1942 a formidable and popular member of 56 Squadron, who had joined it before the war, reappeared on its strength: F\L F. W. Higginson, DFM, known as Taffy. He scored fourteen confirmed victories over France and in the Battle of Britain before being shot down in France in 1941. After a long evasion he was captured, endured several months in two prisons, escaped and returned home in October 1942. On 1 January 1943 his DFC was gazetted.

Like other aircrew who had made successful escapes with the help of members of the Resistance, he was barred from flying over occupied Europe because of his knowledge of this organisation and its escape routes.

In view of the erratic behaviour of the Napier Sabre engine, it was decided to form an engine-handling school for Typhoon pilots at the factory. Taffy was duly appointed to organise and run it. He says, 'The job involved not only desk tuition but I also visited the squadrons to talk to the pilots and see how the pupils who had been with me were getting on. After a time I went seeking help to get back onto an operational squadron.' He did not succeed, but later that year was promoted to squadron leader and, in March 1944, posted to form and command No 83 Group Communications Squadron, which he took to France after the invasion. He retired as a wing commander, joined the aviation industry and was awarded the OBE for his work on guided weapons. Meanwhile Hugh Dundas had been promoted to wing commander and posted to Duxford as leader of a newly formed Typhoon Wing.

Chapter 5
Finding the Typhoon's Ideal Role

While No 56 Squadron was, to use RAF argot, 'looking for trade' across the North Sea, 609 Squadron, commanded by S/L Roland Beamont DFC, maintained standing patrols on England's south coast, where Focke-Wulf fighter-bombers carrying 500kg bombs were making 'tip and run' nuisance raids. These patrols were made by one pair of aircraft at a time, flying back and forth between Ramsgate and Dungeness at under 200ft altitude. Nipping in very low, the FW190s strafed and dropped their bombs at random. Lacking the height to make a visual search for obvious or apparent military targets as they approached the coast or when they crossed inland, they were as likely to hit civilian road traffic (of which there was very little,

fortunately) as military vehicles. Houses, shops, hospitals, schools, churches and people going about their lawful occasions out of doors were in as much danger as RAF airfield buildings, aircraft on the ground, air defence gun pits and anti-aircraft artillery sites.

With both attackers and defenders flying below even the lowest radar cover (Chain Home Extra Low, CHEL), Fighter Controllers at Ground Control Installation (GCI) radar stations and in Sector Operations Rooms could not give much help to the guardian pilots to intercept the intruders. Standing patrols consumed a lot of petrol and engine hours for little return in the way of enemy aircraft destroyed or damaged.

The Royal Artillery's anti-aircraft batteries as well as Fighter Command's Spitfire squadrons repeatedly misidentified Typhoons as Focke-

BELOW: Typhoon prototype P5212. (Philip Jarrett)

ABOVE: The first Typhoon prototype. (Philip Jarrett)

Wulfs. Although sea haze, the speed at which the Typhoon and FW190 flew, and the fact that both types had a round nose and blunt wingtips made identification difficult, especially when there were still very few Typhoons in service, the fact must be faced that the frequent misidentifications were crass. The Typhoon was much bigger than the Focke-Wulf and it bore the distinctive markings on its wings that have already been described and which were promulgated throughout all Allied air, land and sea Services.

There was a typical incident shortly before 1300 hrs on 20 January 1943, when 609 Squadron was stationed at Manston. The airfield was under attack and Spitfires had been scrambled (ordered to take-off). Some of them mistook a Typhoon on its landing approach for a 190 and their leader fired at it. The pilot lowered his undercarriage just in time to avoid being shot down. Beamont, who had taken off to defend Manston, was also attacked by Spitfires but they missed him too.

As instances of adding insult to injury, two perpetrated while 609 were at Manston are classic. The first offender was a thick-skinned gunner officer whom the Squadron Intelligence

Officer telephoned to rebuke for allowing his men to shoot at some Typhoons. This insensitive, tactless ornament of the Army, keen to learn the accuracy of his gun crews, asked if their shells had come close to hitting the aeroplanes. The second was a coastguard: this bi-linguist hailed a Typhoon pilot, who had just been shot down and was wading ashore, by speaking to him in German.

Fighter Command was making offensive as well as defensive sorties. Early in 1941 new types of attacking operations by daylight had been ordered. A 'Circus' meant from twelve to thirty-six bombers escorted by fighter Wings. A fighter squadron's battle strength was twelve and there were three squadrons in a Wing. The escort comprised at least three Wings. The purpose was not so much to drop bombs as to lure the enemy fighters up to do battle with the Spitfires. 'Rhubarbs' were flown by fighters only, in one or two pairs, attacking targets of opportunity such as railway locomotives and military vehicles. Occasionally a pilot would go off on his own. These operations were flown on

ABOVE: First Typhoon prototype in original form. (Philip Jarrett)

days of poor visibilty to give the Hurricanes and Spitfires the best chance to avoid being seen. Casualties on both types of operation were high.

Beamont perceived that the Typhoon's speed, fire power and ruggedness made it well suited to flying Rhubarbs and every other form of ground attack. He was given permission for his pilots to operate in pairs by day, or singly at night by moonlight, against road and rail traffic in France and the Low Countries. On 17 November 1942, he himself carried out the first of these operations – by night, against trains in the Somme area. By the end of April 1943 his squadron had destroyed or irreparably damaged over one hundred locomoties and shot down fourteen FW190s. The Commanding Officer's contribution was fifty-six sorties over France and Belgium, the majority nocturnal.

He went on to become one of the best-known pilots in the aviation world. At the end of 1941 he had spent some time at the Hawker factory, testing Hurricanes and the early Typhoons. When, in May 1943, his second tour of operations ended, he went back to the manufacturer to test the Tempest, the Typhoon's immediate successor. He was given command of the first Tempest Wing, which comprised Nos 3, 56 amd 486 Squadrons, in March 1944. He was shot down by flak and taken prisoner while flying his ninety-fifth

sortie over enemy territory. By then he had shot down ten enemy aircraft and earned the DSO and a bar to his DFC. On release from prisoner-of-war camp, he served briefly at the Central Fighter Establishment before joining Gloster Aircraft as test pilot then moving to English Electric as chief test pilot, where he flew the prototype Lightning and Canberra. With the latter, he set a cross-Atlantic record.

The Typhoon, originally intended to be the RAF's fastest interception fighter, was able to justify this expectation when enemy fighter-bombers swept in at low level to attack targets in southern England. A typical raid was made against a Devonshire village on 26 January 1943 by eight FW190s, about which the succinct *Luftwaffe* report cloaks a barbarous act. The German document gave the following account:

Fighter-Bomber Report No. 1 – 26.1.43
8 Focke-Wulf 190 (start 1515 hours)

Harassment attack on Kingsbridge. Principal target not attacked due to change in wind direction. Alternative target 1600 hrs low-level attack on Loddiswell (5km north-north-west of Kingsbridge). Bombing concentrated on local dwellings. The local church almost completely destroyed. Also cannon attack on Loddiswell.

On leaving the area, more buildings north-east of Start Point were bombarded with cannon fire.

Resistance: during flight medium to heavy flak, accurate. On leaving, about 25km south-east of Start Point 8 Spitfires pursued the formation to mid-Channel.

Lost: 1 Focke-Wolf 190 missing. This one flew on far inland, as its bomb was presumably not released on the first sortie, and thus remained behind the formation.

Weather: ten-tenths at 800–1000 metres. At 200–300 metres patchy cloud.

So much for the enemy viewpoint. The Royal Air Force had something more pertinent to say about this disgraceful event.

The Operations Record Book of 266 Squadron, based at Exeter, states that F/O Bell (flying R8772) and Sergeant Borland (R8804) were scrambled to intercept a FW190 that had crossed the coast near Torquay and was already being chased by Spitfires. Borland had trouble starting, but was close enough behind his leader to see all that happened. Bell saw a FW190 flying south from Dartmouth, overtook it easily as he was 20mph the faster, caught up with it 'at nought feet', gave it three bursts from 660, 300 and 250 yards, and saw it plunge,

smoking, into the sea, some 12 miles SSE of Start Point. One of the Spitfires photographed the wreckage.

The club house of Bigbury Golf Club was damaged. The village devastated by seven bombs and cannonfire was not Loddiswell, but Aveton Gifford, on the Avon between Kingsbridge and Modbury, where 150 people, practically its entire population, were rendered homeless. Miraculously, there was only one fatality – a little girl who was suffocated under the debris of her home.

Yet in Britain, half a century later, post-war generations ignorant of the facts rebuke the RAF for destroying Dresden, a perfectly legitimate target. It had a great railway junction where troops were being mustered for trains to take them into action against Britain's and the USA's ally, the USSR. If RAF Bomber Command had not laid waste the German railway system, including the Dresden complex, the Russians would have been hard pressed and probably forced to give ground. That would have lengthened the war to Hitler's benefit and might even have brought about Russia's defeat. An equally justifiable reason to bomb this sacred cow was not

BELOW: Second Typhoon prototype P5216 armed with 12 machine-guns. (Philip Jarrett)

revealed until decades later: spies there had informed the Allies that the enemy, presuming that reverence for the city's historical and artistic renown would deter air raids, had stored a vast amount of war materiel there. Many of the fires and explosions seen by the bomber crews were caused by secreted German ammunition, from rifle bullets to shells and bombs.

At this time a number of people thought that a fast single-seater equipped with radar would be the ideal night-fighter and in April 1943 trials began that were to prove a complete waste of time and money. In fact it could be said that even Pilot Officer Prune would have noticed it. (Prune was a dim-witted pilot with a low forehead and no chin, who figured in an

Air Ministry publication, *Tee Emm* (*Training Monthly*) issued to all flying stations, ridiculing and warning against dangerous practices.)

The Pruneish undertaking in this instance was a series of trials conducted by a Typhoon (R7881) fitted with Mk IV AI (airborne interception) radar. It was obviously impossible for a pilot to operate this equipment, watch the radar screen as well as his flying instruments and keep a lookout for other aircraft in an increasingly crowded night sky. Since experimental radar was first installed in a few night-fighter Blenheims in the winter of 1939, and in three Defiants, it had been taken for granted that the pilot needed a skilled specialist to operate the 'black box' (as pilots, navigators and air gunners called it in the early days).

This costly, time-wasting experiment in 1943 was made all the more absurd by the fact that the night-fighting variant of the two-seater Beaufighter (the Beau was also used for anti-

Below: Typhoon IA. (Philip Jarrett)

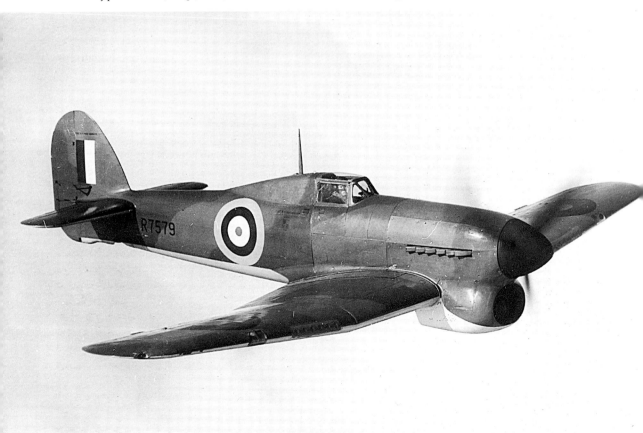

shipping strikes and ground attack) had been operational since 12 August 1940 and was an instant success. There was no need for a single-seat fighter on night operations and the only progressive innovation called for was to instal the equipment in a faster type. The night-fighting Mosquito had already begun to satisfy this demand when it made its first sortie on the night of 27/28 April 1942.

An earlier theory was that a combination of two aircraft would form the deadliest means of intercepting night bombers. Accordingly, eighteen months were wasted experimenting with a radar-equipped Havoc (twin-engine light bomber) fitted with a Turbinlite (1000 candlepower beam) in the nose, flying with a Hurricane one hundred yards to its starboard and one hundred yards astern. The intention was for the Havoc to illuminate an enemy aircraft upon which the Hurricane would immediately swoop and shoot it down. To begin with, nobody who understood the fighter-pilot mentality would have wagered a penny on this method's practicality: no average fighter pilot would tamely lurk behind another aeroplane, waiting for it to light up a target. The instant he spotted exhaust flames that might be an enemy's, or caught a glimpse of a bomber outlined against the moon or cloud, he would have broken formation and charged at it: 'In like Flynn' to use the contemporary RAF phrase. Another strike against its success was, as anyone who has seen the beam cast by a Turbinlite knows, the backwash from this brilliant glare would have dazzled the fighter pilot somewhat. The Hurricane proved too slow, anyway, which was why a Typhoon replaced it; and proved to be so much faster than the Havoc that the two aircraft spent more time hunting for each other than seeking the enemy. In the event, eighteen months of this tomfoolery yielded precisely one victory.

In 1943 the ill-considered practice interceptions with radar in a Typhoon were soon abandoned.

Also starting that April, some sensible tropical trials were done in Egypt with three Typhoons (R8891, DN323 and EJ906) with a modified air circulator system. A Vokes tropical air filter was fitted just behind the radiator and used when the engine was run while the aircraft was stationary on the ground, taxying, taking off and landing; which were the occasions when the slipstream whipped up the greatest amount of dust. The filter was switched off as soon as the aircraft was airborne.

It was Winston Churchill who initiated the investigation into the Typhoon's adaptability to desert and climatic conditions. The aircraft were shipped to Casablanca with their engines in place and the wings, tail units, propellers and cowlings separately crated. Two pilots were detailed to complete the party: F/O Myall, late of 56 Squadron, who had many Typhoon hours in his logbook, and a sergeant (name unknown) who had none. Two experienced fitters accompanied them. Philip Lucas and a Hawker engineer, J. Gale, flew out along the usual England- Lisbon-Gibraltar route.

The first step was assembly of the aircraft at No 145 Maintenance Unit (MU) and Lucas flew DN323 on 7 May. Both the other Typhoons were ready for flight eleven days later. On 22 May Lucas received orders to move to the Canal Zone, so R8891 and DN323 landed at Cairo on 3 June. EJ906 had been forced down by a failure of the supercharger clutch, but was soon flying again as three Sabre engines had been landed at Algiers. No 103 MU at Aboukir now took the three aeroplanes over and modified them to the latest standard. F/O Myall fetched EJ906 from Casablanca, while Philip Lucas arranged for Hawker to despatch two wet-type filters and received them only two days later. The reason for this request was that the existing cleaner was a fire risk because fuel draining from the carburettor drenched it.

No 41 Squadron Royal Australian Air Force, based at Idku and flying Spitfires, was detailed to carry out operational trials in the expectation of being completely re-equipped with Typhoons in due course. These began on 13 June and were flown by nineteen pilots, all of whom were pleased by the aircrafts' performance. On 22 May Lucas left for home and Myall remained to take his place. On 24

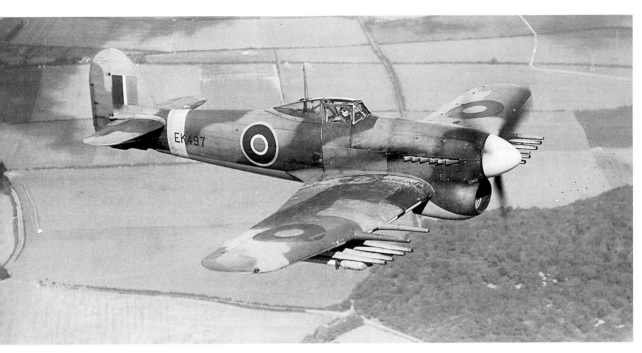

ABOVE: Typhoon armed with four 20mm cannon in the wings and eight 60lb rockets under the wings. (Philip Jarrett)

May Myall and six of the squadron's pilots moved to Landing Ground (LG) 106 at El Daba with DN323 and EJ906, about one hundred miles beyond Alexandria. The intention was for each aircraft to be flown for one hundred hours or so. In the event, 312 hours were accomplished. The trials were deemed successful and the expressed intention was to re-equip the squadron with Typhoons. Mr Gale departed for home on 12 October. Twelve Typhoons modified for desert conditions were ready for despatch to 451 Squadron in October 1943, but delivery was cancelled. No more could be spared for squadrons abroad; all would be needed for operations in Europe after the Normandy invasion.

Later, MN290 was taken to Egypt for Hawker to do cooling tests.

Chapter 6
Typical Operations

Most of the newly formed Typhoon squadrons were in No 10 Group of Fighter Command, which covered south-west England. Their operations meant flying as far as 150 miles over the sea to the target, which required excellent navigation by the formation leader in order to make a precise landfall at the intended place on the coast of France. Inaccurate navigation would mean searching for it and thus inviting the attention of *Luftwaffe* fighters and flak batteries.

Peter Brett made his first sortie in MN172 against the enemy on 29 October 1943, from Predannack in Cornwall. The task was to dive-bomb the enemy airfield at Guipavas near Brest. At briefing the pilots were warned to expect a strong flak defence; but no fighter opposition, as there was no operational squadron there. He remembers 'feeling butterflies in the stomach' – even the most experienced airmen, soldiers and sailors acknowledge the sensation when on the brink of going into action. Many would say that without this anticipatory emotion of apprehension blended with exhilaration, one's senses are not fully alert.

Carrying two 500lb bombs, the Typhoons were to cross the Channel at 'nought feet' (very low), do a battle climb (maximum speed and fully armed) to 12,000ft immediately before reaching the target, then dive at about sixty degrees to 4000ft before releasing their bombs.

BELOW: Typhoon 2B R8224 of 56 and 609 Sqdns showing initial white markings to avoid misidentification as FW190. (Bruce Robertson)

Such a low passage demanded constant vigilance to avoid hitting the sea 20ft below. He was number two in the second four, therefore would be the sixth to attack. At the top of their climb the squadron commander ordered 'Echelon Port. Arm bombs. Go!' Black puffs of smoke began to pock the sky.

The next command was 'Target three o'clock below . . . Diving now,' as the leader peeled off.

'Up to now,' says Brett, 'I had not seen the target and blindly followed my leader into a 135 degree bank and down into what seemed at the time a vertical dive. Looking ahead, I then realised that I was looking down on a grass airfield with hangars and other buildings. I pointed the nose of the aircraft at the centre of the field, glanced at the altimeter, which was unwinding very fast, and as it passed 4000ft I eased the nose up a trifle and pressed the bomb release button on the throttle lever.'

He pulled the stick back and came out of the dive gradually enough to avoid blacking out. When, flying level again, he looked around for his companions, he eventually spotted them some 4000ft above. 'I don't think I have ever felt so alone since.'

He later became adept at pulling just the right amount of G to lose vision but remain conscious during the pull-out. This time, he had to thrust the throttle into emergency boost and put the propeller into fine pitch in order to rejoin the formation.

On 2 November eight Typhoons set out on a shipping reconnaissance in the Goulet de Brest area (a *goulet* is an inlet or the narrow entrance to a harbour etc). The weather was showery and cloud base about 2000ft. They were flying at about 250ft when they spotted two ships in line astern about five miles west of Camaret-sur-Mer, whereupon the squadron commander ordered four aircraft to attack each of these. P/O Brett was number two in the flight attacking the bigger ship. Both vessels immediately opened fire with 20mm and 37mm anti-aircraft guns. It was his first experience of being under tracer fire, which he understandably 'found rather unnerving'. Although there were, he says, probably only three or four guns on each ship, the fact that

they were clustered in so small an area, towards which the Typhoons were hurtling head-on, 'made it seem very concentrated'. The bombing technique was to release the bombs as one climbed steeply to avoid flying into the masts or rigging. Leaving the scene, they saw that both ships were on fire and one was sinking. F/O Alan Palmer had been hit on the run-in and was killed. They returned to Predannack in formation with a gap where Palmer should have been: the usual way to inform those waiting on the ground how many, and who, were/was missing.

The risks inherent in really low flying are recalled by his next sortie, which was on 5 November. This was another dive-bombing mission, this time against Poulenc airfield, south of Brest. Approaching the French coast with cloud lower than 1000ft, the leader judged it useless to attempt that type of attack, so led the formation back to base. They jettisoned their bombs *en route*. Brett saw an aircraft ahead of him disappear in a cloud of spray and assumed that it had gone into the water. The pilot, however, called to say that he had hit the sea and his aeroplane was vibrating badly. On landing, it was found that two of the three propeller blades had been bent forward six inches from the tips.

At this period two Typhoon squadrons often operated together, one carrying bombs and the other as protective escort. The latter rôle was the more popular; unencumbered by bombs and bomb racks, the aircraft was much more pleasant to fly. This phase was short-lived: Spitfires were more efficient as pure fighters and the Typhoon was now highly regarded as a stable gun platform and able to withstand a lot of battering by the enemy. After the Normandy landings, Typhoons again escorted other Typhoons. Operations on which ground-attack fighters had a fighter escort were given the code name 'Ramrod'. The pilots' duty was made clear: 'The primary aim being to destroy the target'; the implication being that casualties were not a consideration. Among the lesser-known threats to life when defying the law of gravity in a flying machine was that usually inoccuous object, the drop-tank. Why, Peter Brett makes plain. On 3 December 1943, W/C

Denys Gillam, whose Wing now comprised four Typhoon squadrons, led them on a long-range sweep to the Bay of Biscay and back across the Brest peninsula. Sixteen Typhoons were in the van, at 12,500ft. Sixteen others, to their rear, kept station at 12,000ft. The intention was to incite the enemy to try to intercept them. A large formation of Spitfires accompanied them at 20,000ft to deal with the hoped-for Me109s or FW190s.

Gillam was an expert fighter pilot at any altitude, who had shot down eight enemy aircraft in the Battle of Britain and another soon after. Douglas Bader described him as 'the unrivalled maestro of the low-level attack technique'.

When a formation used drop tanks (which each held forty-five gallons), one under either wing, the drill was to take off on main tanks, switch to one drop tank when ordered by the leader, switch to the second when told to and to drop both when the leader gave the signal. Using drop tanks involved guesswork, as there were no gauges to tell a pilot how much of the auxiliary fuel he had used; and it was impossible to make an accurate mental calculation because the rate of consumption depended on the engine revolutions and boost, which varied during a sortie. On this occasion, when W/C Gillam signalled his pilots to release their burdens, containing petrol vapour and the dregs of their contents, the sixteen pilots at 12,000ft found themselves in an air space cluttered with falling aluminium cylinders from the sixteen ahead and above. Taking violent evasive action to avoid these,

BELOW: Typhoon IB on rocket trials September 1943. (Bruce Robertson)

they were in considerable danger of colliding with one-another. To make matters more uncomfortable for Brett, his empty tanks resisted all attempts to get rid of them. The Wing leader allowed him to break formation over base and land first.

It was routine for a pilot to fly two operations a day across the Channel from bases in the west of England, so both attackers and defenders soon got to know each other's habits. This necessitated introducing variety to an occupation that was by its nature restricted by inherent parameters. The intricacies of low flying and of dive bombing reveal ingenuity within these limits on the part of both the attackers and the defenders.

Typhoon pilots soon found that when doing shipping reconnaissance or fighter sweeps, if they flew low and too close to the French coast and parallel to it, the German heavy coastal artillery would open fire: not in the expectation of scoring any hits, but so that the shell bursts would throw up huge quantities of water, which compelled the pilots to increase their altitude enough for the light flak to have a go at them. There was an element of mischievousness about this as well as murderous intent.

Set patterns of dive bombing enabled the flak gunners to anticipate the Typhoons' next move and line up their gunsights accordingly. As Peter Brett explains: 'These dive-bombing attacks on Noball (the code name for attacks on V-1 and V-2 flying bomb launching sites) targets were now getting to be routine affairs and the German AA gunners were becoming wary of any formation of aircraft approaching the area. Consequently the flak was gradually becoming heavier and more accurate.'

Varying the method of attack was the obvious riposte. The standard fighter formation by now was two pairs of aircraft in the slighty staggered line abreast of a finger four; two finger fours, one astern of the other, were the usual number involved. The dives before bomb release were made in echelon. Obviously, when the attackers changed formation the defenders knew that they were about to bomb. S/L Dring, commanding 183 Squadron, devised a drill for attacking in finger fours. This was done by

flying past the target, then calling 'Ready . . . Ready . . . Go!' On the executive command he half-rolled, then pulled out on the bombing angle. The rest of his four would follow in the order three, four, two. At the instant when the CO's number two began his roll, the leader of the second four would lead them down in the same order. Having practised it thoroughly, when they put it into effect they found that they could get all aircraft into a dive within six or seven seconds. In consequence, the gunners could not concentrate on any one aircraft but were forced to put up a barrage, when luck played a large part in their prospects of hitting any. The fact that the aircraft were diving close behind one another did not affect the bombing accuracy, as they were all doing the same speed at the same angle of dive and each pilot could safely ignore the others while he aimed his bombs. All each of them had to do was make sure he did not start his pull-out before the man in front of him: if he did pull out prematurely, the one in front might pull out into him.

Ian Ross, of 404 Squadron operating from Needs Oar Point, tells of flying MN369 as number two in a pair on an armed reconnaissance on 14 June 1944, carrying two 1000lb bombs. He and his number one attacked a road system south-west of Caen from a height of 100ft. The fuses should have been set for six seconds delay, but detonated on impact. He remarks, mildly enough, 'lifting the aircraft about 200ft'. In reality it must have felt like being hurled upwards as though a small volcano had erupted immediately beneath.

The consequence was that the 'engine became uneven and over-heated and some instruments failed including speedometer'. But, the 'aircraft remained flyable and enabled successful landing on large field which turned out to be airfield B3 under construction. Apart from the broken pitot head and minor damage to the skin, only the unserviceable engine would have prevented it from taking off again.'

B3 was the first newly built airfield in Normandy to become operational.

Ian Ross was fortunate not to be flying the same aeroplane on 26 July 1944, when it blew up entering a dive at Rocancourt, Calvados.

On 12 July 1944, now a member of 193 Squadron and based at airfield B15, in France, he was taking off on another armed reconnaissance as number two to the Wing Leader when his port tyre burst, 'causing the aircraft to spin off runway 360 degrees'. The port undercarriage collapsed and the propeller blades buckled. The Typhoon came to rest on a wingtip, the propeller and the starboard wheel. The port bomb casing was grazing the ground. The runway was immediately declared non-operational and the mission aborted. The Engineer Officer reported virtually no serious damage to the mainframe. The aircraft, DN256, was later transferred to No 56 Operational Training Unit and pursued its existence until 27 July 1946, when it was struck off charge.

Before joining 197 Squadron as a flight commander in January 1945, F/L G. B. Hartley had been flying Spitfire VBs, spotting for the naval bombardment that was a prime component of the massive D-Day assault on Normandy.

The Typhoons carried two bombs under each wing which were dropped with a slight delay between them so that the first one exploded the second one while both were in the air. There was a perforation in the second bomb through which the blast of the first one passed and caused a striker to detonate it. In this way, anti-personnel shrapnel was scattered.

'Unfortunately,' he recalls, 'the striker would detonate the bomb when dropped "safe" as it hit the ground: so anybody with a misfiring engine had to turn away at low level to avoid being blown up by his own bomb.'

Chapter 7
The Typhoon's Armament

An accurate dive-bomber able to carry two 1000lb bombs, a formidable strafer of troops, road vehicles, tanks and railway locomotives with its four 20mm cannons, the Typhoon reached its apogee of destructive capability as a launcher of eight rockets, which could be fired in pairs or a salvo of all eight simultaneously. These offered a variety of warheads: the 60lb explosive, 60lb phosphorus incendiary, 40lb armour-piercing and 40lb anti-personnel. The design of this last was fiendishly ingenious. It had a small propeller in the nose, which, when the missile was fired, rotated to unscrew a thread that released a three-foot telescopic probe. The front end of the probe hit the ground first, which prevented the rocket burying itself before the charge exploded, thus ensuring the maximum blast effect.

ABOVE: An armourer fitting the electrical plug to a rocket by which it will be fired. (Philip Jarrett)

BELOW: An armourer tightening the outer casing of a Typhoon's cannon. (Philip Jarrett)

The fire power of a salvo was considered equal to a broadside from a light cruiser.

Aiming a rocket was easier than bomb aiming. The gunsight used when firing the cannons could be adapted for rockets and various angles of dive; and whereas a shell or bullet is subject to the pull of gravity from the instant it is fired, a rocket, for the first two or three seconds, maintained a virtually level path. The recoil of four 20mm cannons reduced an aeroplane's speed by 40mph. A rocket's trajectory depended on the speed at the instant it was fired. The missile itself travelled at some 600mph while burning. To that was added the speed of the Typhoon, which might be anything from 200 to 400mph. In level flight, of course, the weight and bulk of rockets and their rails, and on occasion long-range tanks as well, had an adverse aerodynamic effect that greatly reduced speed; but their weight increased it in the dive.

An outstanding exponent of rocketry, who

CAP BLANC NEZ   TARGET XII/5

Observatory

Building surrounded by masts

Monument

TARGET   CAP BLANC NEZ

Light A.A.

ABOVE: Example of target photograph for Typhoon squadrons. Radars indicated here are 2 Giant *Würtzburgs* and a *Freya*. (Bruce Robertson)

displayed his skill to great effect when flying Typhoons, was a Belgian, Raymond Lallement, known as 'Cheval'. Having escaped from Belgium, he joined 609 Squadron in July 1941

as a sergeant pilot, was commissioned and won a DFC. He converted to Typhoons in 1942. After six months at the Napier factory as a works pilot, followed by a period as a flight commander in 198 Squadron, he took command of 609 in 1944. His favourite targets were tanks, about which he wrote: 'The real point was to trace the tanks and kill them before they could run for shelter. When they were in the open a vertical dive was best, but not all pilots could put their aircraft into such a position, since one always gains the impression within the aircraft that the dive is steeper than is really the case.' The method he recommended of checking that an aircraft was in a

LEFT: Rear view of cockpit canopy fairing in moulded Perspex. (Philip Jarrett)

ABOVE: Typhoon JP853 of 486 Sqdn. (Philip Jarrett)

vertical dive was to do a roll: if the attitude was less than vertical, the pull of gravity would be felt when the aircraft was on its back. In a vertical dive one did not experience such an effect. A stringent injunction indeed.

When a vertical or near-vertical dive was impossible, pilots made a shallow one from a height between 300 and 500ft, fired from a range of 500 yards and climbed away immediately with four or five seconds to gain a height at which they would avoid splinters when the rocket exploded.

This form of armament had three advantages: accuracy, as when aiming a gun; the explosive force of a bomb; and the penetrative power of a shell.

Chapter 8

Preparing for the Normandy Invasion

In Britain, during the spring and early summer of 1944, the civilian population as well as the men and women of the British and Allied forces stationed there, knew they must be on the brink of a climactic event that had to achieve the defeat of Germany. If it failed to do so, Britain and the rest of Western Europe (with the exception of resolutely neutral Sweden and Switzerland) would be doomed under the rule that Germany had tried to impose in 1870 and again in 1914. Security was tight, but common sense and a growing atmosphere of expectancy indicated that the invasion of Continental Europe must be imminent.

Second Tactical Air Force (2 TAF) had been formed on 1 June 1943 to prepare for the event and several Fighter Command squadrons were posted to it. On 5 November 1943, Fighter Command's name was changed to Air Defence of Great Britain. This was unpopular because of the magnificent reputation this Command had won in the war's early years and the fact that it was still aggressive as well as defensive. On 15 October 1944 its former – and proud – nomenclature was restored.

Typhoons figured prominently in the work of interdiction, destroying bridges and other features in France, Belgium and Holland to hinder road and rail traffic. The Typhoon squadrons had been much engaged on 'Noball' operations. Now enemy coastal radar stations were prime targets: not only those that would otherwise detect the aircraft that were to cover the invasion, but also others on different parts of the coast, to mislead the enemy about the probable invasion area. All six of the long-range stations south of Boulogne were destroyed before D-Day and fifteen others so badly damaged that they were unserviceable.

When Typhoons operated in squadron strength it became usual for one flight to carry rockets and the other, bombs.

Peter Brett's logbook shows that the radar station on Cap d'Antifer was 183 Squadron's first target of this kind, on 24 May 1944; but they found 10/10 cloud over it, so had to abort. Next day, when he flew JP382, they attacked two on the same trip. The first was on the northern outskirts of Boulogne and the second at Hardelot, just south of the port.

'Both were our first low-level attacks. Since we knew that Boulogne would be heavily defended, the CO decided that we would fly inland well north of Boulogne, turn back and pick up the railway tracks then follow this down to just south of Wimereux, when we would turn out to the coast and, we hoped, hit it at the site of the radar station. We would then attack with cannon and fire four of our rockets. After the attack we would carry on heading straight out to sea, turn south when out of sight of the coast, fly by dead reckoning until we were opposite Hardelot and then turn into the coast again where, once again, we should strike our target and attack using cannon and our four remaining rockets. Everything worked out perfectly. The defences at Boulogne were caught by surprise and most of us had completed our attacks before the flak started. When it did, we were followed out to sea by a veritable hail of 20mm and 37mm tracer. The gunners at Hardelot were also not fully alert. We once again managed to start our attack before the flak reacted. Since this time we were coming in from the sea, the gunners could see us much earlier. Luckily there was not such a concentration of guns. Nobody was hit and

Opposite page: Type of target photograph for Typhoon squadrons on Rhubarb operations. This, taken 31.12.43 was updated as annotation shows. (Bruce Robertson)

both stations were put out of action for at least twenty-four hours.'

On 27 May they were sent to attack a 'Freya' station at Fruges, but there was a thick haze and even down at 2000ft they could not find it. (Freya was a type of German radar.) However, on 2 June they were able to attack the radar at Cap d'Antifer, which was a major one that covered the whole of the approaches to the intended invasion area. Brett flew MN576.

Other squadrons in the Wing also made frequent attacks on radar sites, including several that were far from the true invasion

area, to bluff the Germans.

The variety of targets allocated to the squadron is typical of the operations carried out by all Typhoon Wings and F/O Brett's recollections of them are clear. On the morning of 10 June he was flying as number two to W/C J. M. Bryan on an armed reconnaissance southeast of Caen, when, as they swung round south of the city, Bryan evidently saw something of interest below and peeled off in a steep dive to starboard. They went down to about 600ft, where Bryan went into a steep starboard turn, Brett about 20ft above him. Suddenly there was a burst of flame and the Wing Commander's aircraft rolled onto its back and dived into the ground. Brett broke violently to port and pulled up. As he climbed away a stream of tracer followed him, just missing his starboard

Below: 174 Sqdn, France 1944. Aircraft wearing Invasion stripes. Pilots L to R: F/Sgt Adams, P/O Boucher, F/L Moore, S/L Pitt-Brown, F/L Grantam, F/L Montgomery, F/Sgt Hodges. (Bruce Robertson)

wing. Instinctively he turned starboard into the gunfire. Afterwards, the number three told him that the tracer suddenly swung to port at the same instant and missed him widely. He had been advised at Operational Training Unit always to turn into flak: the gunner, trying to follow the target, would over-correct. It worked.

That afternoon's mission was an attack on a convoy of armoured fighting vehicles (AFVs). The formation attacked from low level, all eight of Brett's rockets hit a tank and blew its turret off – it was hurled into the air above him. On 15 June he led an attack on a ferry at Le Havre, which was hit and caught fire. His next three sorties were abandoned owing to thick haze or low cloud.

On 8 July he landed in France for the first time, at Advanced Landing Ground (ALG) B8, near Bayeux. His introduction to these airstrips was typical of the general experience. Landing caused billows of dust. Take-offs were extremely hazardous for everyone except the first pair. Taxying from the dispersal area was dangerous enough, with every pilot on a zig-zag course to peer through the dusty haze

whipped up by the preceding aircraft. When his squadron took off to attack armoured fighting vehicles reported to be south-west of Caen, he was leading the second four. Two pairs took off ahead of him, which reduced his visibility to 20ft. As he and his number two opened the throttles and surged forward, the haze grew so thick that he could not see ahead at all and very little on either side. With the help of the gyro compass he managed to steer fairly straight, hoping that he would not run off the pierced steel planking (PSP) runway before he felt the aeroplane lifting. He was not able to see clearly until he had reached 200ft.

On 12 July the squadron flew from their base at Hurn. Their first target was again the Giant Würzburg radar at Cap d'Antifer, on which the squadron commander, S/L Felix Scarlett, flying MN806, was to lead a four-aircraft formation. This time, he ordered a new form of attack. Brett would climb to 8000ft, leading the other two, and begin a gentle turn just inland of the target. Scarlett would attack at zero feet, intending to hit the base of the aerial. When he was in position for the run-in he would call Brett, who would begin a sixty-degree dive.

BELOW: 56 Sqdn Typhoons on 21 April 1943. (Philip Jarrett)

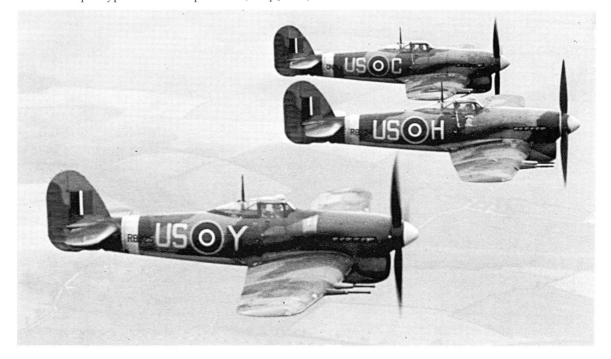

ABOVE: Typhoon IB fully armed with four 20mm cannon and eight 60lb rockets. (Bruce Robertson)

The plan was to co-ordinate their attacks in the hope that while the anti-aircraft gunners concentrated on the three Typhoons overhead, Scarlett would be able to dart in unmolested and rocket the target. The timing of the two run-ins was accurate, but instead of aiming at the three that were diving from 8000ft the flak was directed at the CO: his aircraft burst into flames and crashed into the base of the aerial with a huge explosion. The other three Typhoons' rockets struck within the target area. It was only when a newspaper mentioned his death that the squadron became aware that their popular commander was 'the Honourable' younger brother of Lord Abinger.

They stayed overnight at B8 in order to make another attack on the Le Havre ferry the following morning. This was the last sortie of Peter Brett's first tour of operations.

David Ince was one of several volunteer Army officers who were seconded to the RAF. They were destined for tactical reconnaissance (Tac-R) squadrons and aerial photography was part of their course. Ground attack was what he really wanted to do. Completing his training on Hurricanes and Spitfires, he was about to go on to Mustangs and a posting to a Tac-R squadron when he saw an opportunity to convert to Typhoons: the fighter he most ardently wished to fly. 'If you don't ask, you don't get,' the saying goes; so he asked and, to his delight, he got to fly Typhoons for the rest of the war. This meant further training before he joined a squadron. He has written with lyrical sensitivity about flying in general. Of the 'Tiffie' he says robustly in *Combat and Competition* (Newton Publishers 1992): 'What a splendid brute of an aircraft. At plus-7 [boost] and 3700rpm the sense of power was exhilarating. The acceleration fairly pushed you in the back . . . The sheer size and weight, and the performance, demanded respect . . . Aerobatics took up a lot of sky and the spin was quite violent . . . Downwind in the circuit and the yawing effect from the undercarriage was quite pronounced . . . There was a marked increase in drag when the big twenty-four cylinder engine was throttled back and the flaps were very powerful . . . Steep approaches would be the order of the day.'

He had almost finished his conversion to the

type when fighter reconnaissance (recce) squadrons began to acquire camera-equipped Typhoons. He was given the task of delivering several of the first of these to 268 Squadron. This was followed by an interview with the formidable Denys Gillam, who was now a group captain with a DSO and the first of two bars, a DFC and two bars and an AFC. F/O Ince was posted to No 193 Squadron commanded by S/L Johnny Button. Before long the squadron was at B3, St Croix-sur-Mer, with the rest of No 146 Wing, comprising 197, 257 and 266 Squadrons, soon to be joined by 263, under Gillam with W/C Johnny Baldwin as Wing Leader. 'Baldwin,' David Ince says, 'seemed such an unemotional man, so very different from his colourful predecessor [Reggie Baker, killed in action and awarded a posthumous DSO], yet his skill and his unruffled confidence was an inspiration to all around him. In the air you sensed an exceptional and considerate leader'.

Winter came, Johnny Baldwin was due for a rest and 'Bomber' Wells took over. No 35 Wing, flying Mustangs and the camera-carrying Typhoons that David Ince had delivered, re-equipped with Spitfire XIVs. Denys Gillam kindly gave the abandoned, elderly photographic aeroplanes a good home. Not surprisingly, F/L Ince was one of the pilots detailed to fly them on unescorted sorties; the other was F/L Gerry Eaton of 257 Squadron. The aircraft were fitted with three cameras in the starboard inner gun bay, one oblique and two vertical. Their pilots had an unattractive part to play: unescorted, they made their photographic runs immediately after an attack on a heavily defended target; the madly incensed survivors in the target area retaliated by bringing every possible weapon to bear on the solitary photographer. Initially Eaton and Ince agreed to use the vertical pair of cameras only.

Low cloud compelled the latter to abandon his first sortie. Following an attack on the Headquarters of the German 15th Army at Dordrecht, which was photographed by 35 Wing, his next photographic sortie was to the *Gestapo* HQ at Rotterdam. He orbited high above the target until the Typhoons had delivered their rockets and bombs and quit the scene, and the flak had (momentarily) stopped. Then he dived at the badly damaged target (in which the records had been destroyed). The 88s opened fire again at once and he was hit. Oil spread across the windscreen and fumes invaded the cockpit. Down to 2500ft he was 'rocketing blind across the centre of Rotterdam'. Photographs taken, he scooted low across the flat landscape, still under fire and 'deluged with hot oil', making for the nearest airfield, Gilze-Rijen, which had been alerted. 'Oil continued to flood over the windscreen, obscuring my goggles and, when I raised them, stinging my eyes'. His aeroplane had been hit in the spinner and the constant speed mechanism was badly damaged.

The following weeks saw him engaged again on the Typhoons' customary tasks of attacking a variety of ground targets and working up different photo recce methods using the oblique camera. Soon, going close in and making a steep turn, these sorties were producing good results, but at even greater risk to the pilots. Then came the notion of fitting a forward-facing camera to an aircraft. 'The [photographing] technique would be very similar to low-level bombing. It would require no special training and should give really close target pictures.'

He was posted to 257 Squadron as a flight commander and resumed work on his photographic suggestion with the help of Sergeant Stan Carr, who was in charge of 6913 Servicing Echelon. After some experimenting, they achieved their objective by using a camera with a twenty-inch lens. The results were outstandingly good and resulted in the immediate development of forward oblique camera installations in the belly tanks of 35 Wing's photo recce Spitfire XIVs.

'Examples of these first "forward obliques" were forwarded to Group HQ. They requested one hundred copies which were circulated widely. Rumour had it that 35 Wing, in the person of their Commanding Officer, were not amused. We were stealing their thunder!' Imitation is the sincerest form of flattery: 35 Wing duly fitted a forward-facing camera to the belly tank of a Spitfire XIV and also circulated its photographs.

The Aircraft and Armament Experimental Establishment at RAF Boscombe Down had done some trials with napalm. F/L Ince's next new experience came when the squadron was charged with working out the best way of dropping napalm bombs. These were modified ninety-gallon drop tanks, which of course had no fins and were bound to tumble. After another member of the squadron had made one abortive trial with napalm bombs and Ince had made a satisfactory one by dropping them at very low level, the squadron was ordered to use them in an attack. The target was 'a strong point near Arnhem'. Unfortunately, instead of releasing these crude bombs at the height that David Ince had proved was the only way to deliver them accurately, the squadron commander led the way in a shallow dive to release them at 2000ft. 'The bombs tumbled all over the place.' This was the only napalm attack the RAF made in Europe. In Burma, Thunderbolts (P-47) often dropped modified droptanks containing napalm. A risky business if one of the attachments broke and one end of the tank sagged, spreading napalm under the aircraft. It happened sometimes.

Before the war, royalty and other VIPs were flown by The King's Flight, stationed at Benson in Oxfordshire. During the war it became The Photographic Reconnaissance Experimental Unit (PREU), but for security reasons was known as the Station Flight. Trials at high and low level were done with every type of British and American aircraft that could be fitted with a camera.

Ron Sewell was a Fitter II, who did the daily inspections of the engines. He says: 'They were awkward to work on and absolute bastards to start. The Koffman cartridge starters were a dead loss but our Spitfire PRU [Photographic Reconnaissance Unit] pilots who tested the cameras thought they were wonderful.' (The two words above, expressive of total disapproval, figured largely in the RAF's wartime vocabulary. One of the best known dance bands was conducted by Joe Loss. Hence the vituperation 'Who are you, Joe Loss's brother, Dead Loss?')

During July and August 1944 the unit experimented with two Typhoons that were ultimately fitted with three cameras 'one each

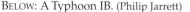

BELOW: A Typhoon IB. (Philip Jarrett)

side and one underneath. Some controls had to be re-routed to enable the cameras to fit flush'.

Sewell continues: 'Having worked on Spitfires previously, I considered them a pain in the neck for the following reasons: (1) We had no proper work stands and all work had to be done from a pair of steps. (2) The engine cowlings were rather heavy and required two to lift them off and on. (3) The Koffman cartridges made the stainless steel and porcelain pipe so hot that it burnt out after ten to twelve cartridges and when this happened it was too hot to handle for about twenty minutes. (4) We had trouble with the sleeve operating mechanism on the Napier engine, usually through lack of oil. The Napier experts had to be called. (5) You couldn't change a wheel in one minute, as you could on a Spitfire with six backs under a mainplane [lifting it]. (6)

One of the Typhoons had trouble with the magneto harness. Instead of bitumen between the leads and around the sheath, it had been filled with grease, which melted and ran all over the place and made the radio u/s (unserviceable). Sabotage was suspected and we were surrounded by the SIB (Special Investigation Branch) for a week.

He ends, rather ruefully, 'My one highlight was to taxi a Typhoon from the hangar to dispersal – the nearest I got to being a pilot.'

There was no reason to disparage this frequent task, which demanded skill and care. Many a pilot has taxied his aeroplane into another or some equally unresilient obstacle with dire consequences – for the man in the cockpit, the aircraft he was in and whatever it barged into.

Chapter 9
Normandy and Onwards

First light at 0445 hrs on 6 June 1944, D-Day for the invasion of France, better known as the Normandy landings, saw the first fighters streaming across the English Channel. The advance airborne troops (by towed glider) and paratroops had begun their landings and drops soon after midnight on the 5th. Typhoons, Tempests, Mustangs and some Spitfires were on ground attack while other Spitfires flew high to protect them from enemy fighters. On reconnaissance at 1330 hrs on 6 June, S/L P. H.

Beake of 164 Squadron, flying JP846, was credited with a FW190 destroyed and another that was shot down was credited to the squadron. Soon after, twelve Typhoons of 183 Squadron were attacking tanks when twelve Me109s appeared out of cloud and shot down and killed three of them: F/O A. R. Taylor in R8973, F/L R. W. Evans in MN432 and F/O M. H. Gee in MN478.

On D-Day plus 1, at 1600 hrs, 182, 145 and 247 Squadrons were sent to back up 61 Brigade

BELOW: Typhoon IB's rockets and cannon. (Bruce Robertson)

2nd TAF Typhoon Squadrons Order of Battle
5 June 1944

83 Group
121 Wing W/C C. L. Green
Squadrons & Aircraft On Strength
174 (18) S/L W. Pitt-Brown
175 (19) S/L J. R. Pennington-Leigh DFC
245 (18) S/L J. R. Collins DFC*
Based at Holmesley South, Hampshire

124 Wing W/C E. Haabjoern DFC
Squadrons & Aircraft On Strength
181 (16) S/L C. D. North-Lewis DFC
182 (18) Maj D. H. Barlow SAAF
247 (19) S/L R. J. McNair DFC
Based at Hurn, Hampshire

129 Wing
Squadron & Aircraft On Strength
184 (19) S/L J. Rose DFC
Based at Westhampnett, Sussex

143 Wing RCAF W/C M. T. Judd DFC AFC
Squadrons & Aircraft On Strength
438 (17) S/L F. C. Grant DFC
439 (16) S/L H. H. Norsworthy
440 (18) S/L W. H. Pentland
Based at Hurn, Hampshire

84 Group
123 Wing W/C R. E. P. Brooker DFC
Squadrons & Aircraft On Strength
198 (19) S/L J. Niblett DFC
609 (18) S/L J. C. Wells DFC
Based at Thorney Island, Hampshire

136 Wing W/C J. M. Bryan DFC
Squadrons & Aircraft On Strength
164 (18) S/L P. H. Beake DFC
183 (19) S/L F. H. Scarlett
Based at Thorney island, Hampshire

146 Wing G/C Gillam D.E. DSO DFC* AFC*
Squadrons & Aircraft On Strength
193 (19) S/L D. G. Ross DFC
197 (19) S/L D. M. Taylor
257 (18) S/L R. H. Fowkes DFM
266 (19) S/L J. W. E. Holmes DFC AFC
Based at Needs Oar Point, Hampshire

and 41 Commando, which were having difficulty in capturing Port-en-Bessin. Eight aircraft attacked a site where artillery was well dug in, while fifteen others smashed the pillboxes that surrounded the area. This enabled troops to take the port and join up with the Americans on their flank at Omaha beach.

Cloud base was about 1000ft. This made the fighter bombers highly vulnerable to light flak, which shot down fifteen Typhoons during their 493 sorties that day. Many more sustained varying amounts of damage.

Between 7 and 16 August fighting was concentrated on the Falaise pocket, a salient thirty-five miles deep and about the same at its widest part, which protruded into the area held by the Allies between Caen and twenty miles due south. On 7 August rocket-firing Typhoons were engaged all day in support of General Patton's armour. On 245 Squadron's first mission, F/L R. G. F. Lee of 245 Squadron, in MN459, was wounded by flak as he fired his rockets at some tanks. He fainted from loss of blood and, of course, lost control of his aircraft. It crashed upside-down in an area between the nearest American and German troops. He regained consciousness to find that he was hanging head-down in the cockpit. Releasing himself from his harness, he fell into the hole that the Typhoon had dug, then blacked out again. Hot oil from his engine burned his back. From time to time he became conscious, but was unable to extricate himself. Through a narrow space between the rim of the cockpit and the ground, he saw some Germans. They, taking it for granted that there was nobody lying under the wreckage, put empty tins on the aeroplane's wings and amused themselves by shooting at them. Some of their bullets hit Lee's legs. He endured his predicament for a week, subsisting on emergency rations, before American soldiers heard him hammering on the side of the fuselage and rescued him. His weight had diminished from fifteen stone to a little over nine and his legs were crippled.

In war the energy and resilience of young men are used and abused. They are the expendable material of politicians, generals, air marshals and admirals, just as much as are guns, ammunition, tanks, ships and aircraft. On 18 August there was a plethora of accidental killings by RAF and USAAF fighter-bombers using cannon, rockets and bombs: friendly fire again among the Allies caused fifty-one casualties to ground troops and demolished twenty-five vehicles.

On 14 August, F/L Cedric Henman, a flight commander in 175 Squadron, flying JR388, had to bale out near Falaise when his aircraft was hit by flak and caught fire. To discourage the anti-aircraft gunners, F/L Ambrose strafed them; which proved not to be altogether a good idea. When Henman hit the ground he hid in undergrowth and a wood, but the enemy found him and tied him to a tree preparatory to shooting him. Luckily, a German officer (and manifest gentleman) ordered them to release him. It happened that the pilot's brother, Dick, who was in a tank regiment, saw him abandon his aircraft. Cedric's troubles were not over yet, however. He was again bound to a tree and about to face summary execution when, once more, he was saved by the appearance of an enemy officer who again exhibited due regard

for the niceties of civilised warfare. Next, he was bundled aboard a lorry and driven off in a convoy – which was soon under air attack. Even ambulances were not entirely immune from being fired at: in their frenzy to get away from the forward area, German lorry drivers often put a Red Cross flag on the roof. In consequence, genuine ambulances were attracting attack. It was also on 14 August that the Supreme Allied Commander ordered that pilots were not to shoot at ambulances except in self-defence if these fired first.

Owing to the inefficiency of a naval officer, a Typhoon squadron unwittingly perpetrated the killing and wounding of comrades-in-arms by the score in a disgraceful episode that was concealed from public knowledge for decades. As a display of the Typhoon's awesome fire power, the incident would have had a profoundly daunting effect on the enemy if it had been directed at them and news of it had spread. Instead, if the truth about what

BELOW: *Fiji 6* presented by that country. (Bruce Robertson)

ABOVE: 263 Sqdn Typhoon IB MN524. Shot down by flak off St Malo 24 June 1944. (Bruce Robertson)

happened had become known, it would have wrought havoc with the morale of the Royal Navy and with the other British armed forces.

Following the invasion, Allied ships at anchor off Normandy were attacked night after night by midget submarines, E-boats (an inexplicable British nomenclature for the inshore German gunboats called *Schnellboote* – fast boats . . . so why not S-boats?) and torpedo-bombers. Enemy aircraft sowed mines in the Channel and off the Normandy coast. Royal Navy minesweepers were at sea from dawn to dusk clearing a passage for friendly shipping.

Le Havre was still in enemy hands, but on 18 August 1944 a flotilla of six began to sweep a minefield near there. This was a priority task that would enable a battleship and two cruisers to approach and shell this major port. On 26 August, during a twenty-four-hour rest, the

flotilla leader, a lieutenant-commander, received a signal ordering him to revert next morning to his previous assignment, which was to sweep betwen Portsmouth and Arromanches. In view of the importance attached to clearing the passage to Le Havre, he was perplexed by this sudden and unexpected change of task, so he sent his navigating officer to the Headquarters Ship to verify the new order. There, this officer was told that there had been a mistake, the order was now rescinded and the flotilla was to carry on sweeping the minefield that protected Le Havre. He was also assured that a new signal would be made (the naval term for 'sent') to all the other Allied armed services, cancelling the first signal and informing them that sweeping the Le Havre approaches would continue.

All Allied shipping activities were required

to be notified well in advance to all the other Allied forces. The HQ Ship should therefore have warned them immediately, but failed to inform anyone at all. Among the authorities who should have been told about the second change of task was the Flag Officer British Assault Area, a rear-admiral.The only signal the HQ Ship did transmit was the one ordering the commander of the minesweeper flotilla to continue sweeping the approach to Le Havre.

Only four ships in the flotilla were, in naval language, 'in all respects ready for sea'. Of the others, one had been damaged by a mine and another was undergoing an engine repair. Those that did sail were *Jason*, *Britomart*, *Salamander* and *Hussar*. Two trawlers accompanied them to lay buoys marking the swept channel. During the early afternoon *Hussar*'s gear developed a fault and she had to stop sweeping, but remained at sea with the others. It was a hot, sunny day and the sailors off duty basked in the sunshine.

At 1330 hrs everyone aboard the six small ships heard aircraft approaching. They were led by one of the most experienced Typhoon pilots in the RAF, W/C J. R. 'Johnny' Baldwin DFC and bar, (later also DSO), who had commanded Nos 609 and 198 Squadrons. He had shot down sixteen enemy aircraft on Typhoons, the greatest number of victories achieved with this type. Later given command of No 146 Wing, he survived the war but was killed in Korea.

The order to carry out this attack had astonished him. It was well known that the Navy had been sweeping the Le Havre area for the past week, so how could enemy craft be doing the same job? And why? He queried the order as soon as he was airborne and three times more. When he closed on the ships he again had great doubts about their identity but there was no option: he had to obey orders.

Immediately the aeroplanes opened fire, *Jason* reported the attack to Headquarters. Two minutes later her captain saw that two of his flotilla had been hit and were heeling sharply. The Typhoons came in for a second run. *Jason* fired the correct recognition signals (Very light flares) but even Baldwin's reporting these as the correct colours of the day had no effect; he

was again assured that the minesweepers were German. The Typhoons raked the flotilla again, so *Jason*'s two Oerlikons opened fire on the attackers. *Salamander*, *Hussar* and *Britomart* were burning, hit by rockets. One of the trawlers, *Colsay*, had stopped.

Eleven minutes after their first salvoes, the Typhoons flew back to base, leaving two ships sinking and one listing badly. One of the minesweepers sent her launch to pick up survivors, but it had been holed by cannon shells and soon sank. An RAF high speed launch came racing up at 45 knots three minutes later and was soon joined by two minesweepers in picking up the dead, wounded and living.

The total casualties were seventy-eight officers and ratings killed and 149 wounded. The survivors were forbidden to say anything about the event. To make the tragedy an even greater example of inefficient Staff work and communications, an RAF aircraft had flown over the flotilla and reported their identity ninety minutes before the attack.

This horrifying episode struck such guilt and shame into the Admiralty, and so great was the horror felt by the Air Ministry, the War Office the Prime Minister and, presumably his Cabinet – no doubt also by the King – that no mention was made of it in any official record that is available for scrutiny by the public. The matter is treated as though it never happened.

When John Shellard, who ended the war as a flight lieutenant, joined 263 Squadron on 1 January 1944 the Command to which it belonged was Air Defence of Great Britain (ADGB), whose squadrons, as explained elsewhere, were previously part of Fighter Command. Squadrons' bombing techniques varied. The practice of this squadron was to dive from between 8000ft and 9000ft and release between 2000ft and 3000ft. His logbook shows that on one occasion he released as low as 1500ft. He says: 'The system, prior to joining TAF in August 1944, was to fly the Channel at zero feet, climb over the coast to dive height and commence the wing-over when the target appeared behind the wing roundel. At release point, one let the nose come through the target and allowed three seconds before pressing the button. Speed at this point was usually well over 500mph.'

Describing his first operational sorties, he recalls that on low level attacks pilots flew below the top of the target whether it were a ship or a building and 'held it there until you felt that you had left it too late to avoid flying into it, then released the bomb and pulled up sufficiently to go over the top. Climbing away or pulling up too high was thought to be asking for trouble.

'Until about May 1944 when rockets were introduced, 250lb or 500lb bombs were carried. The C.O. and one other pilot went on a course for a week, came back and told us how it worked, fired at some rocks off Bolt Head and that was it.' Normally 60lb heads were used, but when, on 15 June 1944, flying MN295, he took part in an attack on a submarine docked at St Peter Port, Guernsey, it was with 25lb solid head rocket projectiles (R/P).

On 6 August the squadron joined 146 Wing, 2nd TAF at B3. The bridgehead was safe but the Army was stuck half-way to Caen whilst Patton was sweeping round towards the east and back. The main trouble about attacks, John

Shellard recalls, was that it was difficult to assess the result: 'e.g. [he quotes from his logbook] Aug 8th, attack on red smoke pinpointing troops. (The flying time was thirty-five minutes, which indicates how close we were to the front line). Often B Flight took off as eight aircraft and came home in twos as and when targets were found. On Aug 13th [flying MN407] we had an armed recce over the Falaise area. This lasted one hour, so we were searching a large area when we found some tanks and trucks. The tanks were attacked at a thirty degree angled dive, holding the speed to the recommended level. The tanks were in a line, nose to tail, under some trees and I fired in pairs [of rockets] as did the other three Tiffies (I think). Certainly when we came round again at a low level, three were on fire so we cannoned the truck and the wreckage before pulling up to 1000ft to return to base.'

On 16 August the Wing took off in force to attack a château. His log book records that this was near Bernay, but that, he says, might have been a phonetic spelling. '263 were the last to attack and I was last in 263 [flying JR382]. We were using R/P and when I went down, again thirty degrees, the place was covered in smoke. Suddenly there was a clearance of the smoke and there in the centre of what looked like a

BELOW: Fighter Reconnaissance (FR) Typhoon IB EK427 of 268 Sqdn. (Bruce Robertson)

Above: Typhoon MN974 of AFDU, CFE and FLS. Written off at Tangmere 13.6.45: lost power on take-off, so pilot retracted undercarriage. (Bruce Robertson)

courtyard was a small building. Using that as the aiming point, I fired a salvo and pulled up to rejoin. At debriefing, Johnny Baldwin, our W/C, asked who had been the last man in from 263 and what he had fired at. I told him and he asked if I'd seen the result. I confessed that I hadn't as I was too busy looking out for five squadrons (minus me) milling around. "Pity," he said, "you blew the damn place up." I must have hit the ammo store. The château was a German HQ.'

On the 18th, in a formation of four, he was on an hour's armed reconnaissance in JR382 when they spotted some tanks and transport near a crossroads. Such sorties were flown at 1000ft so that the pilots could see what was going on. Zero feet would have been useless over the *bocage*, with its trees, hedges and sunken roads. They set two vehicles on fire and blocked the crossroads. Control warned them that twenty-plus FW190s were in the area, but these were not seen; they were probably at 20,000ft.

On the same day, 'on a recce of forty-five minutes, everywhere I looked there were burning vehicles. We reckoned that we added about twelve to the general chaos but the sight from the air was a great morale booster as we seemed to be stuck around Caen, and this showed that we were kicking the Hun where it hurt'.

The squadron spent the next few months attacking railways, bridges, airfields and enemy-occupied buildings, until the day of the Rhine crossing.

The intensity of the air battle, whether air-to-air or air-to-ground, and the burden carried by the Typhoon squadrons are starkly revealed in the statistics for the period 6 June to 1 September 1944.

	Losses	Total Force Engaged	%age lost	Initial Force	%age lost
Spitfire	804	1954	41	1166	68
Hurricane	4	31	13	29	12.9
Mustang	229	462	49.6	233	98
Mosquito	128	398	32.8	282	35.4
Typhoon	491	383	28	874	56.2

S/L R. E. G. Sheward DFC was one of the many Britons resident in Argentina who returned to England, where he had been educated, to volunteer for the armed forces. He had flown Hurricanes and Spitfires before joining No 266 (Rhodesia) Squadron, in 146 Wing, 2nd TAF on 1 November 1944 at Antwerp. His first sorties were to rocket railway trucks, enemy-occupied buildings and road and rail bridges in Flanders and Holland. On 19 November he was given command of A Flight and on the 26th was posted to 263 Squadron, in the same Wing, as B Flight commander.

Next day the Wing, commanded by G/C D. E. Gillam, was ordered to destroy the *Gestapo* Headquarters in Amsterdam, where records naming members of the Resistance were kept. The attack had to be made between 1230 and 1330 hrs, when the children at a school nearby would be at home for lunch. The attack was led by the Wing Leader. Four of 263's aircraft, each carrying two 1000lb bombs and led by their C.O., S/L R. D. Rutter DFC, were given the *Gestapo* building as their target. F/L Sheward and two Canadians, F/O Hamilton and F/O Woodward, made up the section. The rest of the Typhoons were detailed to other targets or to set fire to what remained of the *Gestapo*

BELOW: June 1944. F/L Moran (killed August 1944) and his ground crew. Right to left: George 'Pad' Crump, Photographic member of squadron, 'Chalky' White, 'Jacko' Jackson. (Mrs Ann Crump)

ABOVE: LK427, Typhoon FRIB of 268 Sqdn, seen at 5MU Kemble, March 1945. (Bruce Robertson)

premises with incendiary rockets. Ronnie Sheward recalls: 'Our eight bombs went straight through the front of the building'.

Three days after this, 146 Wing made a similar attack on the *Gestapo* H.Q. in Rotterdam, on which Sheward led a formation of eight against the anti-aircraft defences in the dock area.

On 1 January 1945 Rutter was sent on rest and handed over to S/L Rumbold DFC who went on leave a day later, which left F/L Sheward, the senior flight commander, in command of the squadron. His first task that day was Army support, on which he was about to take off with seven other Typhoons, when the proceedings were interrupted by the arrival of eight FW190s and eight Me109s. These made a poorly executed attack, flying straight and level instead of weaving. Two were shot down by Mustangs that happened to be on reconnaissance and anti-aircraft guns claimed nine.

Soon after midnight on New Year's Eve 1944 the *Luftwaffe* made a large-scale onslaught: launched from the air, it was the equivalent of the intensive shelling that in the Great War had been called a 'Hate'. In those days the 'PBI' (poor bloody infantry) in their damp, rat-infested, malodorous trenches and dugouts were the victims. Now, it was aimed at 2nd TAF's airfields. The Operation was codenamed *Bodenplatte*, which literally suggested the use of a flat-iron on the ground and is the equivalent of the English expression grand slam. The ground in question lay in Belgium and Holland. The objective was to destroy so many Allied aircraft that some respite from their constant battering of the German Army would be achieved, even if only for a short time.

Eindhoven, where 124 and 123 Wings, each comprising four squadrons, were based, suffered worst.

Attacking Force, Operation *Bodenplatte*

Strength	Types	Target	Comment
I, II, III/JGI 69 a/c	Me109G 109K		
	FW190A FW190D	St Denis Westrem	Lost 22
I, II, III/JG3 65 a/c	Me109G 109K	Eindhoven	Lost 17
I, II, III/JG6 64 a/c	Me109G FW190D	Volkel	Lost at least 12
I, II, III/JG26 60 a/c	FW109G 109K	Brussels-Evere & Grimbergen	Lost 20 to 22
& IIIJG/54 17 a/c	Me109G & 109K	Same targets Brussels-Melsbroek	Total lost by both JG
I, II, III, IV/JG27 55 a/c			
& IV/JG54 17 a/c	Me109G & FW190D	Same target	29 a/c
I, II, III/JG77	Me 109K	Antwerp-Deurne	Lost 11

In addition to the Typhoon squadrons on these airfields, there were three French and three Polish squadrons of the RAF flying Spitfire IXs.

Deployment of Typhoon Squadrons on the Above Airfields

B78 Eindhoven, Holland
165 Typhoons. Squadrons Nos 137, 168, 181, 182, 247,438 RCAF, 439 RCAF, 440 RCAF. 141 Typhoons had to be written off.

B89 Volkel, Holland
146 Typhoons and Tempests. Typhoon squadrons: 174, 175, 184 pus four Tempest squadrons. Eleven Typhoons had to be written off.

B70 Antwerp-Deurne
162 Typhoons plus three RAF French Spitfire squadrons. Ten Typhoons had to be written off.

Metz-Frascaty, in France, and three Belgian airfields, where USAAF P-47 fighters were based, Le Culot, St Trond and Asche, were also attacked.

The enemy lost 193 aircraft. This was a last desperate fling by the *Luftwaffe*. Many of the pilots had as little as sixty flying hours. They had to keep formation and follow an experienced leader (of whom there were few) and flares fired from the ground served as signposts en route. For its ambitious but hopeless bravado in the small hours of New Year's Day, the *Luftwaffe* had some 800 aircraft serviceable. Those pilots who were not fully trained flew only in formations led by an experienced fighter pilot or bomber crew. The *Luftwaffe* statistics available are in round figures: some 280 Allied aircraft were destroyed on the ground, 100 damaged and about eighty shot down. Losses were: 300 aircraft shot down, 170 pilots killed and sixty-seven taken prisoner. The significant factor was that, whereas the Allies had plenty of aircraft and combat-experienced aircrew with which to replace them, Germany had hardly any.

The verdict of *Generalleutnant* Adolf Galland, Commander of Fighters, was: 'In this total effort we sacrificed our last substance'.

The air operation had been a corollary to a massive, desperate and nearly successful offensive in the Ardennes. Known as the Battle of the Bulge, it had been ordered by Hitler and

BELOW: Typhoon IB EK183 served in 56 and 609 (as shown) Sqdns. (Bruce Robertson)

was commanded by *Feldmarschall* von Rundstedt. It opened with an artillery barrage along the chosen front from Monschau to Trier and the Germans were relying on bad weather to keep the Allied air forces grounded. The ultimate objective was Antwerp, which the British 11th Armoured Division had entered on 4 September. The land battle continued until the third week of January, when the Germans began to fall back.

The efficacy of the Typhoons' tactics and their pilots' courage were acknowledged by General Speidel, *Feldmarschall* Rommel's Chief of Staff. 'During the German endeavour to break the siege of our forces, we were continuously subjected to massive attacks by Typhoons. Our convoys were decimated because the Typhoon tactics were to hit both the head and the tail of our columns, then to wreck the immobilised armour caught in the trap.' In one day eighty-four tanks were destroyed, thirty-five heavily damaged and twenty-one damaged. Three Typhoons were shot down.

General Bayerlin, commanding the *Panzer Lehrer* Division reported: 'Our Division was denied use of main roads and our movements were totally interrupted by daytime as a result of the heavy losses sustained after the terrible and repeated attacks made by rocket Typhoons.'

On 5 January 1945 while eight Typhoons with Sheward at their head were waiting to take off on a reconnaissance requested by the Army, a Typhoon arrived overhead and set about trying to dislodge a hung-up bomb. It was more destructive than the enemy had been four days earlier: the bomb fell on the airfield, exploded and damaged four of the waiting aircraft. Flying Control suggested abandoning the operation, but not wishing to let the soldiers down, Ronnie Sheward led the four surviving aircraft off, as requested by the Army, and did some successful strafing of roads and buildings.

On 7 March R. E. G. Sheward was promoted to squadron leader and returned to 266 as Commanding Officer.

Chapter 10
The Servicing Crews

The general public and many who served in the wartime RAF have never heard of the RAF's Servicing Commandos. It is common knowledge that on the strength of every squadron there have always been technicians – in RAF language, technical tradesmen – who maintain the aircraft in airworthy condition: fitters, riggers, flight mechanics, armourers, electricians, instrument repairers, radio mechanics, radar mechanics *et al.* In those fighter squadrons, however, that had to operate from forward bases as soon as possible after a beach landing, their ground crews and all the workshop equipment could not go ashore until the Army or the RAF Regiment had secured an airfield, or an RAF airfield construction squadron and the Royal Engineers had built one.

The RAF therefore formed servicing commando units (SCU) consisting of trades-men who were given rigorous ground defence training and issued with rifles or Sten guns. After taking part in a landing they were entitled to wear the Combined Operations badge.

The runways at temporary airstrips, also known as landing grounds, were made from PSP: interlocking rectangles with holes in them to reduce weight and enable the maximum to be transported. All ranks lived in tents.

On the Normandy beach-head dust was the bugbear of pilots and those who kept the engines in working order, because it clogged the carburettor. Vokes, the manufacturers of this component, quickly designed an air filter and the Typhoons were flown in turn to England for these to be fitted. On the return journey each brought two eighteen-gallon barrels of beer attached to the bomb racks under the wings: the usual practice when aircraft were returning from a visit to England.

George Ellis was an armourer in 3209

BELOW: Typhoon JR193 of 182 Sqdn and (as seen) coded PA of No 3 Tactical Exercise Unit. (Bruce Robertson)

Servicing Commando. He writes: 'We were selected to service the Typhoons before the Normandy landings.' For the Typhoon pilots to practise rocket-firing, these weapons were fitted with concrete war heads instead of explosive ones. 'Loading the rockets entailed sliding them onto the rails, putting a piece of thick copper wire into the necessary bracket, bending it U-shaped as a retainer for the rockets. After that we had a five-pin testing lamp which we put in the appropriate plug. If the bulb lit up we knew the switch was on in the cockpit: a mishap by the pilots at times. When the pilot pressed the firing button the rockets shot off, severing the copper wire.'

Arthur Carkeek, a mechanic in 184 Squadron, reminds us that 'the Typhoon or Tiffy was not an easy engine to work on, very difficult to start and in the winter had to be run up during the night to be kept warm'. The squadron moved from landing ground B5 to Beauvais and on to Antwerp. 'The second week here the German Army brought up 88mm guns. They were only a mile away and could

hit anything on the ground. Our squadron got hit hard in one attack. One Typhoon blew up and others were damaged. All ground crew escaped, we had been working on them at the time the warning came to take cover. The next attack saw one Spit, one Typhoon and one Thunderbolt all receive direct hits as they came in one at a time. All three had their wheels on the runway when the shells hit. All three pilots escaped. One evening HQ gave orders for four Typhoons to attack the 88s. Up went the Auster spotter followed by the Typhoons. Spotter then moved away and down the Typhoons went, rockets gone, a quick end to the 88s, no more trouble after that.'

An armourer's trade was probably more subject to accidents than any other: throughout the history of military aviation, guns, bombs and rockets have caused death and injury by firing or exploding while being handled. When the squadron reached Volkel, in Holland, Carkeek recalls that, 'during November we had an accident in which one of my mates died of injuries from the blast of four rockets'. When

BELOW: Tempest I HM599 in Feb 1943. Originally Typhoon II, one of two prototypes ordered as latter marque. (Bruce Robertson)

eight Typhoons operated together, it was common practice for a ninth to follow astern in case anyone had to withdraw on account of some defect in engine, radio etc. If none suffered a fault, the spare man returned to base at about half-way to the target. 'We sent out eight plus one on this op, but it was cancelled before take-off. All the aircraft returned to dispersals, where the armourers unplugged the rockets. I saw LAC Ken Wolfreys [twenty years old] go to one Typhoon. He did the rockets on the starboard wing and went to the port wing to do the same thing. Must have been an electrical fault here, as the four rockets left the racks just as he was about to unplug them. He was taken to hospital at Eindhoven but died a short while after from the injuries he received.'

Gwyn 'Tich' George, an engine fitter, recalls that in Normandy and on many British airfields: 'We didn't have the luxury of a petrol bowser. High octane (100) fuel was in two-gallon cans. In Normandy they were brought up from the beach-head in DUKWs [amphibian American vehicles known as 'ducks'] and when refuelling took place each can was handed up to a chap standing on the wing. He punched two diagonally opposed holes in the can by means of a commando-type dagger with which we had been issued. The fuel was then poured into a square funnel lined with chamois leather in order to filter out any moisture caused by condensation.'

This primitive method of fuelling aircraft on campaign was common. The most valued perquisites when Desert Air Force took possession of an abandoned German airstrip in North Africa were the cleverly designed petrol cans, easy to pour from, that the enemy left behind; hence the name 'jerrican'.

Another Normandy veteran, Jack Clabburn, who was a corporal armourer, reports: 'We had been briefed on the essential need for a quick turn around of the Typhoons, as they would be a prime target whilst on the airstrip. Preparation was important, so we had prepared the rockets fitted with 20lb warheads, a supply of test lamps and belts of 20mm cannon ammunition. We also had to prepare ourselves for the dust storm conditions we would have to work in. I had a German field

cap pulled down over my ears, gas goggles and a scarf around my mouth.

'When the first Typhoon started up its engine we tested and plugged in the eight rockets. As it taxied away the dust enveloped the next aircraft, we had to walk towards it until we could see its propeller emerge from the dust.

'We did have first sight of a Typhoon in action over the air strip. The Canadians had organised a film show in a large tent. While we were waiting for the show to start, somebody dashed in and said that there was a dogfight overhead. We went out and saw a Me109 with a Spitfire on his tail. The Me109 did a very tight turn with vapour streaming off its wingtips into a cloud. It came out again right in front of a Typhoon which let go a burst of cannon fire. The German pilot promptly rolled his plane over and baled out, landing in a field nearby. The Canadians raced over to him, we thought to capture him. Instead the first one took his Luger and they all trooped back, leaving the bewildered German pilot standing in the field.'

George Bentham, an engine fitter who was in 6263 Echelon, which serviced 257, 263 and 266 Squadrons, remembers that 'getting the cowling off the radiator assembly needed two men to handle it. The biggest problem was in taking the Glycol/oil/air intake assembly off. You could drain the oil, but this still left some in the connections which had to be split. To get at them, you were in direct line of fire when the remaining oil came out, covering you with about a gallon of dirty oil. The only way to get this off was to get your mate to throw a gallon of petrol over you, then go and wash. A very dangerous practice.

'The other regular problem was getting started with a Koffman cartridge, the engine very often backfiring through the air intake and causing a fire, so you had to have somebody standing by with a fire extinguisher. We used to have bets on getting it started with one cartridge.'

When the unit arrived at airfield B3 at St Croix-sur-Mer, it was shelled by an 88mm gun at Le Havre. A rocket attack by Typhoons silenced it.

'Our longest and worst period of attack was at an ex-*Luftwaffe* airfield at Berchem near

ABOVE: MN454 of 183 and 164 Sqdns, latter based Thorney Island. Shot down on D-Day by FW190s near Caen 6.6.44. Here seen on King George VI's inspection at Northolt. Third and fourth Air officers from left, ACM Sir Trafford Leigh-Mallory and AM Sir Hugh McEvoy. (Bruce Robertson)

Antwerp, during the latter part of 1944, by V-1s and V-2s.'

One night a careless armourer crossed some wires, which caused two armour-piercing rockets to fire. They went straight through George Bentham's billet [hut]. It was his half day, but he was changing the propeller on an aircraft; otherwise he would have been in there, getting ready to go out.

On New Year's Eve he was on night duty, which entailed periodically running up the engines of six Typhoons on account of the cold weather. At midnight the airfield was bombed and 'I can remember standing in the middle of all the aircraft blazing away at them with my issue Bren gun'.

He thinks that while at B3 he and another engine fitter must have set the record for a complete engine change. A Typhoon taking off at 0900 hrs suffered a major oil pipe burst, but managed to fly a circuit and land just before the engine seized solid. They worked all night while their corporal brought them food and drink, and were able to finish and test the engine for the aircraft to take off next morning at 0900 hrs.

In RAF slang, airmen were referred to by their trade followed by 'basher'. G. T. Roberts, a Leading Aircraftman instrument repairer, introduces his contribution to the Typhoon story with 'I was a Group 1 LAC instrument basher'. (Storemen were storebashers, but, oddly, wireless operators were not Morsebashers but wops.) He goes on to explain that after nearly two and a half years in Nova Scotia and sundry movements in the United Kingdom, he was posted to 2 TAF to await despatch to Normandy as a casualty replacement. Some three weeks after D-Day he arrived at Juno Beach. From there he joined the Headquarters Squadron at airfield B6, where 124 Wing was based. 'Most of our time was spent repairing flak damage, replacing sections of pipeline and electric leads.' As well as working on the Wing's aeroplanes, they took care of those based in England which operated from the airstrip and returned to their permanent bases at the day's end.

'A well remembered day,' he writes, 'was 7 August when a strong thrust of *Panzers* set off for Avranches under cover of mist which prevented air attack. Mid-morning the fog lifted and the Tiffies moved in and we spent the day rearming and refuelling. The pilots were very enthusiastic and rushing to get back into the fray.'

'Quite often,' he remembers, 'our Typhoons were attacked by fighters who apparently found difficulty in distinguishing them from [FW]190s.' He tells a pleasantly ironical story about one such event. 'One day our "Groupie" [group captain] sent a signal of protest to the C.O. of a nearby Thunderbolt Wing. [The American "T-bolt" (P-47) also had a round nose and blunt wings.] The reply was posted for all to see. "You should worry. One of my boys shot me down this morning." '

Chapter 11

The Origin and Deployment of 2nd Tactical Air Force

Desert Air Force (DAF), which was the RAF's first tactical air force, had earned a scintillating reputation in North Africa and Italy. When a new tactical air force for the invasion of Continental Europe was formed, the experience DAF had gained was a solid foundation for the new formation's organisation and operations.

The Chief of Air Staff (CAS), Air Chief Marshal Sir Charles Portal (later a peer and Marshal of the RAF), however, insisted that the air's most important contribution to Operation Overlord (the Normandy landings) would be to establish air superiority over the beachheads. Air Marshal Sir Trafford Leigh-Mallory, who had commanded No 12 Group of Fighter Command in the Battle of Britain and risen to be that Command's Commander-in-Chief, was appointed to command the Allied Expeditionary Air Force when it was formed. DAF consisted not only of fighter squadrons but also bomber and transport. Most of the squadrons were fighter. Similarly, Second Tactical Air Force, formed on 1 June 1943, comprised air superiority fighter, fighter-reconnaissance, ground-attack and photographic reconnaissance squadrons. All these constituted 83 Group.

On 21 January 1944 Air Marshal Sir Arthur Coningham was appointed Commander of 2nd TAF. This was an obvious choice for the post: he had commanded Desert Air Force before and after it was given that title and when it was Northwest African Tactical Air Force. The name DAF was restored in Italy, where it was not uncommon to see 'with the compliments of DAF' painted on a ruined building.

Location of Typhoon Squadrons 1941–1945
And names of Commanding Officers.
All but two were of Squadron Leader rank.
(* denotes bar to decoration)

No 1 Squadron
First Typhoon delivery 21.7.42. Operational 9.42.
Disposed of Typhoons April 42
J. A. F. MacLachlan DSO DFC* 7.41 – 8.42
R. C. Wilkinson OBE DFM* 8.42 – 5.43
A. Zweighburgh DFC 5.43 – 4.44
Location: Acklington from 8.7.42. Biggin Hill from 9.2.43. Lympne from 15.3.43. Martlesham Heath from 15.2.44. North Weald from 2.4.44.

No 3 Squadron
First Typhoon delivery 1.2.43. Operational 16.5.43.
Disposed of Typhoons 4.45
F. de Soomer 9.42 – 8.43
S. R. Thomas DFC AFC 8.43 – 9.43
R. Hawkins MC AFC 9.43 – 10.43
K. A. Wigglesworth DFC 10.43 – 8.44
Location: Hunsdon from 21.8.42. West Malling from 14.4.43. Manston from 11.6.43. Swanton Morley from 28.12.43. Manston from 14.2.44. Bradwell Bay from 6.3.44. Ayr from 6.4.44. Bradwell Bay from 14.4.44.

No 4 Squadron
First Typhoon delivery 1.10.44. Operational 11.10.44.
Disposed of Typhoons 2.45
C. D. Harris St John DFC
Location: B61 St Denis Westrem, Belgium from 27.9.44. B70 Deurne, Belgium from 11.10.44. B77 Gilze-Rijen, Holland from 23.11.44.

No 56 Squadron
First Typhoon delivery 11.9.41. Operational 29.5.42.
Disposed of Typhoons 5.44
P. P. Hanks DSO DFC AFC 6.41 – 12.41
H. S. L. Dundas DSO* DFC 12.41 – 11.42
A. C. Johnstone 12.42 – 6.43
T. H. V. Pheloung 6.43 – 9.43
G. L. Sinclair DFC* 9.43 – 5.44
Location: Duxford from 26.6.41. Snailwell from 30.3.42. Matlaske from 24.8.42. Manston from 22.7.43. Martlesham Heath from 6.8.43. Manston from 15.8.43. Bradwell Bay from 23.8.43. Martlesham Heath from 4.10.43. Scorton from 15.2.44. Acklington from 23.2.44. Scorton from 7.3.44. Ayr from 7.4.44. Newchurch from 28.4.44.

No 137 Squadron

First Typhoon delivery 1.44. Operational 8.2.44.
Disposed of Typhoons to No 174 Squadron 8.45
J. R. Dennehey DFC 12.43 – 4.44
G. Piltingrud DFC 4.44 – 9.44
E. T. Brough DFC 9.44 – 12.44
R. V. G. Barraclough 12.44 – 3.45
D. Murray DFC 3.45 – 8.45

Location: Colerne from 2.1.44. Lympne from 4.2.44. Manston from 1.4.44. B6 Coulombs, France from 13.8.44. B30 Creton, France from 29.8.44. B48 Amiens/Glissy, France. B58 Melsbroek, Belgium. B74 Eindhoven, Holland from 22.9.44. B86 Helmond, Holland from 13.1.45. B106 Twente, Holland from 11.4.45. B112 Hopsten, Germany from 13.4.45. B120 Langenhagen, Germany from 17.4.45. B156 Lüneburg, Germany from 30.4.45. B118 Celle, Germany from 7.5.45. B160 Kastrup, Denmark from 11.4.45. B172 Husum, Denmark from 21.6.45. B158 Lübeck, Germany from 11.7.45. Warmwell from 20.8.45.

No 164 Squadron

First Typhoon delivery 1.44. Operational 20.3.44.
Disposed of Typhoons 6.45
H. à B. Russell DFC 9.43 – 5.44
P. H. Beake DFC 5.44.- 8.44
W. E. van Lierde DFC* 8.44 -1.45
P. L. Bateman-Jones 1.45 – 8.45

Location: Twinwood Farm from 4.1.44. Fairlop from 13.1.44. Twinwood Farm from 11.2.44. Acklington from 8.3.44. Llanbedr from 11.4.44. Thorney Island from 22.4.44. Fungtington Sussex from 17.6.44. Hurn from 21.6.44. B8 Sommervieu, France from 20.7.44. B7 Martragny, France from 20.7.44. B23 Moraineville,

France from 3.9.44. B35 Baromesnil, France from 6.9.44. B53 Merville, France from 13.9.44. B67 Ursel, Belgium from 30.10.44. B77 Gilze-Rijen, Holland from 26.11.44. Fairwood Common from 17.12.44. B77 Gilze-Rijen, Holland from 29.12.44. B84 Chievres, Belgium from 1.1.45. B77 Gilze-Rijen, Holland from 19.1.45. B91 Kluis, Holland from 21.3.45. B103 Plantlunne, Germany from 17.4.45. B116 Wünstorf, Germany from 26.5.45. Turnhouse from 12.6.45.

No 168 Squadron

First Typhoon delivery 23.9.44. Operational 12.10.44.
Disposed of Typhoons 2.45
Flight Lieutenant A. M. Barbour
(acting Commanding Officer)

Location: B66 Diest, Belgium from 20.9.44. Eindhoven, Holland from 2.10.44.

No 174 Squadron

First Typhoon delivery 8.4.43. Operational 14.7.43.
Disposed of Typhoons 9.45
W. W. McConnell DFC 8.42 – 2.44
J. Pitt-Brown DFC* AFC 2.44 – 8.44
J. C. McIvill 8.44 – 1.45
D. T. N. Kelly 1.45 – 3.45
R. R. Monk DFC 2.45 – 4.45
D. Murray DFC 8.45 – 9.45

Location: Gravesend from 5.4.43. Merston from 12.6.43. Lydd from 1.7.43. Westhampnett from 10.10.43. Eastchurch from 21.1.44. Westhampnett from 4.2.44. Holmesley South from 1.4.44. B2 Bazenville, France from 19.6.44. B24 St André, France from 27.8.44. B42 Beauvais, France from 1.9.44. B50 Vitry-en-Artois, France from 4.9.44. B70 Deurne, Belgium from 17.9.44. B80 Volkel, Holland from

---

BELOW: Servicing a Typhoon's starboard wheel. (Mrs Ann Crump)

30.9.44. Warmwell from 10.11.44. B80 Volkel, Holland from 21.11.44. B100 Goch, Germany from 20.3.45. B158 Lübeck, Germany from 26.8.45. Warmwell from 9.9.45.

No 175 Squadron
First Typhoon delivery 10.4.43. Operational 12.6.43.
Disposed of Typhoons 9.45
J. R. Pennington-Lee DFC* 3.42 – 7.43
R. T. P. Davidson 7.43 – 9.43
M. R. Ingle-Finch DFC 9.43 – 11.44
W. Campbell 11.44 – 9.45

Location: Colerne from 8.4.43. Lasham from 24.5.43. Appledram from 2.6.43. Lydd from 1.7.43. Westhampnett from 9.10.43. Eastchurch from 24.2.44. Westhampnett from 8.3.44. Holmesley South from 1.4.44. B3 St Croix, France 20.6.44. B5 Le Fresney, France from 24.6.44. B42 Beauvais, France from 4.9.44. B50 Vitry-en-Artois, France from 4.9.44. B70 Deurne, Belgium from 17.9.44. B80 Volkel, Holland from 30.9.44. Warmwell from 21.11.44. B80 Volkel, Holland 4.12.44. B100 Goch, Germany from 21.3.45. B110 Achmer, Germany from 11.4.45. B150 Hustedt, Germany from 19.4.45. Warmwell from 28.5.45. Manston from 11.6.45. B164 Schleswig, Denmark 13.6.45. B160 Kastrup, Denmark from 22.8.45. B164 Schleswig, Denmark from 5.9.45.

No 181 Squadron
First Typhoon delivery 7.9.42. Operational 10.2.43.
Disposed of Typhoons 9.45
D. Crowley-Milling DSO DFC* 9.42 – 8.43
W. M. Jensen DFC* AFC 8.43 -11.4
J. G. Keep 11.43 – 8.44
C. D. North-Lewis DSO DFC* 5.44 – 8.44
A. E. S.Vincent DFC 8.44 – 12.44
W. H. B. Short DFC 12.44
D. R. Crawford 12.44 – 2.45
H. Ambrose DFC* 2.45 – 8.45

Location: Duxford from 1.9.42. Snailwell from 10.12.42. Cranfield from 1.3.43. Snailwell from 8.3.43. Gravesend from 24.3.43. Lasham from 5.4.43. Appledram from 2.6.43. New Romney from 2.7.43. Merston from 8.10.43. Odiham from 31.12.43. Merston from 13.1.44. Eastchurch from 6.2.44. Merston from 21.2.44. Hurn from 1.4.44. B6 Coulombs, France 20.6.44. B30 Creton, France from 31.8.44. B48 Amiens/Glisy, France from 3.9.44. B48 Melsbroek, Belgium from 6.9.44. B78 Eindhoven, Holland from 23.9.44. Warmwell from 13.2.45. B86 Helmond, Holland from 3.3.45. B106 Enschede, Holland from 3.3.45. B106 Enschede, Holland from 11.4.45. B112 Hopsten, Germany from 13.4.45. B120 Langenhagen, Germany from 18.4.45. B156 Lüneburg, Germany from 1.5.45. B158 Lübeck, Germany from 7.5.45. B160 Kastrup, Denmark from 6.7.45. Manston from 20.7.45. Warmwell from 21.7.45. B160 Kastrup, Denmark from 3.8.45. B166 Flensburg, Denmark from 5.9.45. B164 Schleswig, Denmark from 8.9.45.

No 182 Squadron
First Typhoon delivery 16.9.42. Operational 3.1.43.
Disposed of Typhoons 9.45
T. P. Pugh DFC 9.42 – 8.43
D. R. Walker 8.43 – 10.43
M. E. Reid 10.43 – 4.44
Maj D. H. Barlow SAAF 4.44 – 7.44
G. J. Gray DFC* 8.44 – 3.45
J. D. Derry DFC 3.45 – 9.45

Location: Martlesham from 25.8.42. Sawbridgeworth from 7.12.42. Snailwell from 17.1.43. Sawbridgeworth 20.1.43. Martlesham Heath from 30.1.43. Middle Wallop from 1.3.43. Zeals from 12.3.43. Middle Wallop from 13.3.43. Fairlop from 5.4.43. Lasham from 29.4.43. Appledram from 2.6.43. New Romney from 2.7.43. Wigtown from 18.9.43. New Romney from 22.9.43. Merston from 12.10.43. Odiham from 31.12.43. Eastchurch from 5.1.44. Merston from 21.1.44. Hurn from 1.4.44. B6 Coulombs, France from 20.6.44. Holmesley South from 22.6.44. B6 Coulombs, France from 3.7.44. B30 Creton, France from 30.8.44. B48 Eindhoven, Holland 12.9.42. B86 Helmond, Holland from 13.1.45. Warmwell from 3.2.45. B86 Helmond, Holland from 21.2.45. B106 Enschede, Holland from 11.4.45. B108 Rheine, Germany from 13.4.45. B120 Langenhagen, Germany from 17.4.45. B156 Lüneburg, Germany from 1.5.45. B158 Lübeck, Germany from 7.5.45. B160 Kastrup, Denmark from 11.7.45. Warmwell from 5.8.45. B160 Kastrup, Denmark from 19.8.45. B166 Flensburg, Denmark 5.9.45. B164 Schleswig, Denmark from 8.9.45.

No 183 Squadron
First Typhoon delivery 1.11.42. Operational 4.43.
Disposed of Typhoons 6.45
A. V. Gowers DFC 11.42 – 10.43
W. Dring DFC 10.43 – 4.44
F. W. Scarlett 4.44 – 7.44
R. W. Mulliner DFC 7.44 – 1.45
H. M. Mason 1.45 – 2.45
J. R. Cullen DFC 2.45 – 10.45

Location: Church Fenton from 1.11.42. Cranfield from 1.3.43. Snailwell from 8.5.43. Church Fenton from ???. 12.3.43. Colerne from 26.3.43. Gatwick from 8.4.43. Lasham from 3.5.43. Colerne from 30.5.43. Harrowbeer from 5.6.43. Tangmere from 4.8.43. Perranporth from 18.9.43. Predannack from 13.10.43. Tangmere from 1.2.44. Manston from 15.3.44. Thorney Island from 1.4.44. Funtington from 18.6.44. Hurn from 22.6.44. Eastchurch from 14.7.44. B7 Martragny, France from 25.7.44. B23 Morainville, France from 3.9.44. B53 Merville, France from 11.9.44. B67 Ursel, Belgium from 29.10.44. B77 Gilze-Rijen, Holland from 25.11.44. A84 Chievres, Belgium from 1.1.45. B77 Gilze-Rijen, Holland from 19.1.45. B91 Kluis, Holland from 21.3.45. B103 Plantlunne, Germany from 17.4.45. B116 Wünstorf, Germany from 27.4.45. Milfield from 16.6.45.

No 184 Squadron
First Typhoon delivery 24.12.43. Operational 25.4.44.
Disposed of Typhoons 9.45
J. Rose DFC 12.42 – 8.44
J. W. Wilson DFC 8.44 – 11.44
W. Smith DFC 11.44 – 8.45
Location: Detling from 12.10.43. Odiham from 6.3.44. Eastchurch from 11.3.44. Odiham from 3.3.44. Westhampnett from 23.4.44. Holmesley South from 13.5.44. Westhampnett from 20.5.44. Holmesley South from 17.6.44. B10 Plumetot, France from 27.6.44. B5 Le Fresney, France from 14.7.44. B24 St André, France from 28.8.44. B42 Beauvais, France from 2.9.44. B50 Vitry-en-Artois, France from 4.9.44. B70 Deurne, Belgium from 17.9.44. B80 Volkel, Holland from 30.9.44. B100 Goch, Germany from 21.3.45. B110 Achmer, Germany from 11.4.45. B150 Hustedt, Germany from 19.4.45. Warmwell from 7.5.45. B164 Schleswig, Denmark. B160 Kastrup, Denmark. B166 Flensburg, Denmark.

No 186 Squadron
First Typhoon delivery 16.11.43.
Never became operational.
Disposed of Typhoons 2.43
F. E. G. Hayter 8.43 – 1.44
W. H. Ireson 1.44 – 4.44
Location: Ayr from 3.8.43. Tain from 7.1.44.

No 193 Squadron
First Typhoon delivery 22.1.43. Operational 1.4.43.
Disposed of Typhoons 8.45
W. H. A. Wright
G. W. Petre DFC AFC 1.43 – 2.44
D. G. Ross DFC 2.44 – 6.44
J. C. Button DSO DFC 6.44 – 8.44
J. M. G. Plamondon 8.44 – 11.44
C. D. Erasmus DFC 11.44 – 3.45
D. M. Taylor DFC 4.45 – 8.45
Location: Harrowbeer from 18.12.42. Gravesend from 17.8.43. Harrowbeer from 18.9.43. Fairlop from

20.2.43. Thorney Island from 15.3.44. Llanbedr from 6.4.44. Needs Oar Point from 11.4.44. Hurn from 3.7.44. B15 Ryes, France from 11.7.44. B3 St Croix, France from 15.7.44. Manston from 8.9.44. B51 Lille, France from 11.9.44. Fairwood Common from 18.9.44. B70 Deurne, Belgium from 6.10.44. B89 Mill, Holland from 8.2.45. B111 Ahlhorn, Germany from 30.4.45. R16 Hildesheim, Germany from 8.6.45.

No 195 Squadron
First Typhoon delivery 27.11.42. Operational 8.3.43.
Disposed of Typhoons 2.44
D. M. Taylor DFC 11.42 – 1.44
C. A. Harris 1.44 – 2.44
Location: Duxford from 16.11.42. Hutton Cranswick from 21.11.42. Woodvale from 12.2.43. Ludham from 13.5.43. Matlaske from 31.7.43. Coltishall from 21.8.43. Fairlop from 23.9.43.

No 197 Squadron
First Typhoon delivery 27.11.42. Operational 31.1.43.
Disposed of Typhoons 8.45
P. O. Prevot DFC 11.42 – 6.43
A. H. Korkett 6.43 – 7.43
M. P. C. Holmes DFC 7.43 – 1.44
D. M. Taylor DFC 1.44 – 7.44
A. H. Smith 7.44 – 1.45
H. C. Curwen DFC 1.45 – 2.45
J. Harding DFC 2.45 – 8.45
Location: Drem from 25.11.42. Tangmere from 28.3.43. Manston from 1.4.44. Needs Oar Point from 10.4.44. Manston from 2.9.44. B51 Lille, France from 11.9.44. B70 Deurne, Belgium from 2.10.44. B89 Mill, Holland from 8.2.45. B105 Drope, Germany from 16.4.45. B111 Ahlhorn, Germany from 30.4.45. R16 Hildesheim, Germany from 8.6.45.

No 198 Squadron
First Typhoon delivery 8.12.42. Operational 28.3.43.
Disposed of Typhoons 9.45
J. W. Villa DFC* 12.42 – 5.43

BELOW: Typhoon engine being run up. A Mustang stands on the right and a Mitchell B-25 far right. (Mrs Ann Crump)

71

J. Manak 5.43 – 8.43
J. M. Bryan DFC* 8.43 – 11.43
J. Baldwin DSO DFC* 11.43 – 4.44
J. M. Bryan DFC* 4.44 – 5.44
J. Niblett DFC 5.44 – 6.44
J. J. Davies DFC 6.44
Y. P. E. H. Ezano CdeG 8.44 – 10.44
A. W. Ridler 10.44 – 12.44
N. J. Durrant 12.44 – 9.45

Location: Digby from 8.12.42. Ouston from 23.1.43. Acklington from 9.2.43. Manston from 24.3.43. Woodvale from 15.5.43. Martlesham Heath from 5.6.43. Bradwell Bay from 19.8.43. Manston from 23.8.43. Tangmere from 17.3.44. Llanbedr from 30.3.44. Thorney Island from 6.4.44. Funtington from 18.6.44. Hurn from 22.6.44. B5 Le Fresny, France from 1.7.44. B10 Plumetot, France from 11.7.44. B7 Martragny, France from 29.7.44. B23 Morainville, France from 3.9.44. B35 Baromesnil, France from 6.9.44. B53 Merville/France from 11.9.44. B67 Ursel, Belgium from 30.10.44. Fairwood Common from 6.11.44. B67 Ursel, Belgium from 21.11.44. B77 Gilze-Rijen, Holland from 26.11.44. A84 Chievres, Belgium from 31.12.44. B77 Gilze-Rijen, Holland from 19.1.45. B91 Kluis, Holland from 21.3.45. B103 Plantlunne, Germany from 17.4.45. B116 Wünstorf, Germany from 27.5.45.

No 245 Squadron
First Typhoons delivery 31.12.42. Operational 28.2.43. Disposed of Typhoons 8.45
S. S. Hordern 10.42 – 9.43
J. R. Collins DFC* 9.43 to 8. 44
A. Zweighbergh DFC 10.44 – 8.45

Locations: Charmy Down from 26.10.42. Peterhead from 29.1.43. Gravesend from 31.3.43. Fairlop from 28.5.43. Selsey from 1.6.43. Lydd from 30.6.43.

Westhampnett from 10.10.43. Holmesley South from 1.4.44. Eastchurch from 25.4.44. Holmesley South from 30.4.44. Eastchurch from 12.5.44. Holmesley South from 22.5.44. B5 Le Fresney, France from 27.6.44. B24 St André, France from 28.8.44. B42 Beauvais, France from 2.9.44. B50 Vitry-en-Artois, France from 4.9.44. B70 Deurne, Belgium from 17.9.44. B80 Volkel, Holland from 1.10.44. Warmwell from 24.12.44. B80 Volkel, Holland from 6.1.45. B100 Goch, Germany from 21.3.45. B110 Achmer, Germany from 11.4.45. B150 Celle, Germany from 19.4.45. B164 Schleswig, Denmark 28.5.45. Warmwell from 16.6.45. B164 Schleswig, Denmark from 3.7.45.

No 247 Squadron
First Typhoons delivery 11.1.43. Operational 11.3.43. Disposed of Typhoons 8.45
J. C. Melville 5.42 – 8.43
E. Haabjoern (Norway) DFC 8.43 – 1.44
S. McNair DFC 1.44 – 8.44
B. G. Stapleton DFC 8.44 – 12.44
J. H. Bryant DFC 1.45 – 6.45

Location: High Ercall from 21.9.42. Middle Wallop from 1.3.43. Fairlop from 5.4.43. Gravesend from 28.5.43. Bradwell Bay from 4.6.43. New Romney from 10.7.43. Attlebridge from 7.8.43. New Romney from 13.8.43. Merston from 11.10.43. Snailwell from 23.10.43. Merston from 5.11.43. Odiham from 31.12.43. Merston from 13.1.44. Eastchurch from 1.4.44. Hurn from 24.4.44. B6 Coulombs, France from 20.6.44. Hurn from 23.6.44. B30 Creton, France from 30.8.44. B48 Amiens/Glisy, France from 3.9.44. B58 Melsbroek, Belgium from 6.9.44. B78 Eindhoven, Holland from 22.9.44. B86 Helmond, Holland from 13.1.45. Warmwell from 21.2.45. B86 Helmond, Holland from 7.3.45. B106 Twente, Holland from 12.4.45. B112 Hopsten, Germany from 13.4.45. B120

BELOW: Odiham, early 1944. Typhoon EK218. B-25 in background, Mustang's tail on right.

Langenhagen, Germany from from 17.4.45. B156 Lüneburg, Germany from 2.5.45. B158 Lübeck Germany from 6.5.45. Chilbolton from 20.8.45.

No 257 Squadron

First Typhoon delivery 15.7.42. Operational 31.8.42.
Disposed of Typhoons 3.45
P. G. Wykeham-Barnes DSO* OBE DFC* AFC 5.42 – 9.42
G. A. Brown DFC 9.42 – 4.43
C. L. C. Roberts 4.43 – 5.43
P. H. Lee 5.43 – 7.43
R. H. Fowkes DFC DFM 7.43 – 6.44
W. C. Ahrens 6.44 – 7.44
W. J. Johnston DFC* 7.44 – 10.44
D. P. Jenkins DFC 10.44 – 1.45
A. G. Todd DFC 1.45 – 3.45
Location: High Ercall from 6.6.42. Exeter from 21.9.42. Warmwell from 8.1.43. Gravesend from 12.8.43. Warmwell from 17.9.43. Beaulieu from 20.1.44. Tangmere from 31.1.44. Needs Oar Point from 10.4.44. Hurn from 2.7.44. B3 St Croix, France from 15.7.44. Fairwood Common from 11.8.44. B3 St Croix, France from 30.8.44. B23 Morainville, France from 6.9.44. B51 Lille/Seclin, France from 11.9.44. B70 Deurne, Belgium from 2.10.44. B89 Mill, Holland from 8.2.45.

No 283 Squadron

First Typhoons delivery 2.12.43. Operational 1.2.44.
Disposed of Typhoons 8.45
G. B. Warnes DSO DFC 12.43 – 2.44
H. A. C. Gonay (Belgian) 2.44 – 6.44
D. Rutter DFC 6.44 – 1.45
T. S. Rumbold 1.45 – 8.45
Location: Warmwell from 12.7.43. Ibsley from 5.12.43. Fairwood Common from 5.1.44. Beaulieu from 23.1.44. Warmwell from 6.3.44. Harrowbeer from 19.3.44. Bold Head from 19.6.44. Hurn from 10.7.44. Eastchurch from 23.7.44. B3 St Croix, France from 6.8.44. Manston from 6.9.44. B51 Lille/Vandeville, France from 11.9.44. B70 Deurne, Belgium from 2.10.44. Fairwood Common from 13.1.45. B89 Mill, Holland from 10.2.45. B105 Drope, Germany from 16.4.45. B111 Ahlhorn, Germany from 30.4.45. R16 Hildesheim, Germany from 10.6.45.

No 266 (Rhodesia) Squadron

First Typhoon delivery 5.1.42. Operational 29.5.42.
Disposed of Typhoons 7.45
C. L. Green DFC 10.41 – 7.43
A. S. Macintyre 7.43 – 8.43
P. W. Lefevre DFC 8.43. – 2.44
J. W. E. Holmes DFC AFC 4.44 – 7.44
J. D. Wright DFC 7.44 – 10.44
J. H. Deall 10.44 – 3.45
R. A. G. Sheward DFC 3.45 – 7.45
Location: Kings Cliffe from 24.10.41. Duxford from 29.1.42. Warmwell from 21.9.42. Exeter from 2.1.43. Gravesend from 7.9.43. Exeter from 10.9.43. Harrowbeer from 21.9.43. Bolt Head from 7.3.44.

Harrowbeer from 12.3.44. Acklington from 15.3.44. Tangmere from 22.3.44. Needs Oar Point from 10.4.44. Snaith from 27.4.44. Needs Oar Point from 6.5.44. Eastchurch from 29.6.44. Hurn from 13.7.44. B3 St Croix, France from 17.7.44. B25 Morainville, France from 6.9.44. Manston from 8.9.44. Tangmere from 9.9.44. B51 Lille/Vendeville, France from 11.9.44. B70 Deurne, Belgium from 2.12.44. B89 Mill, Holland from 8.2.45. B105 Drope, Germany from 16.4.45. Fairwood Common from 27.4.45. B111 Ahlhorn, Germany from 4.6.45. R16 Hildesheim, Germany from 8.6.45.

No 268 Squadron

First Typhoon delivery 2.7.44. Operational 8.8.44.
Disposed of Typhoons 12.44
A. S. Mann DFC
Location: Odiham from 27.6.44. B10 Plumetot, France from 10.8.44. B4 Beny-sur-Mer, France from 13.8.44. B27 Boisney, France from 1.9.44. B31 Fresney Folncy, France from 5.9.45. B43 Fort Rouge, France. B61 St Denis Westrem, Belgium from 27.9.44. B70 Deurne, Belgium from 11.10.44. B77 Gilze-Rijen, Holland from 25.11.44.

No 609 (West Riding) Squadron

First Typhoon Delivery 4.42. Operational 30.6.42.
Disposed of Typhoons 9.45
G. K .Gilroy DSO DFC* 3.41 – 6.42
P. H. M. Richey DFC 6.42 – 10.42
R. P. Beamont DSO DFC* 10.42 – 5.43
A. Ingle DFC AFC 5.43 – 8.43
P. G. Thornton-Brown 8.43 – 12.43
J. C. Wells DFC* 12.43 – 6.44
L. E. J. Geerts (Belgian) 6.44 – 8.44
A. F. Lallemant (Belgian) DFC 8.44 – 9.44
T. Y. Wallace DFM 9.44 – 11.44
C. J. G. de Moulin (Belgian) DFC 11.44 – 12.44
E. R. A. Roberts DFC 12.44 – 3.45
L. W. F. Stark DFC* AFC 3.45 – 9.45
Location: Duxford from 30.3.42. Bourn from 26.8.42. Duxford from 30.8.42. Biggin Hill from 18.9.42. Manston from 2.11.42. Matlaske from 22.7.43. Lympne from 18.8.43. Manston from 14.12.43. Fairwood Common from 6.2.44. Manston from 20.2.44. Tangmere from 16.3.44. Acklington from 21.3.44. Thorney Island from 1.4.44. B2 Bazenville, France from 18.6.44. Hurn from 22.6.44. B10 Plumetot, France from 1.7.44. B7 Martragny, France from 19.7.44. B23 Morainville, France from 6.9.44. B53 Merville, France from 11.9.44. B67 Ursel, Belgium from 30.10.44. B77 Gilze-Rijen, Holland from 26.11.44. A84 Chevres, Belgium from 31.12.44. B77 Gilze-Rijen, Holland from 19.1.45. B91 Kluis, Holland from 21.3.45. B103 Plantlunne, Germany from 17.4.45. B116 Wünstorf, Germany from 27.5.45. Lasham from 2.6.45. Fairwood Common from 4.6.45. B116 Wünstorf,Germany from 23.6.45.

No 438 Squadron RCAF

First Typhoon delivery 12.1.44. Operational 3.44.

Disposed of Typhoons 8.45
F. G. Grant DSO DFC 11.43 – 7.44
J. R. Beirne 7.44 – 10.44
R. F. Reid 10.44 – 12.44
Flight Lieutenant P.Wilson 12.44 (acting commander)
J. E. Hogg 1.45 – 3.45
J. R. Beirnes DFC 3.45 – 6.45
R. A. Brown 6.45
P. Bissky 6.45
M. Harrison 6.45
Location: Ayr from 1.44. Hurn from 3.44. Funtington from 4.44. B9 Lantheuil, France from 6.44. B24 St André, France from 8.44. B48 Amiens/Glisy, France 9.44. B58 Melsbroek, Belgium 9.44. B78 Eindhoven, Holland from 9.44. Warmwell from 3.45. B100 Goch, Germany 4.45. B110 Osnabrück, Germany 4.45. B150 Celle, Germany from 4.45. B166 Flensburg, Denmark from 5.45.

No 439 Squadron RCAF

First Typhoons delivery 2.44. Operational 3.44.
Disposed of Typhoons 8.45
W. M. Smith 1.44 – 3.44
H. H. Norsworthy 3.44 – 9.44
K. J. Fiset DFC 9.44 – 12.44
R. G. Crosby 12.44 – 1.45
J. H. Beatty 1.45 – 8.45
Location: Ayr from 1.44. Hurn from 3.44. Funtington 4.44. Hurn from 4.44. Hutton Cranswick 5.44. Hurn from 5.44. B9 Lantheuil, France from 6.44. B24 St André, France from 8.44. B48 Amiens/Glisy, France 9.44. B58 Melsbroek, Belgium 9.44. B78 Eindhoven, Holland from 9.44. B100 Goch, Germany from 3.45. Warmwell 4.45. B150 Celle, Germany from 5.45.

No 440 Squadron RCAF

First Typhoon delivery 2.44. Operational 3.44.
Disposed of Typhoons 8.45
W. H. Pentland 2.44 – 10.44
A. E. Monson 10.44 – 12.44
H. O. Gooding 12.44 – 3.45
R. Coffey 3.45 – 7.45
A. E. Monson DFC 8.45
Location: Ayr from 2.44. Hurn from 3.44. Funtington 4.44. Hurn from 4.44. B7 Martragny, France 6.44. B9 Lantheuil, France from 6.44. B24 St André, France from 8.44. B48 Amiens/Glisy, France 9.44. B58 Melsbroek, Belgium 9.44. B78 Eindhoven, Holland from 9.44. B100 Gosh, Germany from 3.45. B110 Osnabrück, Germany 4.45. B150 Cell, Germany 4.45. Warmwell from 4.45. B150 Cell, Germany 5.45. B166 Flensburg, Denmark from 5.45.

No 485 Squadron RNZAF

First Typhoon delivery 3.45.
Did not become operational.
Disposed of Typhoons 4.45
K. J. McDonald OBE DFC
Location: Predannack 2.45 – 4.45.

No 486 Squadron RNZAF

C. L. C. Roberts 3.42 – 4.43
D. J. Scott DSO OBE DFC 4.43 – 9.43
D. Waddy 9.43 – 1.44
J. H. Iremonger 1.44 – 12.44
Location: Wittering from 4.42. North Weald from 9.42. West Malling 10.42. Tangmere 10.42. Beaulieu from 1.44. Castle Camps 3.44. Ayr 3.44. Castle Camps from 3.44.

BELOW: Eindhoven, March 1945. 168 Sqdn ground crews. (Mrs Ann Crump)

Chapter 12
Hard Pounding

At the crucial stage in the Battle of Waterloo, when the British infantry were hard pressed by French cavalry, the Duke of Wellington's urbane and ungrammatical comment to his staff was: 'Hard pounding this, gentleman, let's see who will pound the longest'. His sentiment could be applied to the whole experience of flying Typhoons in preparation for, and during, the Normandy invasion: a pounding that the RAF's most formidable ground-attack fighters endured for nearly two years, not one day, after the Normany landings and had endured two hard years before that.

F/L T. T. Hall DFC of 175 Squadron had come from the opposite ends of the earth to be there. As he found out, if you flew Typhoons the pilots of air superiority fighters on your own side were almost as likely to shoot you down as the enemy.

He did his flying training in his native Australia and was sent to England by sea, via America. Like many of his countrymen, he was posted to an RAF squadron, not the Royal Australian Air Force (RAAF). Numerous New Zealanders, Canadians, Rhodesians and South Africans who were destined for Britain also found themselves in the RAF, not their national air forces.

Ground-attack pilots were subjected to the heaviest damage by both light and heavy flak, but the Typhoon was the sturdiest of fighters. (The Tempest was also big and tough – but V-1s and V-2s couldn't shoot at their pursuers!) So was the American P-47 Thunderbolt, but that was essentially an air superiority fighter: the Mark XP72 could achieve 490mph at 25,000ft and was reckoned the world's fastest piston-engine 'pursuit ship'.

The famous German 88mm gun was a magnificent anti-aircraft and anti-tank weapon that caused the Allied armies and air forces much distress in the desert and Italian campaign. It was equally destructive and abhorred by them all the way from Normandy to Berlin. Flying a Typhoon towards the target, pilots could hear the predictors on the 88mm flak sites ticking in their earphones. Tom Hall DFC writes: 'If you kept on a straight and level course for too long, a number of rounds of 88mm shells would explode in black bursts right on your track or very close to it. So the

BELOW: Tom Hall, Oct 1943. (Tom Hall)

technique was to change course, altitude and speed continually (it was called 'jinking') and although it made navigation a bit harder it dissuaded the enemy from wasting shells. But it also put a strain on new chums to the squadron as they would be slow to react and not anticipate such changes and would be almost continually out of position from the standard finger four formation which required each one to scan their allotted segment of air space as they kept position. In catching up to get back in position they would invariably fly well behind everyone else.

'As the target approached we would be echeloned out and then dive on the target. As we were going pretty fast, the gunners (light flak) would almost always under-deflect on the leading aircraft and the 20mm shells would pass behind you, so it was fatal to fly directly behind anybody. As a result many pilots were knocked down in their first few days of combat flying. In the actual attack the most dangerous position was to be the last aircraft to attack, as by that time there was no element of surprise and all the defences would be lined up and concentrated on the last ones in.'

For all air force, naval and army pilots of any nation, the essence of their profession is the sheer joy of flying. Going into action takes some of the shine off youthful, high-spirited and heady self-indulgence.

'Until my first op, the war had been a big game, all good fun for a young bloke with a fast aircraft and plenty of low flying, skylarking etc. On D-day, twelve aircraft went on an RP attack for heavy gun positions near Cabourg in France and I was number twelve in that attack, which was very successful despite a lot of flak. Pulling out of the dive, I heard a loud bang on the aircraft but it continued to fly OK. When I got back to England I found that a 20mm shell had gone through the fuselage just behind my head. This really woke me up that it was now for keeps, the big game was over and I took things a lot more seriously.

'My second attack [MN986], on 7 June 1944 was with long-range tanks in the Caen-Falaise area. We paired off to look for targets (I was with Kelly Kelasik [JR502]) and we found some MT and a tank. I gave it [the tank] a burst of

cannon and fired a pair of rockets just in front of it. It was firing small stuff from a four-gun turret and hit me three times in the starboard wing, which, apart from damage to the aileron, hit nothing vital.

'This confirmed for me that luck was ninety per cent and ten per cent was for experience, know-how and ability; and at the end of my flying career nothing had happened that changed my view. I recall a wonderful pilot with us, F/L Vernon-Jervis, OC of A Flight. He was tour-expired with us. On his next tour he was killed in an attack when his tail was blown off.' [This officer, whose initials were E.C.H.,won a DFC, was given command of 168 Squadron in February 1945 and killed in the same month, flying RB270, when shot down by flak.]

'On the day's second operation on 18 August '44, when we were attacking a lot of tanks and transport south of Vimoutiers, a West Indian took a solid hit and three-quarters of his port aileron was blown off. The aircraft flew with a thirty-degree list, but he got back safely – full marks for the toughness of the good old Tiffie.'

In pace with the Army's progress, 2nd TAF's operational bases advanced, keeping behind the bomb line. No 175 Squadron moved to Antwerp on 17 September 1944.

Tom remembers: 'It was great to land on a

BELOW: Landing Ground B3, 13 June 1944. 175 Sqdn's first landing in Normandy. Tom Hall extreme left, Stud Foley third left, S/L Ingle-Finch, F/L Jack Davies. Background W/C Charles Green in steel helmet, 3rd on his left S/L Pitt-Brown. (Tom Hall)

former civil aerodrome. The field engineers had done a good job of patching up the bomb holes. We had just completed taxying to our designated squadron area, when German artillery opened up from about four miles away on the other side of the Albert Canal.

'We had personal belongings stuffed in the gun bays and didn't have a chance to take anything out of the aircraft, just run for the slit trenches. The barrage continued for some time.'

On the 23rd 'The Germans were dropping isolated artillery shells on the aerodrome as well as holding up our troops on the road to Eindhoven. My aircraft [MN986] received a direct hit and caught fire. It was one of the first Typhoons with a four-bladed propeller, a pleasure to fly and had logged only nine and three-quarter flying hours. Not long after catching fire, it blew up and some of the rockets took off. One hit a NAAFI van on the far side of the aerodrome and killed a number of people who were getting a cup of tea. It took a while for the remaining rockets and 20mm cannon ammunition to explode and I have a memento of a 20mm shell case which was the largest piece of metal left after the fire and explosion.

'Later that day we did two attacks, the first under VCP control on the artillery guns in the forest overlooking the Eindhoven road. There was bags of flak, the VCP [Visual Control Post – described in a later chapter] controller was very pleased with the attack. The second attack was on troops in the village of Walkensward. All RPs in the target area. On 22 September we successfully attacked the Antwerp fort number one. Plenty of flak. Paddy Moore hit and crashed in our lines but walked back.' The record shows that he flew MN986 and Moore flew MN376, while the squadron commander flew MN194.

On 24 October 1944, the squadron attacked a factory at Maashees with a chimney that was being used as an observation post. It was stressed that the Canadians were very near it and the pilots must take great care when approaching the target. Indication smoke would be laid to help them. Eight aircraft took part and Tom Hall was flying number three to the squadron commander. When they arrived at the target they found much smoke and haze

ABOVE: Tom Hall and Typhoon, France 1944. (Tom Hall)

on the scene. The CO ordered them into echelon starboard and signalled that he was going down, but did not mention that it might be only to check conditions before firing rockets.

F/L Hall recalls: 'I concentrated on the target and got a lovely strike. The rest of the squadron followed, the chimney was knocked down and nothing much was left of the factory. When we formed up again, the C.O. and his number two had not fired their rockets. As we returned home he did a bit of pointing at me and shaking his head. After we had landed and stopped our engines, he rushed up to me and said that I was going to carry the can for what he termed 'the bloody black' [making a serious error was known as 'putting up a black'], as he was pretty certain that the Canadians had occupied the factory! I didn't feel too happy but asked why he didn't mention some doubt as he carried out the normal attack procedure. I said "Surely you realise I cannot watch what you are doing if I have no time to line up the target."

'At the debriefing he was in earnest conversation with the Wing Commander, both of them glaring at me from time to time. Before the Intelligence Officer got going, the Wingco said it looked as though we had put up a great black and he had signalled HQ to see what the position was at the target area. He intended to wait until he got a reply before taking further action. When my turn came with the I.O. I told him that all procedures for an attack were carried out as normal and if the C.O. had had any doubts he should have warned us and I would have kept an eye on him. As debriefing finished, a corporal came in with a signal for the Wingco. He read it, then showed it to the C.O. before reading out: "Great attack, Canadian forces have now advanced beyond target area." The two of them departed after the Wingco had commented that we were off the hook.

'A few days later at briefing for an op the C.O. remarked that I had been quiet and asked if anything was the matter. I replied that I was sure that he knew. In early November he was tour-expired and replaced by Rollo Campbell, a great bloke who flew with me until he was genned up ['gen' meaning correct information, correct procedure, genuine fact etc].

The high esteem in which the ground forces held the Typhoon pilots was expressed many years later in the Correspondence columns of *The Times*. A member of what had once been a cavalry regiment, wrote: 'Dr [name omitted here] is right in giving credit to the rocket-firing Typhoons for "smashing the enemy's spearhead" in Normandy in early August 1944. But it was in the subsequent advance across northwest Europe that the aircraft came into its own. As the 7th Armoured Division's recce regiment, we in the 8th Hussars had a set procedure whenever we came across German rearguard Tiger tanks or 88mm anti-tank guns, we'd call up the Tyffies (*sic*), watch their rockets destroy the obstacle and then carry on advancing. Thanks to the RAF, many crews' lives were saved and the momentum of Monty's advance upheld.'

Ronnie Sheward, who figures elsewhere in

BELOW: 175 Sqdn, Volkel, Holland, on edge of a bomb crater. (Tom Hall)

this book, submitting this cutting from the newspaper, adds: 'I thought this was rather nice, a thank you from the "Brown Jobs" – not often experienced, though I do remember in a bar in Brussels an enormous Canadian Army chap came up to me and asked "Are you a Typhoon pilot?" And on saying that I was, he thumped me on the back and said "What will you have, Buddy? You're doing a great job and saved our skin on many occasions".'

F/L Hall continues: 'Another indication of the toughness of the Typhoon happened on 10 November 1944 when we carried out an armed recce of the Goch – Wesel – Geldern area looking for motor transport. We passed up two trucks that we saw for the alternative target, which was at Wesel. I led the squadron and after putting our rockets into the factory we copped some heavy flak from Goch. We got some height and circled to check that we had really got the factory, as the smoke and dust started to clear. An 88mm shell burst straight under me and the aircraft seemed to be thrown about fifty feet up and on its side. The port 'D' door – one of the two doors covering the retracted undercarriage – was blown off along with some holes in the fuselage and the aircraft flew port wing low. Other than the scary tendency to flick over to port, the hydraulics and undercarriage were undamaged and other than a bit more throttle on and a bit nose up the aircraft landed reasonably well.'

W/O Bob Merlin of 175 Squadron, had been shot down over France some ten months before this attack and was rescued by the French Resistance organisation. After D-Day, when the squadron was at B5, he arrived there driving a *Kugelwagen* (the German equivalent of a jeep) with an Alsatian dog that had belonged to a German major whom the Maquis had killed. After a short leave in England and familiarisation training on the Typhoon, he rejoined 175 in November 1944. On Christmas Day he flew number two (JP918) to Tom Hall, who was leading the squadron on an armed reconnaissance for motor transport east of Malmédy. Attacking some trucks, they were

fired on by light flak. It hit Merlin under the engine, from which glycol began to leak copiously. Tom Hall ordered the rest of the squadron to return to base, which was 'a fair distance away', while he and Merlin would cut across the bomb line to get the damaged aeroplane down as soon as possible. Merlin kept asking if they were near the bomb line, but they still had a good way to go. As they had enough altitude and flames were belching from under the damaged engine, Tom repeatedly told him to bale out; but he wouldn't. Soon he was losing power and height. Wheels up, Merlin made a good, flat crash-landing. Plants, foliage and dirt were thrown up as the Typhoon slithered through tall bushes until it exploded in flames. Hall circled the spot for some time but saw no movement, so he climbed and transmitted for a D/F (direction finder) fix in order to pinpoint the position of the accident. He says, 'I got back to base and reported that he had bought it.'

At dinner 'in our rough mess' next night, in walked W/O Merlin, his face still smoke-blackened.

He had landed about 600 yards from the Germans. As soon as he hit the ground he undid his straps. The port side of the fuselage had been ripped away and he was thrown into an empty water channel while the wreckage continued to travel forward until, a good distance from him, it blew up. Tom Hall could not see him, because the bushes that his crash had parted had closed again. Presently Merlin heard a noise, then saw a British soldier crawling towards him, motioning him to keep quiet and follow. Bullets from the burning Typhoon kept whipping over them. Merlin was sent home on leave and then posted to another theatre of operations. Tom has no fond memories of the Alsatian, which bit him and left a lifelong scar on his hand.

All too often in war a triumphant moment is marred by an unforeseen, because rare, consequence. A narrow avoidance of death is even rarer. On 21 February 1945 F/L Hall [MN988] was leading the squadron on an armed reconnaissance in the Heek area, where, it had been reported, V-2s were stored and firings had been observed. As they approached, they noticed some buildings close to the railway line and saw, near them, a cleared space where stood an upright V-2 venting vapour. They formed echelon and as they dived out of sun-light flak opened fire from the building and the surrounding woods. When Hall and his number two finished their attack he looked back and saw 'a terrific explosion'.

'When we formed up, [P/O] Joe Swift [SN407] (an Aussie and a great mate) who was Blue Section leader, was missing. Neither his number two nor anybody else had seen what had happened to him. I assumed that he had been blown up in the explosion of the V-2.

'Some time later we found out that he had been hit by flak, and had crashed some distance away and was a PoW.'

Tom Hall recalls without rancour occasions when he was subjected to 'friendly fire'. The several measures taken to make the Allied identity of Typhoons conspicuous had always failed to have total success. One of these well-meant markings was itself a hazard: when spinners were painted white, they proved to be an excellent aiming mark for flak gunners.

'We had been bounced by Spitfires on 18 December 1944 when returning from a target east of Aachen – a lot of cloud was around. Again, on the morning of 25 December we did an armed recce looking for motor transport south of Cologne and on the way back we were bounced by Tempests. Again we didn't see them because of cloud. In both cases they identified us – the black and white invasion stripes helped.

'On 31 December I led the squadron on an armed recce to attack transport on the roads south of St Vith and Aachen. We had one long range tank and six rockets. The weather in the target area was not expected to be too good. Half way across France a squadron of what looked like Mustangs was sighted at two o'clock about four or five thousand feet above us and a few miles away. I kept on course and

we kept an eye on them, as, if they were Yanks, you had to assume that they would have their usual blood lust up whereby they never seemed to be able to identify any aircraft, despite Allied markings – just wanting to shoot something down.

'The Mustangs had slightly altered course and were now at about five o'clock. I couldn't wait any longer as it could be risky, so I got the boys to drop their long-range tanks and warned them to be prepared to break starboard on the call.

'Just after we got rid of the tanks the Mustangs winged over and dived at us. At the right time we broke to starboard and passed under them. They were American Mustangs and passed overhead and continued on course, obviously recognising us.

'We got back on course but being well short of the target area and the weather becoming worse – down to zero – we returned home with the rockets. Another wasted abortive operation.

'At debriefing I reported the Mustang incident with the time and exact location of the anticipated attack. The Intelligence Officer took it up with Allied Air Headquarters but all that we got back was that no U.S. aircraft were operating in the reported area at that time.'

In a speech to the USA Senate in 1917, Hiram Johnson had declared: 'The first casualty when war comes is truth'. As the RAF was to find throughout the war, the validity of this was frequently manifested.

Wild, gung-ho shooting at friendly aircraft mistakenly assumed to be hostile was rife. Tom Hall records an instance: 'On 14 January 1945 F/O Chapman of 121 Squadron in our Wing, was shot down by an American Thunderbolt.'

'"Ashes" Ashman [JR376] was killed on 27 February 1945 as a result of an abortive show which should never have been put on. Because of the general clamp in the weather, no operations were being conducted and 175 Squadron was on call. There certainly was a hush when a signal came through for four aircraft to make an effort to see if any targets could be caught moving on the roads in the

Steinhuder Lake area. This looked a dicey show from the start and it was decided to draw three low cards to make up the three to go with the C.O. I had 120 operations up and Ashes had 103. Normally a tour was completed after one hundred operational sorties, but replacement pilots were slow coming through, hence our excess numbers of sorties. The C.O., Rollo Campbell, said that we didn't need to be in the draw for the trip. We both declined his offer. The three lowest were P/O Ainsley and, would you believe it, Ashes and myself. Apart from

our normal cannon armament we had six rockets and one long-range petrol tank. We climbed up on a rough course, heading through the overcast on instruments which weren't too accurate, due to the constant knocking around that aircraft had been receiving on normal operations.

'Eventually we got out of the cloud at about 6000ft and joined up, with Ainslie number two to the C.O. and Ashes and I on their port side. We set course over the overcast for the target area. All round the target area there was not one break in the overcast and after dropping the long range tanks we dived down into it, but as we weren't out of cloud by a safe altitude (really dicey with the lag in instruments) we pulled up and when we came out of the overcast we were well scattered and only three in number. It was very touchy getting back through the overcast, which was still a bad clamp. The C.O. and I got into our base but Bob Ainslie overheated and landed at Eindhoven. Some months later Ashes's aircraft was found crashed on a hill in the area where we dived. Fortunately all three of us had evidently dived into the valley.'

ABOVE AND BELOW: Memorial to Typhoon pilots killed during Battle of Normandy. (Tom Hall)

Not the least discomforting and discomfiting performers on the air war scene are those technical experts, most often involved with electronics, who are known to the RAF as 'boffins'. Apart from the nerve-racking and general emotional wear and tear of daily combat, these learned scientists impose peculiar burdens on the tolerance of air crew with experiments.

Tom Hall and his Typhoon JR517 fell into their clutches towards the end of his tour of operations.

'In the week prior to 18 February 1945 it was arranged for me to meet some boffins who had a modified radar which they proposed to use for directing Typhoon attacks in extreme weather conditions in which Typhoons would not normally operate.'

The purpose of this secret apparatus was to prevent the movements of enemy supply vehicles, which always increased when bad weather grounded the Typhoons.

'I was to carry out the practical tests as required at suitable times between operational sorties. It would involve flying under Group Radar Control (GRC) on a special radio telephone (R/T) channel, on courses and at set heights, speeds and rates of turn on gyro settings to arrive at a speciific target point from a set angle of dive. Short flights were also to be undertaken for the calibration of the radar equipment.

'In discussions I stressed the difficulties in taking off and returning to base in adverse weather conditions in which GRC would operate. Our attrition rate was already quite high [a tactful way of saying that a lot of Typhoon pilots were being killed in action as it was] and it seemed that it would increase if the new system was introduced.

'However, the first test was on 10 February 1945 on a trip which lasted eighty minutes. I did my best on following instructions as called, but didn't arrive at the anticipated target point as described by the controller.

'I never mentioned what the project was about, but it had been leaked by someone, as I received a lot of ribbing from the squadron boys to make certain that the new system wasn't too successful!

'I always tried my best, but to me the aircraft speed seemed to be the main problem, as a warning from GCC of a turn and rate of turn always led to a final disparity in diving on the correct target point.

'I was pretty certain that the whole exercise was aimed at a future propaganda release to bluff the Germans with Typhoons flying over roads and railway lines at specific targets in adverse weather conditions to reduce German activities.

'I did the last radar calibration with GCC on 11 March 1945 – a fifteen minute flight and later the same day a radar exercise of eighty-five minutes.

'I always moaned after each exercise, as GCC would advise 'end of exercise' and switched off, never giving me a course to steer back to base. Consequently it took me a long time to get reorientated.

'These trips did not count as operational.They were the last ones that I had while with 175 Squadron at Volkel. I had completed 122 operational trips and was posted to 83 GSU at Dunfold to give replacement Typhoon pilots some operational training and then lead a ferry flight of them in new replacement aircraft to Typhoon squadrons on the continent. When calling at Volkel I always enquired about the project I had been on but it had never continued – possibly because of the better war outlook.'

Chapter 13
The End in Sight

Ronnie Sheward, who had been promoted to command No 266 Squadron on 7 March 1945, led it on 19 March against an important target on an operation about which the news media rhapsodised: 'A smashing blow was struck during the afternoon at the enemy ability to equip and refit armoured fighting vehicles for the big battle that cannot be long delayed on the British sector of the Western Front. A repair depot near Emmerich capable of dealing with over 500 tanks and other fighting vehicles was wrecked by Typhoons. A reconnaissance pilot said, "It was a miniature Falaise. I don't think one vehicle escaped".'

The Rhine crossing, on 24 March 1945, Operation Varsity, was the Allied air forces' last big show of the war. It took two and a half hours for the 1500 RAF and USAAF aeroplanes and 1300 gliders that set off from England to pass any given point. They carried 17,000 troops, 800 vehicles and guns and 600 tons of ammunition.

No 146 Wing by now comprised five squadrons. 266 Squadron's first mission was to take out a fortified farmhouse on the German side of the frontier. From S/L Sheward's description, it was evidently a classic attack: 'We all had direct hits with salvoes of R/P, leaving the place wrecked. The next task was to silence the flak. The pilots operated in pairs, taking the two rôles in turn: one drawing fire while the other looked out for the flashes and dived on a gun position as soon as he spotted it.' This seems to be pushing the principle that *"Non nobis solum nati sumus . . . We are not born for ourselves alone"* a trifle far. As Sheward, wryly remarks in retrospect decades later, 'An ideal pastime for anyone who was tired of living'.

F/L John Shellard's recollection of that epic day when 1500 aeroplanes and 1300 gliders, loaded with paratroops, glider-borne soldiers of all arms, vehicles and ammunition crowded the air space, carries a note of awe. 'Hundreds of aircraft all in a couple of square miles and at roughly the same height, in a thick cloud of grey/brown murk thrown up by the artillery, mortars and general conflagration. All we could feel was the prop wash from aircraft we couldn't see and which suddenly appeared in front somewhere.'

The aircraft he flew that day were RB232 against an SS Headquarters, on an air test and an armed recce and MN738 on an anti-flak patrol.

The sky was cluttered with aircraft of many types at low, medium and high levels, among bursting anti-aircraft shells. This operation, and the similar one carrying troops to the Normandy landings on the night preceding the dawn of D-Day and on that day itself, must have borne the greatest collision risks of the war.

On 26 April John Shellard, F/L Gus Fowler, P/O David Morgan and Warrant Officer (W.O.) Jock Barrie had just strafed a train near the German/Danish frontier when Morgan radioed that he had to make a forced landing. Barrie warned that two Me262 jet fighters were about to attack. The leading one overshot and Barrie fired at it, then turned to cover Morgan. Shellard fired next and saw that the enemy aircraft at which he had shot was burning. He gave the other one a burst, then turned again to watch the first one go down. Fowler also fired at the second one but it departed, climbing. This engagement was the last time Typhoons shot down a German fighter.

On the evening of 4 May 1945 the German armies in north-west Germany, Denmark and Holland surrendered. On 7 May the war in Europe formally ended.

Second Tactical Air Force Final Order of Battle

83 Group
121 Wing
B150 Hustedt
W/C J. G. Keep DSO
Squadrons: 175 184 245

124 Wing
B158 Lübeck
W/C M. R. Ingle-Finch DFC AFC
Squadrons: 137 (detached to 125 Wg)
B118 181 182 247

143 Wing
B150 Hustedt
W/C F. G. Grant DSO DFC
Squadrons: 438 439 440

123 Wing
B103 Plantlunne
W/C J. C. Button DFC
Squadrons: 164 183 198 609

146 Wing
B111 Alhorn
W/C J. C. Deall DFC
Squadrons: 193 197 263 266
(at Fairwood Common, Armament Practise Camp)

Chapter 14
Specimen Intelligence Summary and Extracts from Pilots' Logbooks

121 WING INTELLIGENCE SUMMARY

B. 100   *Dawn to Dusk 26 March 1945*   *No. 85*

WING OPS

The day started with 2 armed recces,followed by V.C.P. with 4 a/c on cab rank every 15 minutes until the light failed. On the whole the weather was kind to us though some afternoon sorties were rather spoiled by heavy rain clouds in the Battle Area.

The number of sorties reached a second high record – 192. Serviceability was again magnificient and losses small – 1 Typhoon Cat [category] E. W/O Wyper, the pilot of this aircraft had to bail out after being hit by flak. His parachute had only just opened when he landed, fortunately with only superficial injuries.

The score for the day was as follows:-

Sqd	TNK	MET	Strong Points	Ops	Suspicious Woods	H.Q.	Rly Sheds
174	1–2	9–7	4	1	1	–	–
175	–	1–0	9	–	1	–	–
184	2–1	6–26	4	–	3	–	–
245	1–2	7–1	7	–	1	–	–
Totals	4–5	23–34	24	1	6	1	1

Perhaps the most interesting sortie of the day was led by F/O Walker – 184 Squadron. He was briefed in the air to attack SP guns in buildings near a railway crossing, but he was warned that our troops were very close. He saw our line and it was only 40 yards from his target. He claimed one SP [self-propelled] gun [usually 88mm] destroyed and, in 3 further attacks which he made from low level,

considerable damage was done to houses, one of which produced an explosion. Interrogation had only just been completed when a message came from the Battalion Commander of the infantry to say that Walker's attack had been completely successful and it had enabled our troops to walk in and capture what had been a very strong point.

W/C Keep led a very successful sortie in which two tanks were left smoking and their trailers on fire; these were probably SP guns with ammo trailers. He also destroyed 5 and damaged one MET [mechanical enemy transport].

P/O Wheatcroft (184) destroyed 3 MET and 1 tank as well as damaging 6 MET and 1 tank.

These are three examples of successful sorties in which the results were observed; but the vast majority of sorties showed no result to the pilots though doubtless they were of immense advantage to our troops on the ground.

174 Squadron

Flying 44 sorties today 174, together with the rest of the Wing, continued picking out the spots in the enemy's geography where it hurts, and punching hard. Numerous results of first-rate attacks were confirmed, and so we go merrily on.

From the Pilots to the Ground Crew

For three days the pilots of 174 have witnessed one of those spectacles that reach the heart, and make the game of life worthwhile. It has seen a body of men in the hour of necessity reacting in the best impulse that human nature knows – the sense of absolute responsibility. The effort that has kept our aircraft to such a pitch of serviceability has not been the mere daily work of a number of men. It has been the willingness by one and all to, at any time, do anything, anywhere, with the maximum of efficiency and expedition.

Ground Crew we thank you, and at the same time solemnly promise that we will take full advantage of your every well-spent minute on the ground, to bring to the squadron in the air, honour and a brave name.

175 Squadron

The weather holding out the programme of Hun-bashing was continued. ('Our target was a tank in a wood. Well we hit the wood anyway.') The Hun contrived to concentrate his animosity during the morning and Jock Wyper got hit. He managed to cross the Rhine before baling out. Trying to bunt out of the kite he struck his knee on the windschield and eventually got free at about 1000 feet with the undoubted help of his patron saint and his horoscope in the Sunday Press. The brolly opened too close to the ground for comfort but far enough away to keep him in one piece. After being provided with strong drink by the Army he returned to the Squadron the same morning. Congratulations, Jock, and nice work!

In the afternoon the C.O. was going to and fro on his lawful occasions in the Battle Area and with microscopic eye and eagle glance of a Sherlock Holmes was sniffing out some Huns. Unfortunately he was at 3000 feet at the time. Very promptly some flak removed the greater part of the port aileron and port tail-plane! Minus hood he managed to land at base wheels down, and, efficient to the last detail, smartly taxied the remains to Echelon! [servicing echelon].

No other extraordinary excitement graced the day.

Between sorties several bods [bodies i.e. people] were at work building roofs to their foxholes. At least these are probably rainproof if nothing else.

We seem to cross the Rhine very frequently these days, without the pastimes of the three German officers of 14–18. [A scabrous First World War song: 'Three German officers crossed the line/To woo (putting it politely) the women and drink the wine . . .']. In fact life on the ground waxes very quiet.

184 Squadron

Another very successful day for the Wing and the Squadron. Again we were able to do more sorties and fire more rockets than any other Squadron, which only goes to show how far a little co-operation between pilots and ground crew can go. Our C.O. arrived back from leave more than a little annoyed at having missed part of the big show. He gave vent to his feelings by doing two shows in rapid succession, and as far as we can gather, intends to do a whole heap more at the earliest opportunity. In addition, we welcome two new pilots to the Squadron – Sgt. Turner and Sgt. Manchett. Consequently we are well up to strength which will doubtless lead to even better results in the future. An early night was had by all in anticipation of another big day tomorrow.

We notice that the odd slit-trench has been constructed in view of last night's disturbance. We have our doubts as to whether their constructors will be the first to occupy them in times of emergency. The organised hunt in the woods by our E.O. [Engineer Officer] proved rather fruitless, but perhaps it will have frightened off any unwanted intruders who might have been lurking within.

245 Squadron

PILOTS' GEN. Another splendid day of close support where many well-directed rockets and cannon fire caused further confusion and despondency amongst the hostile natives.

F/O Glossold on the first scout of the morning was unfortunately hit by a poisoned arrow and was forced to take to his parachute, which he did most successfully. He was last seen running towards a track in Indian Territory, about 6 miles in front of our forward troops. We all wish him the best of luck and a speedy return.

Weather deteriorated somewhat late in the afternoon, thunder clouds and lightening [sic] being encountered.

Aircraft serviceability was again maintained up to its normal high standard.

A quiet evening was spent inside our stockade. Our only sorrow is the entire absence of squaws.

Armament. Yet another record-breaking day. Yesterday, three more expenditure records set up. Our Wing ammunition record was shattered by no less than 15,000 rounds. 184 Squadron was the first Squadron ever to fire more than 400 rockets in one day, and 174 Squadron the first to fire more than 17,000 rounds during the same period.

One complete R.P. weighs 100lb. One hundred 20mm rounds weigh 56lb. Bearing these weights in mind we feel that no praise is too high for the boys who rearmed this weight of explosive. By the end of a twelve-hour day a rocket seems to weigh 200lb. And the last cannon re-arm, done with the aid of a box of matches (Equipment please note) just about breaks the proverbial camel's back.

Yesterday's results [rockets and shells fired] were:-

Squadron	R.P.	20mm
174	337	17,412
175	328	12,713
184	405	14,046
245	284	13,980

WHO BUILT OUR STRIP? Since we began operating from this strip we have flown on three successive days a number of sorties greatly in excess of our previous record. It will be of interest to everyone that No 13 Airfield Construction Group who have made this excellent strip for us were originally intended to complete by 31 March. Fortunately for us Col. Rankin and his staff did a first-class job in many days less than target date and enabled us to fly in on the 21, settle down, and operate to maximum effort at the beginning of the battle. Those who made the strip share the success of these days with us – and to them our thanks.

OPERATIONAL & TACTICAL CONSIDERATIONS. The last three days' intensive operations of respectively 209, 160 and 192 sorties per day have all been Wing records and despite this, aircraft serviceability has remained at an extremely high level due to the ideal arrangements as far as pilots and ground crew are concerned of four aircraft per squadron per hour. Under these conditions daylight is the only limiting factor on operations.

The 'Cab Rank' system has worked extremely smoothly and the close support targets given have all been easy to find due to excellent controlling on the part of either advanced contact cars or advanced G.C.C. The lack of flak in the close support and red smoke areas has been very welcome, giving all pilots plenty of time to do really accurate shooting when near our own forward troops.

After the fifteen minutes on 'cab rank' should no target materialise the aircraft press on to the back areas searching for any movement. There is a lot of scattered MET to be found and pilots find that 3000 to 4000 feet is reasonable height, although at times it is necessary to come down much lower especially where roads run through woods. On this type of work four a/c is the ideal formation as it is very flexible and has considerable hitting power.

There is still plenty of flak in the rear areas but until an attack has commenced it does not often open up, presumably because it took a considerable beating on the first day and is rightly scared of a repetition.

MILITARY SITUATION. The least that can be said about the 2nd British and 9th American Armies' bridgeheads is that they are going according to plan. Considerable advances have been made and rapid re-grouping is taking place. PoWs are still staggering into the cages especially from the eastern sector i.e. N and NE of Wesel. The 9th Army's bridgehead is nine miles deep on a broad base.

The Remagen area is becoming interesting and the bridgehead has grown to 30 miles by 20 deep. Two smaller bridgeheads have been made further up the Rhine and then further south still General Patton expanding his bridgehead rapidly has swung N and then E to Frankfurt. Great developments are to be expected in this area if the weather is at all reasonable.

27 March 1945. Signed by the Senior Intelligence Officer [a flight lieutenant] No 121 Wing Headquarters.

Pilots' entries in their logbooks are unequalled in the terse way that they convey the reality of battle. T.S.Eliot's declaration, 'Human kind/Cannot bear very much reality' is disproved in war. Airmen, sailors and soldiers have no option but to bear what duty demands: airmen perhaps most of all, for there has never been conscription into the flying branch of the RAF.

S/L R. E. G. Sheward DFC had flown many ground attack and escort operations on Hurricanes before going on to Typhoons. Here are some extracts from his log with additional notes made by him, while he was a flight commander in 263 Squadron and commanding 266.

1.1.45 Runway frozen. Watched 8 Fw190s & 12 Me109s fly over our drome, Deurne B70 Antwerp. They flew straight and level. Strafed a few aircraft but put up a very poor show. AA got 9, Mustangs 2. If only we could have taken off we could have murdered them. I have my flight down at dispersal for the early morning show which was Army Support E of Dordrecht. Later on led 8 a/c with RPs on 20-plus invasion barges. We had 7 direct hits and strafed. Wizard prang no flak, which made a change.

4.1.45 Army Support E of Dordrecht. 8 a/c RPs strafed Sliedrecht factory where 600 Huns were stationed & invasion barges. Good results. Bags of flak.

5.1.45 Army Support Schouwen Zierikjee with 266 and 257. Destroyed Army H.Q. house in orchard. Wizard results.

5.1.45 Taxied out to lead 8 a/c on request from the Army, to make a recce to see how strong the enemy was, when I saw a Typhoon flying over our heads trying to dislodge a bomb which was stuck. It came off, exploded and damaged 4 of my a/c, which were unable to take off. Flying Control called me to abandon the mission. I felt I couldn't let the Army down, so after finding out that 4 of us were OK I led the remaining a/c and we strafed houses and roads where Army requested, with good results.

24.2.45 Led 9 a/c, cloud 8–9 10s over target area. RPs target one house demolished S of Calcar.

18.3.45 Attacked HQ Gorssel of General Blaskowitz. 62 staff were eliminated.

7.4.45 Found 20-plus trucks in main yard at Assen. Got a direct hit – blew up smoke to 2500ft 2 more direct hits and 20mm strikes.

10.4.45 Armed recce NE Emden 1 hr 45 mins. 3-ton lorry, 1 large lorry and staff car destroyed. One of my pilots called 'Transport below' & I led my section down to attack but when I saw it was horse-drawn I called the attack off. One of my pilots asked 'Why did you do that, Boss?' and I said they didn't ask to be in this war & anyway I love horses too much to kill them in cold blood.'

F/L Derek Lovell's logbook entries are typical of all pilots' – cryptic. Space did not allow room for much elaboration on events, but a reader's imagination dwelling on these matter-of-fact statements is free to conjure up the buffeting of explosions as flak bursts around the aeroplane and the pilot's own bombs detonate close beneath it; the engine noise and effects of 'g' in a tight turn, the total concentration on hitting the target and avoiding a mid-air collision, the sensation of pulling into a steep climb at the bottom of a dive. Only the familiar smells that linger in aircraft are missing: remember that the first thing a Typhoon pilot had to do when he entered the cockpit was to switch on the oxygen supply.

The entries below are taken at random and the gaps between dates do not mean that Derek Lovell did not fly on those days.

August 1944
2 From Tangmere to B3 1hr 5 mins.
2 Fighter cover. Cover to 266 Sqn. Rockets. Uneventful. 1.05.
3 Close support Ramrod. Attacked an ammo dump SE of Caen. Good prang.
6 Armed recce. 0.55. Attacked a wood. Black smoke otherwise uneventful.
7 Close support Ramrod. O.45. Bombed a wood S of Vire. Strafed 4 MT [motor transport] 1 flamer.
8 Close support Ramrod. 0.35. Bombed château nr Gouvire – good prang.
8 Close support Ramrod. 0.35. Bombed at Poussey. Very good prang.
9 Close support Ramrod. 0.45. Bombed an

ammo dump – very good prang.

12 Close support Ramrod. 0.45. Mortar & gun positions plastered near Le Thiery – very good.

17 Rhubarb. 1.05. With McFee as No 1. Very little seen. I destroyed 1 car and 1 DR [despatch rider].

October

5 Ramrod. Railway junction at Utrecht. Good prang – my dear the flak!!

11 Close support Ramrod. 1.10. Village of Oosberg to be wiped out. Excellent bombing.

11 Close support Ramrod. 0.55. Same target more good bombing.

11 Close support Ramrod. 0.50. Same target with 1000lb low level then anti-flak.

11 Close support Ramrod 0.50. Same target low level then anti-flak again.

15 Ramrod. 1.10. Railway crossover at Geldern. V good prang. Attacked a train. Engine damaged.

21 Ramrod. 0.50. Rail junction N of Breda – 4 direct hits, accurate-flak.

24 Ramrod. 1.10. 15 Army [enemy] HQ Dordrecht. Wing show, good prang.

24 Close Support Ramrod. 0.35. Village of Bath holding up troops – good prang.

28 Close Support Ramrod. 1.10. Factory at Wemkirk – good prang. Mahaffy forced down.

29 Close Support Ramrod. 0.50. Guns near Flushing – excellent prang – debris 3000ft. Peter attacked a barge – sunk.

Chapter 15
Close Control System

The organisation for providing air support was quick and efficient. The Army allotted the priority of targets and the RAF dealt with them in order.

An immediate response was also made possible by the Cab Rank system. This had been originated by Desert Air Force in North Africa, was also used by DAF in Italy and by 2nd TAC in the France and Germany Campaign.

Every day at dawn a ground attack pilot known as the controller took post as near the front line as possible, from which he had a good view of the battle area. Originally he was in a tank but this was soon changed to a truck in which he was accompanied by a driver, a wireless mechanic, an RAF radio-telephone (R/T) operator and an Army R/T op. In the advance that followed the Normandy landings an armoured vehicle was used.

A 'cab rank' of ground-attack fighters at low level orbited a point close behind the forward control post (FCP). In DAF these were usually six Mustangs, Hurricanes or Spitfires; in 2nd TAF, four Typhoons.

The controller and pilots had special large-scale maps gridded in 500x400 metre rectangles, numbered from south to north and lettered from west to east. This made the target's position quick and easy to communicate: e.g. 'square 2D', without having to waste time on six-figure co-ordinates. The controller then gave a visual and precise description of the target, which was promptly attacked. If no target was offered after fifteen minutes, the cab rank departed to seek objectives for their attention and were replaced by four more Typhoons. This went on until dusk.

The United States Army Air Force adopted the system in Italy and carried it on from Normandy to VE Day.

Chapter 16
The Typhoon Compared With its Kin

Shakespeare's statement of the obvious, 'some men are born great, some achieve greatness, and some have greatness thrust upon them' would score zero in a contest of original thinking, but does have relevance to the Typhoon's status as a ground-attack fighter: it was thrust into the rôle when it proved unsuitable for the one it was designed to play.

The Air Ministry ordered another fighter from Hawker: the Tempest, a development of the Typhoon. The Mks I and V were to have Sabre engines, the Mk III a Griffon and Mk II a Centaurus. The first to fly was the prototype Mk V (HM595), a converted Typhoon, on 2 September 1942. HM599, a Mk I, was the next, on 24 February 1943, but flew only as a prototype. The Mk III was abandoned. The Mks II and V therefore were the main production versions.

The first, and major, advantage the Tempest enjoyed over its progenitor, the Typhoon, was the newly designed wing. It was thinner than the latter's, its area was smaller and it had an elliptical planform. These features gave great potential for both improving high-altitude performance and reducing the wing's tendency to buffet at around 500mph.

The Mk V was the only mark to see war service. The first production Tempest (JN729) first flew on 9 May 1944 and 800 were produced by August 1945; the last being SN355. After the war, the RAF bought 142 Mk V.

It was the Tempest that performed a task that would have fallen to the Typhoon if it had been fast enough at the required altitude. Both types had the same armament, but only the Tempest was capable of 466mph at 18,500ft, which enabled it to overtake the V-1 and V-2 flying bombs ('Doodlebugs' to the British public), which usually flew at 1500ft to 2000ft, by both day and night. Fighters shooting them down at a range of 300 yds were able to break away in time to avoid the blast of the explosion. In the dark, they aimed at the missile's bright exhaust. Tempest squadrons shot down some 800.

W/C R. P. Beamont, DSO DFC & bar became Leader of the first Tempest Wing, comprising 3, 56 and 486 Squadrons.

The Tempest squadrons operated over the continent from bases in England until after the Arnhem assault in September 1944. The personnel not only lived in greater comfort than the Typhoon pilots and ground officers and airmen who were under canvas at the beach-head and in makeshift accommodation as they advanced from there, but also, of course, suffered no damage when the *Luftwaffe* made its New Year's Day attacks.

By the war's end seven 2nd TAF and one Fighter Command squadrons were flying Tempests and had shot down 240 enemy aircraft, including Me262s, plus thirteen probables. This compared well with the record of the Typhoon, which could not match its performance at the altitudes at which most fighter combat took place and 'Doodlebugs' flew. Typhoons scored 247 enemy aircraft destroyed plus twenty-seven probables.

Hurricanes, Spitfires, Mustangs and Beaufighters all played an important part in attacking ground targets in various theatres of war, but the Typhoon was adapted to this type of operation, and the Tempest was purpose-designed for it. They are regarded as its joint champions in the campaign across France, Belgium, Holland and Germany.

The squadrons equipped with the Tempest II were Nos 5, 16, 20, 26, 30, 33, 54, 152, 247. With the Tempest V: 3, 33, 56, 80, 222, 247, 266, 274, 287, 349, 486, 501. Tempest VI: 3, 6, 8, 16, 56, 80 39, 213, 249.

Chapter 17
Typhoons Issued to Squadrons and Other Flying Units

Abbreviations

A & AEE	Aircraft & Armament Experimental Establishment
ADF	Aircraft Delivery Flight
AFDU	Air Fighting Development Unit
APC	Armament Practise Camp
APS	Armament Practise School
ASWDU	Air-Sea Warfare Development Unit
ATDU	Air Transport Development Unit
CCDU	Coastal Command Development Unit
CFE	Central Fighter Establishment
CFS	Central Flying School
CS	Communications Squadron
DBF	Destroyed By Fire
DBR	Damaged Beyond Repair
DH	De Havilland
ECDU	Electronic Countermeasures Development Unit
FIDS	Fighter Interception Development Squadron
FIU	Fighter Interception Unit
FLS	Fighter Leaders' School
FPP	Ferry Pilot Pool
GDC	Group Disbandment Centre
GSU	Group Support Unit
Mkrs	Makers
MU	Maintenance Unit
NFD	No Further Data
OTU	Operational Training Unit
RAE	Royal Aircraft Establishment
RR	Rolls-Royce
RSU	Repair & Salvage Unit
SF	Station Flight
TEU	Tactical Exercise Unit

3317 Typhoons were built: 2 prototypes and 15 Mk IA by Hawker and 3300 Mk IA and IB at Gloster's Hucclecote factory. In 1941 the total deliveries were 28. In 1942, 677. 1943, 1131. 1944, 1165. 1945, 299. The RAF did not receive the last one, SQ722, until November 1945. In 1945 and 1946, some were used for target-towing and in the latter year the type was declared obsolete.

Where only an aircraft's serial number and the unit(s) to which it was sent are shown, there is nothing of interest to record and it was ultimately struck off charge or sold for scrap.

Serial No   Delivered To and Significant History

250 IA and IB delivered between December 1941 and July 1942

R7576	RAE/56/RAE
R7577	Mkrs and RAE
R7578	Mkrs and Napier
R7579	CFS/Mkrs
R7580	AFDU/56/59 OTU Spun into ground near Milfield 13.6.43
R7581	AFDU/609
R7581	56
R7582	56
R7583	56
R7584	56
R7585	56 Hit tractor on overshoot near Matlask 24.8.42
R7586	56
R7587	56
R7588	56
R7589	56/266/181/RAE
R7590	266/8MU Undercarriage retracted on landing Little Rissington 22.6.4
R7591	56/59 OTU/FLS
R7592	56 Dived into ground near East Harling, Norfolk 1.11.41
R7593	56
R7594	56
R7595	56/AFDU/609/RAE/3TEU
R7597	56
R7497	56
R7598	56 To synthetic trainer 8.10.42
R7599	56
R7613	56
R7614	RAEE
R7615	56/56 OTU
R7616	56
7617	A & AEE/Mkrs/RAE
R7618	266 Flew into ground in bad visibility

ABOVE: ATC cadets from Stround (Glos) visiting an RAF airfield. (Bruce Robertson)

Serial No	Delivered To and Significant History	Serial No	Delivered To and Significant History
	near Welney, Cambs 11.6.42	R7636	266
R7619	266	R7637	266 Spun into ground near Duxford 7.3.42
R7620	56/De Havilland		
R7621	56/182/59 OTU	R7638	Napier and Mkrs
R7622	266	R7639	266/RR
R7623	266	R7640	609
R7624	266/Duxford/609/182/198	R7641	56/266
R7625	Crashed before delivery 27.1.42	R7642	266
R7626	266	R7643	56/Napier
R7627	266/181/'93	R7644	56 Tail broke off in dive near Spalding, Lincs 18.8.42
R7628	609 Belly-landed Duxford 10.6.42		
R7629	56/182 Overshot landing Martlesham Heath 30.9.42	R7645	266 Abandoned after engine failure 25 miles off Cherbourg 15.9.42
R7630	266/FIU/609/3/59 OTU Crashed on landing Milfield 26.5.43	R7646	Mkrs/56/Mkrs and A & AEE
		R7647	609 Abandoned near Ely 29.5.42
R7631	266/486/181/183	R7648	56
R7632	SOC 2.4.43	R7649	266/181/183/3/59 OTU
R7633	56 Belly-landed at Oulton 27.8.4	R7651	609/FIU/193/55 OTU
R7634	266	R7652	56 Undercarriage collapsed on landing Matlask
R7635	266		

Serial No	Delivered To and Significant History	Serial No	Delivered To and Significant History
R7653	56/182/198 Crashed in forced landing Acklington 26.2.43	R7687	266 Control lost in cloud over Hampshire 28.11.42
R7654	266 Flew into ground out of cloud Gt Casterton, Rutland 24.4.42	R7688	609/182/195
R7655	266 Crashed in forced landing near Duxford 4.6.42	R7689	266/109 Shot down in Channel 15.12.42
R7672 29.6.42	266 Crashed on landing Duxford	R7690	609/198
R7673	A & AEE	R7691	609/182 Crashed on Take-off Martlesham Heath 13.11.42
R7674	266	R7692	Mkrs
R7675	56	R7694	56/Napier Crashed on test flight 26.8.42
R7676	266/181 Spun into ground Duxford 27.9.42	R7695	266 Broke up in air Wooton Glanville, Dorset 24.10.42
R7677	609/182	R7696	266/181/198/181/59 OTU
R7678	56 Shot down by Spitfires off Dover 1.6.42	R7697	Napier
R7679	56	R7698	609/Duxford/198
R7680	609/56	R7699	SOC Oct 43
R7681	609/182/197/55 OTU	R7700	A & AEE and Mkrs
R7682	56	R7701	SOC March 43
R7683	56/182/59 OTU	R7702	56 Undercarriage collapsed on landing Matlask 4.11.42
R7684	56/Duxford/193	R7703	609
R7685	Gloster	R7704	266
R7686	266 Ditched 15 miles E of Torquay 3.2.43	R7706	609/182/197/59 OTU
		R7707	266
		R7708	609 Hit by own AA and abandoned Pegwell Bay, Kent 31.10.4

Below: Typhoon R7700 above cloud. (Philip Jarrett)

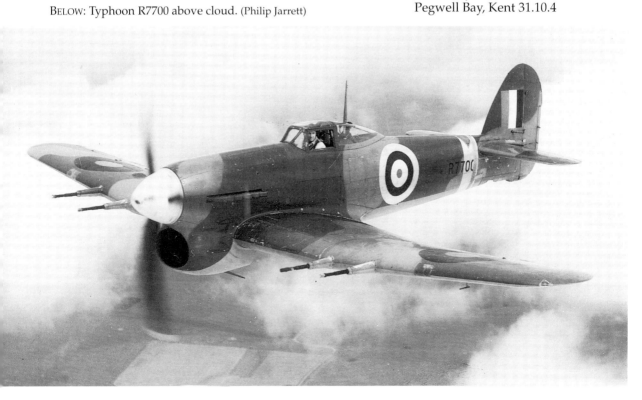

Serial No	Delivered To and Significant History
R7710	609 Collided with R7817 on take-off Duxford 26.6.42
R7711	56 Crashed on landing Coltishall 1.10.42
R7712	Napier
R7713	609
R7714	56 Missing 10.4.43
R7715	266 Engine cut on approach Exeter 13.2
R7739	56 Dived into ground near Oulton 12.4.43
R7752	609/56
R7753	SOC 8.6.43
R7766	486
R7771	Napier/Mkrs/182
R7800	266
R7813	266 Missing (Dieppe) 19.8.42
R7814	266 Collided with Spitfire 16.9.42
R7815	266 Shot down by Spitfires 20 miles S of Dungeness 19.8.42
R7816	609 Crashed in forced landing Catwater Farm, Cambridge 30.7.42
R7817	609 Collided with R7710 on take-off Duxford 26.6.42
R7818	609 Flew into Dover balloon barrage and crashed 5.11.42
R7819	266 Crashed in forced landing Warmwell 8.11.42
R7820	266/247 Shot down by flak near Vimoutiers 18.8.44
R7821	266 Dived into ground Morebath, Bampton, Devon 2.2.43
R7822	266/3ETU Caught fire and crashed, Low Newton, Northumberland 5.6.44
R7823	56 Crashed in forced landing Matlask 24.4.43
R7824	56
R7825	56/181/184
R7826	56
R7829	266
R7845	609
R7846	56 Abandoned in spin Fordham, Suffolk 8.12.42
R7847	266 Undershot landing at Ibsley 15.9.42
R7851	1
R7853	56 Hit by fire from Spitfire and abandoned 10 miles off Dungeness 30.7.42
R7854	56 Lost tail during aerobatics near Brinton, Norfolk 17.1.43

ABOVE: R7881, the only Typhoon night fighter (NF IB) – fitted with AI Mk 5 radar (Mk 14 whose aerials are seen on the port wing). (Philip Jarrett)

Serial No	Delivered To and Significant History
R7855	609 Crashed on landing Manston 16.4.43
R7856	1 Spun into ground 3 miles NW of Tangmere 23.8.43
R7861	1 Missing off Amble, Northumberland 21.10.42. Presumed collided with R7867
R7862	Crashed forced landing near Charterhall 21.11.42
R7863	1 Missing 19.5.43
R7864	Crashed forced landing near Daneshill, Sussex 13.2.43
R7865	1
R7866	486 Crashed forced landing Durrington, Sussex 24.11.42
R7867	1 Missing off Amble, Northumberland 21.10.42
R7868	1
R7869	56/183/3
R7872	609 Shot down by FW190s off Cap Gris Nez 14.2.3
R7876	1 Missing over Channel 29.3.43
R7877	1
R7879	257
R7880	609/245 Crashed on take-off Lydd 4.8.43
R7881	RAE/FIU/3TEU
R7882	266
R7883	609 Belly-landed Duxford 1.8.42
R7889	181/55 OTU
R7914	182/195
R7915	266 Ditched 25 miles SE Start Point, Devon 17.6.43
R7919	1

Above: Typhoon IB R8224, November 1942. (Philip Jarrett)

Serial No	Delivered To and Significant History	Serial No	Delivered To and Significant History
R7921	1		High Ercall 29.7.42
R7922	1	R8634	1 Crashed forced landing Pevensey,
R7923	1		Sussex 28.4.43
R8198	Mkrs/DH	R8635	RAE and Mkrs Crashed in forced
R8199	56 Shot down by Spitfires off Dover		landing Meadfoot Beach, Torquay
	1.6.42		21.5.43
R8200	56	R8636	257/245
R8220	56/609	R837	257 Overshot landing Zeals 24.1.43
R8221	609/182 Hit balloon cable and forced	R8638	257/266 Hit obstruction on runway
	landed 4 miles south Salisbury		during forced landing Portreath
R8222	609		30.7.43
R8223	56	R8639	257
R8224	56/609 Overstressed during	R8642	257
	aerobatics Lympne 13.9.43	R8650	257 Crashed forced landing near
R8225	193		Linstead, Hants 29.11.42
R8226	18MU Crashed in forced landing	R8651	193
	Craigs Marsh, Dumfries 15.1.43	R8652	257/59 OTU Crashed on landing
R8227	197/486 Hit by DN559 while parked		Rearsby 15.8.43
	Tangmere 23.5.43	R8653	257
R8229	181	R8654	257/247
R8230	245 Hit by flak, crash landed near	R8655	257
	Longingen 11.4.45	R8656	257
R8630	1	R8658	257
R8631	1	R8659	257
R8632	257	R8660	486/195
R8633	257 Lost tail and crashed 2 miles SW	R8661	257/59 OTU

Serial No	Delivered To and Significant History
R8663	257 Crashed forced landing Chilframe, Dorset 15.12.42
R8680	257
R8681	486
R8682	486 Swung on take-off and Hit Lancaster R5665 Tangmere 24.2.43
R8683	486 Missing, presumed ditched 2.10.42
R8684	486
R6865	257
R8687	Duxford/247/245/175/184/245
R8688	RAE/247 Shot down by P-47 10 miles NE Arnhem 14.1.45
R8690	1 Crashed forced landing 4 miles NE Longtown 5.9.42
R8691	257
R8692	486
R8693	RAE/266/247
R8694	266
R8696	486/168
R8697	486
R8698	486 Caught fire and crashed, Battle, Sussex 16.10.42
R8699	486
R8701	486 Dived into sea 6 miles SE Selsey Bill 31.10.42
R8702	193
R8703	257
R8704	486

Serial No	Delivered To and Significant History
R8705	59 OTU
R8706	486
R8707	Duxford/198
R8708	1
R8709	Duxford 198/59 OTU Crashed on take-off Milfield 20.5.43
R8710	Duxford/257
R8711	257
R8712	486
R8713	Duxford
R8715	Duxford/609/56
R8720	9FPP Crashed on ferry flight, Brockworth 30.8.42
R8721	56
R8742	181
R8743	266 Ditched 15 miles SE Torquay 20.2.43
R8744	486 Ran out of fuel and crashed Tangmere 14.3.43
R8745	56
R8746	181
R8752	1
R8760	195 Compressed air bottle exploded in flight
R8762	Mkrs/A & AEE/Napier
R8767	266
R8768	257/486
R8772	181/266 Crashed in forest, landing Whimple, Devon 282.43

BELOW: A Typhoon with a sliding hood, R8809. (Philip Jarrett)

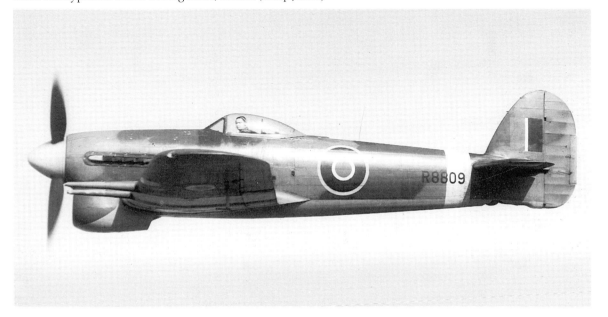

Serial No	Delivered To and Significant History	Serial No	Delivered To and Significant History
R8781	486/609/195/164/266	R8842	182
R8799	182/56/182/56 Dived into sea 40 miles E Great Yarmouth, 10.4.43	R8843	181/164/175/181 Shot down by flak near Goch 29.9.44
R8800	486 Missing 18.12.42	R8844	245/247
R8801	486 Damaged in action 31.10.42	R8845	609 Shot down by P47s near Doullens 21.12.43
R8802	181/266 Crashed forced landing between Etaples and Guincamp 11.1.43	R8861	266 Flew into sea 3 miles S Bold Head, Devon 15.4.43
R8803	Napier/266	R8862	182/181
R8804	266 Hit by flak and ditched off French coast 9.7.43	R8864	266 Crashed in night landing Warmwell 12.10.42
R8809	Mkrs and A & AEE	R8865	56 Forced-landed near The Hague, presumed hit by flak 13.1.43
R8810	609	R8866	181/3/181 Missing 15.7.43
R8811	266 Damaged by Spitfires and abandoned 4 miles ESE Exeter 17.4.43	R8867	181/247/198/247/59 OTU Crashed on take-off Milfield 18.4.43
R8812	609 Flew into hill near Battle, Sussex 23.10.42	R8868	181
R8813	266	R8871	181
R8814	486 Spun onto ground, Willedborough, Kent 25.10.42	R8872	257 Crashed forced landing in circuit, Exeter 22.12.42
R8815	609	R8873	56
R8816	486 Crashed on take-off Tangmere 24.2.43	R8874	609
		R8875	181 Belly-landed Detling 25.9.43
R8819	Duxford/195	R8876	56 Shot down by flak over The Hague 13.1.43
R8822	56 Collided with DN43 and crashed near Blickling, Norfolk 20.1.43	R8877	181
R8823	266 Overshot landing at Warmwell 27.10.42	R8878	266/59 OTU/FLS
R8824	56	R8879	181/3 Shot down by FW190s near Poix 18.5.43
R8825	56 Hit by pieces of DN265 and forced-landed, Barton Lamas, Norfolk 28.4.43	R8880	181 Missing in sea fog off Dutch coast 19.2.43
R8826	182/609/601/609	R8881	486
R8827	56	R8882	1/3 TEU/54 OTU
R8828	181/Snailwell/181	R8883	609 Dived into sea 3 miles ESE Dover 30.4.43
R8829	181	R8884	183/175
R8830	181	R8885	183/197/486
R8832	25	R8886	183/197/486
R8833	181 Shot down by Me109 off Pas de Calais 30.7.43	R888	609 Crashed forced landing Marston, Kent 29.3.43
R8834	182 Shot down by flak Tricqueville 16.4.33	R8889	A & AEE and Mkrs
R8835	181/3 Shot down by FW190s near Poix 18.5.43	R8890	193
		R8891	Mkrs and A & AEE Tropical trials in Middle East
R8836	181	R8892	182
R8837	609 Crashed in sea 15 miles S South Foreland 23.12.42	R8893	182 Crashed while attacking motor transport in Fôret d'Hardelot 28.4.43
R8838	609 Missing near Dunkerque 7.2.43	R8894	198 Hit by flak off Boulogne and presumed ditched 10.2.44
R8839	182 Crashed on take-off Ridgewell 22.1.43	R8895	181/3 Ditched after take-off, Bradwell Bay 22.3.44
R8840	181/164/198	R8896	181
R8841	609/247		

Serial No	Delivered To and Significant History
R8897	439/83 GSU Broke up in air near Milford, Surrey 28.8.44
R8898	609
R8899	609/56
R8900	198/181
R8923	257/263 Collided with MN769 over Belgium 14.10.44
R8924	182 Shot down by flak near Hesdin 25.4.43
R8925	Mkrs
R8926	3/3TEU/183/164
R8927	181/182 Missing 19.8.43
R8928	182
R8929	181
R8930	182 Crashed forced landing near Fairlop 18.4.43
R8931	182 Overshot landing and hit trench Appledram 26.6.43
R8932	181/247 Forced landing after engine cut Achmer 17.4.45
R8933	183/175
R8934	266
R8935	198 Crashed forced landing near Radcliffe, Northumberland 11.3.43
R8936	266/486
R8937	266 Crashed forced landing 1 mile north Topsham, Devon 30.4.43
R8938	195
R8939	198/266
R8940	609/56
R8941	486 Crashed landing Tangmere 8.1.43
R8942	1 Collided with DN615 in cloud and crashed near Benenden, Kent
R8943	RAE/DH/175/247
R8944	183 Ditched out of fuel in Channel 14.5.43
R8945	182
R8946	3 Missing from attack on convoy off Hook of Holland 1.7.43
R8947	182/181
R8966	182/198 Hit by flak and abandoned near B7 Normandy 18.8.44
R8967	FLS Crashed forced landing near Lowick, Northumberland 30.9.44
R8968	55 OTU/TEU
R8969	164
R8970	136 Shot down near Evreux 17.8.44
R8971	438/439 Wg/183 Flew into hill near New Cumnock, Ayrshire 20.2.44
R8972	609 Shot down by flak near Hottot 11.7.44

Serial No	Delivered To and Significant History
R8973	183
R8974	182
R8975	182
R8976	181/183/175
R8977	181/3/609
R8978	183/175
R8979	3 Shot down near Poix 18.5.43
R8980	257
R8981	182 Hit by flak and crash landed near Ford 13.5.43

300 IB delivered between October 1942 and March 1943

Serial No	Delivered To and Significant History
DN241	1 Overshot landing Southampton 9.2.43
DN242	183/175
DN243	183 Overshot landing Sherburn-in-Elmet 27.1.43
DN244	1
DN245	257
DN246	182/3 Shot down by FW190s near Poix 18.5.43
DN247	182 Taxiing accident Middle Wallop 7.1.43
DB248	3/245/183 Missing on sweep near Deventer 1.4.45
DN249	183/198/183/175
DN250	FLS
DN251	5FPP Flew into high ground in bad visibility a mile S Bunbury, Salop 21.11.42
DN252	246
DN253	183/3 Overshot landing Manston 8.7.43
DN254	247/263/59 OTU
DN256	257/193/56 OTU
DN257	183/175
DN258	175/184/181
DN259	181
DN260	247/3 TEU/55 OTU Crashed on overshoot Aston Down 23.4.45
DN261	182 Crashed forced landing 4 miles S Basingstoke, Hants 2.5.43
DN262	266
DN263	183/175 Belly-landed Detling 11.8.43
DN264	197
DN265	56 Broke up in air between Buxton and Lamas, Norfolk 28.4.43
DN266	195
DN267	193/175 Shot down by flak near Aunsey-sur-Odon, 30.7.44

Serial No	Delivered To and Significant History	Serial No	Delivered To and Significant History
DN268	183/175	DN318	257
DN269	9FPP Undershot landing Staverton 20.12.42	DN319	182
		DN320	197
DN270	197/56/609	DN321	197
DN271	183 Hit tree low flying near Weston Turville, Bucks	DN322	197
		DN323	451 Tropical trials aircraft
DN272	3 TEU/55 OTU	DN324	198/609/56
DN273	183/175	DN325	197
DN274	197 Lost 12.8.44 night flying	DN326	59 OTU
DN275	183/175	DN327	195/52 OTU/197/198
DN276	266/257	DN328	195
DN277	56/609	DN329	198/257/609/56
DN278	183 Crashed on overshoot Church Fenton 21.2.43	DN330	56/247/609
		DN331	1/195
DN293	245 Spun into ground attempting to out-turn a Mosquito, Pagham Harbour, Sussex 19.6.43	DN332	198/486
		DN333	197
		DN334	183/175
DN294	609 Shot down by FW190s off Cap Gris Nez 14.2.43	DN335	1 Overshot landing and overturned, Lympne 19.3.43
DN295	257 Crashed forced landing Biddlestone, Wilts 28.2.43	DN336	195
		DN337	181
DN296	266 Missing 16.8.43	DN338	247 Hit by flak, Merville, crashed Lympne 26.7.43
DN297	183 Undercarriage jammed, crash landed Church Fenton 14.2.43	DN339	56/609
		DN340	A & AEE/Mkrs/56 OTU
		DN341	247/198 Shot down by Flak near Zwolle 11.4.45
DN298	609/56		
DN299	198 Dived into sea 5 miles SW Dover 1.4.43	DN335	247
		DN356	198
DN300	609	DN357	3/197 Abandoned after engine cut near Poix 1.7.43
DN301	197		
DN302	195 Crashed landing Hutton Cranswick 20.12.42	DN358	195
		DN359	198/266 Hit by DN62 taxying at Exeter 7.2.43
DN303	486 Crashed forced landing near St Helens, Isle of Wight 29.5.43		
		DN360	609 Damaged by flak from ships off Vlissingen & belly-landed Manston 1.6.43
DN304	195		
DN305	198/609/56		
DN306	195 Crashed forced landing Maltby-in-Marsh, Lincs 23.1.43	DN361	195 Crashed in forced landing Plumstead, Norfolk 6.8.43
DN307	56/609 Matlask	DN362	197
DN308	193	DN363	197/486
DN309	197 Shot down by flak, Airel 10.4.43	DN364	197 Tail broke off in air, East Linton, East Lothian 28.1.43
DN310	193 Spun into ground near Kingston Halt, Devon 12.2.43		
		DN365	197 Crashed on training flight, Drem, Ayr, night flying 24.1.43
DN311	245		
DN312	245 Crashed forced landing Beach Bitton, Glos 17.1.43	DN366	Flew into high ground in cloud, E. Ferresay, East Lothian, 14.2.43
DN313	197 Flew into high ground 4 miles S of East Fortune 12.2.43	DN367	609/56
		DN368	198/486
DN314	195	DN369	486
DN315	195	DN370	195
DN316	486	DN371	197 Abandoned after engine cut 4
DN317	56 Crashed landing Matlask 23.4.43		

Serial No	Delivered To and Significant History	Serial No	Delivered To and Significant History
	miles S Newhaven, Sussex 18.7.43	DN428	486
DN372	193/197	DN429	247
DN373	195 Crashed in forced landing Warton, Lancs 16.4.43	DN430	247 Crashed on take-off Fairlop 28.5.43
DN374	56 Abandoned 35 miles off Happisburg, Norfolk 15.3.43	DN31	247 Missing, presumed shot down by fighters over French coast 15.4.43
DN375	195	DN432	1/164/2TAF CS
DN376	197 Crashed on approach, Tangmere 18.4.43	DN433	198/56 Collided with R8822 and crashed near Blickling, Norfolk 20.1.43
DN377	197/183/197		
DN378	198	DN434	245/247
DN379	198	DN435	198 Crashed during low-level aerobatics, Little Beeling, Suffolk 19.6.43
DN380	245/56/609		
DN381	247/166/83 GSU Spun into ground while low flying 1 mile SE Marks Cross, Sussex 9.6.44		
		DN436	3 TEU/55 OTU
		DN437	198
DN382	247/198	DN438	198 Dived into sea 2 miles off St Annes Pier, Lancs 26.5.43
DN384	59 OTU		
DN385	1	DN439	198 Undercarriage collapsed on take-off, Acklington 16.2.43
DN386	197 In night flying accident 18.4.3		
DN387	245	DN440	195 Engine cut, crashed at Mone 3.4.43
DN388	197 Crashed on take-off Tangmere 4.5.43		
		DN441	195
DN389	195 Damaged by Me109 and not repaired 15.5.43	DN442	257/266/59 OTU/FLS/3 TEU/55 OTU. Collided with MN285 taxying at Aston Down 17.4.45
DN404	247		
DN405	Crashed forced landing Stapton, Bucks 11.3.43		
		DN443	197
DN406	198/257/609/56	DN444	247 Spun into ground in bad visibility Madeley, Salop 193.43
DN407	197 Spun into ground, Patcham, Sussex 7.5.43		
		DN445	247 Crashed in forced landing High Ercall 1.3.43
DN408	183/175 Abandoned after engine cut over Channel 1.7.43		
		DN446	6 FPP Engine cut, crashed in forced landing Henlow 9.3.43
DN409	3 Crashed on take-off Manston 9.6.43		
DN410	197	DN447	56 Abandoned over North Sea 6.7.43
DN411	198/156 Spun into sea off Winterton, Norfolk 24.2.43	DN448	609/56
		DN449	175/245
DN412	195	DN450	3TEU/55 OTU
DN413	198	DN451	1
DN414	198	DN452	245/59 OTU
DN415	198	DN453	247
DN416	609 Ditched off Dover 6.4.43	DN467	198
DN417	55 OTU	DN468	245
DN420	247/245	DN469	609/56
DN421	181	DN470	193 Crashed on landing Harrowbeer 25.2.43
DN422	DFLT Bottisham/Del Flt. Abandoned take-off and hit crash tender Sawbridgworth 16.2.43		
		DN471	245
		DN472	609/56
DN424	Hit railway signal low flying near Burscough, Lancs 9.4.43	DN473	197 Abandoned after engine cut 3 miles off Selsey, Sussex 11.5.43
		DN540	247/245
DN426	198	DN541	245
DN427	198	DN542	247

Serial No	Delivered To and Significant History	Serial No	Delivered To and Significant History
DN543	55 OTU	DN594	174
DN544	195	DN596	486
DN545	197 Spun into ground, Bognor Regis, Sussex 22.4.43	DN597	182
		DN598	3 Shot down by FW190 near Poix 18.5.43
DN546	198	DN599	245 Abandoned over sea 5 miles E Winterton, Norfolk 14.5.43
DN547	609/56		
DN548	197/175/184	DN600	182
DN549	609/181 Sent to repair unit 9.11.44. NFT	DN601	609/56
		DN602	182 Crashed forced landing Blandford Camp, Dorset 27.3.43
DN550	198/174		
DN551	174/247 Shot down by flak attacking destroyer near Kiel 3.5.45	DN603	55 OTU
		DN606	175/183
DN552	198	DN607	197
DN553	182 Missing on sweep to Lille 17.8.43	DN608	245
		DN609	3 Crashed forced landing Laindon, Essex 28.4.43
DN554	257		
DN556	198	DN610	175/183
DN557	59 OTU Crashed on take-off Milfield 15.6.43	DN611	486 Hit by R8697 while parked, Tangmere 3.8.43
DN558	197	DN612	609
DN559	197 Hit R8227 on take-off, Tangmere 23.5.43	DN613	174
		DN614	193
DN560	609 Shot down by FW190 off Ramsgate 25.3.43	DN615	1 Collided in cloud with R8942 Benenden, Kent 6.3.43
DN561	609/3 TEU/55 OTU Crashed forced landing Farnham, Surrey 15.5.45	DN617	174
		DN618	198
DN562	Mkrs and RR/266 Abandoned 5 miles NW Caen 6.6.44	DN619	609 Shot down by flak near Dunkirk 11.4.43
DN576	609/Zeals/1/198/350/123 Wg	DN620	59 OTU/609
DN577	174/193	DN621	174
DN579	175/183	DN622	AFDU/257
DN580	175 Collided with EK134 and crashed, France 30.7.43	DN623	3 Crashed near Dordrecht on shipping strike 13.9.43
DN581	266		
DN582	609	*400 IB delivered between February and July 1943*	
DN583	609/56/268/609	EJ899	193/184/193/263
DN585	1 Missing presumed shot down by FW190s near Douai 16.6.43	EJ900	485
		EJ901	175/183/193/266 Engine cut, abandoned 33 miles off The Lizard, Cornwall 23.9.43
DN586	245/609 Engine cut on take-off Manston 8.7.43		
		EJ902	175/183/193 Shot down by flak near Cherbourg 6.1.44
DN587	198 Abandoned after engine cut off Frinton, Essex 12.6.43		
		EJ903	56 OTU
DN588	247 Crash landed near Enschede 12.4.45	EJ904	485
		EJ905	268/4/198/123 Wg
DN589	3 Missing from attack on convoy off Hook of Holland 1.7.43	EJ906	451
		EJ907	83 GSU Engine cut, belly landed near Dunsfold 29.5.45
DN590	3		
DN591	245 Crashed in forced landing 1 mile SW Eythorne, Kent 28.7.43	EJ909	195 Engine cut on overshoot, belly landed on approach Woodvale 18.2.43
DN592	83 GSU Crashed on take-off Tangmere 15.12.44	EJ910	195/245/175/174/182 Caught fire in
DN593	486		

Serial No	Delivered To and Significant History	Serial No	Delivered To and Significant History
	hangar Luneberg 5.5.43		Barville 24.3.43
EJ911	245/247/181/124 Wg/182	EJ957	182 Engine cut, crashed on approach Woodchurch 31.7.43
EJ912	170/609/56/609/193 Lost panels and crash landed near Wantage, Berks 17.6.44	EJ958	3/257/164/198 Engine cut on take-off Gilze-Rijen 12.2.45
EJ913	245	EJ959	400
EJ914	3/3 TEU	EJ960	400
EJ915	486 Shot down by fighters near Trouville 24.9.43	EJ961	3 Missing, presumed shot down by flak Dunkirk 29.6.43
EJ916	257 Swung to avoid Master on runway on take-off and crashed, Warmwell 8.3.43	EJ962	268/609/56 Lost power and dived into sea 8 miles NE Orfordness, Suffolk 5.2.44
EJ917	266 Engine cut, crash landed Lidshott Common, Surrey 7.9.43	EJ963	181 Air bottle exploded in air. Overshot into ditch Langenhagen 26.4.45
EJ918	175/183	EJ964	3 Hit balloon cable and crashed Dover Harbour 27.6.43
EJ919	175/183/257		
EK921	195 Hit sea after control lost at low altitude 18 miles off Great Yarmouth, Norfolk 24.7.43	EJ965	266/56 OTU Engine cut. Hit house in forced landing 2 miles N Wooler, Northumberland 15.1.45
EJ922	3	EJ966	609/198 Shot down by Me109s near Terneuzen 11.7.43
EJ923	193/175/56 OTU		
EJ924	266/56 OTU	EJ967	193/164 Shot down by flak near Kleve 13.2.45
EJ925	266/268/164		
EJ926	257/245/184 Abandoned after engine cut, Petershagen, Germany 28.5.45	EJ968	3/268/609/3/ TEU/55 OTU
		EJ969	486 Hit by flak and abandoned off Le Havre 16.5.43
EJ927	Tyre burst on take-off, belly-landed Gravesend 13.9.43	EJ970	3 Shot down by FW190s during attack on convoy off Hook of Holland 1.7.43
EJ928	193/197		
EJ929	266/4/485		
EJ930	193/198	EJ971	3/56/609/183/245 Damaged by flak and abandoned near Wesel 25.3.45
EJ931	266 Lost power and abandoned 12 miles S Berry Head, Devon 21.6.43		
EJ932	266 Broke up in air 4 miles S Exeter 3.5.43	EJ972	137/174
		EJ973	486
		EJ974	247/1/3 TEU/55 OTU
EJ934	175/183/193/266	EJ975	485/349
EJ946	175/183/266/168 Missing on sweep near Prum 26.12.44	EJ976	486 Shot down by flak near Le Havre 16.9.43
EJ947	175 Overshot landing Colerne 13.4.43	EJ977	247 Broke up in air near Fairlop 18.5.43
EJ948	486		
EJ949	268	EJ978	56
EJ950	3 Tail became detached. Crashed on approach, Manston 16.8.43	EJ979	175
		EJ980	195 Ran out of fuel and ditched 6 miles N Mardyke 7.11.43
EJ951	193/3 TEU/55 OTU Engine cut. Overshot forced landing and hit tree, half-mile N Elberton, Glos 13.2.45	EJ981	486 Engine cut. Belly-landed near Eartham, Sussex 20.11.43
		EJ982	1 Stalled on take-off Lympne 6.7.43
EJ952	182	EJ983	1/3 TEU
EJ953	288/609/56 Engine cut on take-off Martlesham Heath 12.8.43	EJ984	Napier. Over-stressed during test flight 13.7.43
EJ954	182		
EJ955	266/164/268/4/123 Wg	EJ986	266/56 OTU/FLS/CFE
EJ956	486 Hit by flak, crash landed near	EJ987	247/198/164

Serial No	Delivered To and Significant History	Serial No	Delivered To and Significant History
EJ988	247/198/3 TEU/fls	EK121	56/609 Stalled on landing and wing hit ground, Manston 2.2.44
EJ989	3 Hit by flak and abandoned 20 miles NW Ostend 13.9.43	EK122	Mkrs/Napier
EJ990	175/183/266/e TEU/55 OTU	EK123	198/3 TEU/55 OTU
EJ991	59 OTU/FLS/247	EK124	181
EJ992	59 OTU	EK126	Napier
EJ993	174 Ditched 20 miles NW Le Havre 19.11.43	EK127	164
		EK128	174/137 Shot down by flak, Lingen 1.4.45
EJ994	174/183/193/266/56 OTU/266/268/CFE/FLS Undercarriage collapsed on landing Gravesend 25.4.43	EK129	137/174
		EK130	174
		EK132	193 Crashed during attack in V-1 site near Beauvoir 26.3.44
EJ995	175/183/193/266/56 OTU/266/268 Broke up in air, Goswick ranges, Northumberland 10.11.44	EK133	175/183/193/3 TEU/181/247 Engine cut, crash landed after take-off, Eindhoven railway yards 8.11.44
EK113	1 Flew into hill in bad visibility after overshoot, Hawkinge 7.12.43		
EK114	182 Crashed 15 miles SW Lüneburg 29.4.45	EK134	174 Collided with DN580 over Avekapelle and crashed 30.7.43
EK115	183/175	EK135	485/268/247 Engine cut on delivery flight, crash landed 7 miles NE Louvain 4.11.44
EK116	59 OTU		
EK117	247		
EK119	486 Lost tail while attacking E-boats near Bernival 6.9.43	EK136	56/609/266
		EK137	3 TEU/55 OTU

BELOW: Typhoon IB EK183. US-A of 56 Sqdn. (Philip Jarrett)

Serial No	Delivered To and Significant History	Serial No	Delivered To and Significant History
EK138	175 Collided with Wellington X3595 on landing Filton 16.4.43	EK172	257/181 Destroyed in air raid Eindhoven 1.1.45
EK139	175/183/266/198/1 Engine cut on take-off, hit trees, Lympne 26.1.44	EK173	56 OTU
EK140	59 OTU/FLS/168/245/174/247	EK174	56 Hit by ship's flak and dived into sea 15 miles W Schevningen 20.6.43
EK141	175/183/197 Destroyed when Halifax HX181 hit hangar, Tangmere 19.11.43	EK175	174/164 Broke up in air near Twinwood Farm 2.3.44
EK142	198 Stalled on take-off Martlesham Heath 10.6.43	EK176	1 Engine cut, crash landed 2 miles SE Lydd, Kent 16.8.43
EK144	56/609	EK177	174 DBR in accident NFD
EK145	183/175	EK178	181
EK148	182	EK179	56/609/3TEU Engine lost power, belly-landed on overshoot 1 mile S Aston Down 10.9.44
EK149	3/83 GSU/84 GSU		
EK150	247	EK180	268/4/183/84 Gp CS
EK151	3 TEU Engine cut on take-off Aston Down 10.11.44	EK181	170/609/56/198/263
EK152	Mkrs/55 OTU	EK182	59 OTU/FLS
EK154	A & AEE/RAE/56 OTU	EK183	56/609
EK167	3 Missing on sweep to Menin 18.6.43	EK184	183/175 Missing (Dieppe) 19.6.43
EK168	175/183/266/56 OTU/FLS/257/193	EK186	174 Broke up in air near Redhill, Surrey 4.5.43
EK170	486	EK187	3/56/609/198 Hit by flak and abandoned NE Caen 18.7.44
EK171	175 Overshot landing at Weston-super-Mare 18.5.43	EK189	609/56 Tyre burst on take-off

BELOW: Typhoon IB, EK288 with prominent recognition marking. (Philip Jarrett)

Serial No	Delivered To and Significant History	Serial No	Delivered To and Significant History
	Bradwell Bay, 27.9.43 DBR		Predannack and crashed in sea 3.4.45
EK190	59 OTU	EK243	266/84 Stalled and dived into sea, Studland Bay, Dorset 13.8.44
EK191	268		
EK194	247	EK244	182
EK195	182 Damaged by flak near Les Hayons 21.6.43	EK245	175/183/266/198/1 Engine cut, ditched 7 miles NE Orfordness, Suffolk 23.3.44
EK196	268/349		
EK208	Napier/FLS Hit by Wellington NB855 while parked Tangmere 8.8.45	EK247	268/4
		EK250	55 OTU
EK209	609/56 Damaged by flak and crash landed 20.11.45	EK252	485
		EK266	182
EK210	1/609/193	EK267	268
EK211	59 OTU/609/263 Hit church tower after take-off, Harrowbeer 28.5.44	EK268	609/56/Mkrs/183 Shot down by flak off Cap d'Antifer 23.44
EK212	268/3 TEU/55 OTU Engine cut on take-off, hit fence and undercarriage collapsed Aston Down 23.4.45	EK269	198
		EK270	181/137/247
		EK271	RAE
EK214	195 Lost power and belly landed Ludham 16.5.43	EK272	486 Ditched off Barfleur 3.10.43
		EK273	195 Shot down by flak from ship off Dutch coast 6.7.43
EK215	59 OTU		
EK216	18 MU Engine lost power. Crash landed 5 miles SE Dalbeattie, Kirkudbright 22.5.43	EK285	609/56
		EK287	3 TEU/55 OTU
		EK288	1
EK217	3 Undercarriage collapsed on take-off, Tangmere 7.7.43	EK289	609/56/137/182 Shot down by flak near Aeltre 8.9.44
EK218	56/609/198 Engine cut, ditched S of Isle of Wight 23.6.44	EK290	AFDU/56 OTU
		EK321	3/56/609 Overshot landing Lympne and overturned 4.9.43
EK219	168/438/439/440		
EK220	184 Tyre burst on take-off, Warmwell 17.5.45	EK322	175/183/257/609 Damaged at No 1 FP 9.4.45
EK221	59 OTU	EK323	268
EK222	56 OTU	EK324	3 TEU/55 OTU
EK223	195/164/247 Engine lost power during ground attack, crash landed near Bostrum 13.10.44	EK325	56 OTU
		EK326	609/56/55 OTU
		EK327	RAE/268
EK224	247 Hit by flak, crashed Schelde, near Nieue Sluis 8.7.43	EK347	485/135 Wg/485
		E348	56 OTU Abandoned in bad weather near Wooler, Northumberland 14.2.45
EK225	174/486 Shot down by flak near Le Havre 16.9.43	EK364	56 OTU Undercarriage dropped recovering from dive. Aircraft flicked over and crashed, Ilderton, Northumberland 27.3.45
EK226	182/156		
EK227	3 Shot down by flak near Menin 2.6.43		
EK228	1 Lost tail in dive, Paddlesworth, Kent 15.7.43	EK369	174 Stalled on landing, Lydd 25.8.43 DBF
EK229	Mkrs/RAE/A & AEE/Mkrs/DH	EK370	3 Shot down by flak Zeebrugge 23.2.44
EK232	3 TEU Engine cut, crash landed near Cerne Abbas, Dorset 27.4.45		
		EK371	Zeals/3/247
EK233	268	EK372	268/4/193/266
EK236	193 Hit by flak and abandoned near Breda 24.2.45	EK373	3 TEU/55 OTU Bounced on landing, undercarriage collapsed. Aston Down 6.3.45
EK239	55 OTU		
EK240	268/349 Overshot landing at	EK374	DBR in flying accident 6.4.44 NFD

Serial No	Delivered To and Significant History	Serial No	Delivered To and Significant History
EK380	268/4/609 Shot down by flak near Xanten 3.3.45		Clermont 5.2.44
		JP370	182/3 TEU/55 OTU
EK382	DH/168/175 Flew into ground near Münster 30.3.45	JP371	268
		JP372	268/4/146 Wg
EK383	268/4	JP373	268/4
EK384	83 GSU Damaged 30.10.44 NFT	JP374	197 Spun into ground Hambrook, Sussex 16.10.43
EK385	56		
EK395	182 Shot down by flak Dunkirk 2.8.43	JP375	183/609/257/609 Engine cut, crash landed near Wünstorf 22.8.45
EK412	3 TEU/55 OTU		
EK413	3 TEU 55 OTU	JP376	175 Hit by flak and abandoned near Bois Carré 4.1.44
EK246	268		
EK427	268	JP377	Mkrs
EK418	268	JP378	175 DBR in accident 8.7.45. NFD
EK429	268/4 Hit by flak and crash landed near Kessel 18.11.44	JP379	175 Engine cut on take-off, Lydd 8.9.43
EK431	83 GSU	JP380	182/56 OTU
EK432	168/83 GSU Dived into ground near Dunsfold 26.6.45	JP381	182/247 Engine cut, abandoned 1 mile S Flers 15.2.44
EK436	268/4/35 Wg	JO382	257/183/175/55 OTU Engine cut, crashed forced landing near Chepstow 3.2.45
EK439	268/84 GSU Engine cut, hit trees forced landing 8 miles S Oldham		
EK440	268/4	JP383	183 Tyre burst on take-off Predannack 14.1043 DBR
EK481	245		
EK491	A & AEE	JP384	257/183/257
EK492	135 Wg/349	JP385	175 Hit by flak, forced landed near Evreux 5.2.44
EK494	56 OTU		
EK497	Mkrs and A & AEE/183 Shot down in Circuit by P-51 Y29 (USAAF) Asche 1.1.45	JP386	257/183 Hit by flak, ditched 3 miles S St Mathieu 11.11.43
		JP387	175 Tyre burst on take-off, belly landed Dettling 2.9.43
EK498	183 Shot down by flak near Xanten 28.2.45	JP388	257/183 Damaged by FW190s. Overshot landing Harrowbeer 13.7.43
EK500	Napier/257/FLS/263/56 OTU 13.3.36		
EK506	245	JP389	257/182/609/268/198 Tyre burst on take-off, swung and undercarriage collapsed, Plumetot 9.8.44
EK512	485/349		
EK535	3 TEU/55 OTU		
EK536	3 TEU/55 OTU	JP390	56/109 Hit by flak, ditched off Deal 8.8.43
EK537	3 TEU/55 OTU		
EK538	247	JP391	182 Overturned on landing, New Romsey 24.9.43
EK539	3 TEU/55 OTU		
EK541	56 OTU	JP392	257/56 Shot down by flak near Leiden 3.7.43
		JP393	183 Tyre burst on take-off, undercarriage raised to stop, Harrowbeer 28.7.43
600 IB delivered between June and December 1943			
JP362	164 Crashed landing Wünstorf 27.5.45 DBR		
		JP394	175/193
JP363	164	JP395	182/55 OTU
JP367	164 Damaged by explosion of V-1, Gilze-Rijen 7.2.45 and not repaired	JP396	183 Shot down by flak Cherbourg 24.10.43
JP368	183 Hit by flak and belly-landed Warmwell 24.10.43	JP397	175/182
		JP398	266 Shot down by FW190 over Guipavas 15.8.43
JP369	175 Missing from sweep near		

ABOVE: Typhoon IB JP504. OV-Z of 197 Sqdn. (Philip Jarrett)

Serial No	Delivered To and Significant History	Serial No	Delivered To and Significant History
JP399	266 Shot down by FW190 Guipavas 3.8.43	JP432	245 Engine cut after take-off, crashed near Ivychurch, Kent 10.7.43
JP400	182 Shot down by flak near Amiens 19.8.43	JP433	193/3 TEU/55 OTU Collided with Anson DJ471 on approach, Aston Down 20.3.45
JP401	182/266		
JP402	183 Ditched 25 miles N Brest 28.1.44	JP434	245 Missing, presumed shot down by fighters near Evreux 4.10.43
JP403	182 Engine cut. Crashed in forced landing 1 mile SW New Romney, Kent 15.8.43	JP435	181 Shot down by flak, Caen 25.10.43
		JP436	181/124 Wg Shot down by FW190 near Beauvais 11.9.43
JP404	183 Spun into ground near Harrowbeer, 7.7.43	JP437	195/164/247/181
JP405	195 Hit obstruction while low flying, Potter Heigham, Norfolk 8.7.43	JP438	195
		JP439	3/181/3 Shot down by flak 2 miles NE Middleburg 25.9.43
JP406	245/3 TEU/55 OTU		
JP407	195/164/609 Shot down by flak, Laigle 29.7.44	JP440	3/184/175
		JP441	175/266 Shot down by flak near Breskens 21.10.44
JP408	3/3 TEU/263/266		
JP425	193/609/1/609 Shot down by FW190 near Bapaume 2.1.44	JP442	198 Undershot landing at Lympne 16.8.43
JP426	197 Missing near Yvetot 23.7.43	JP443	174/AFDU/3 TEU/247 Forced landed on sweep near Holten-Lochem 31.3.45
JP427	183/164/182 Shot down by flak near Orbec 18.8.44		
JP428	183 Shot down by flak, Cherbourg 24.10.43	JP444	174 Shot down by flak, Amiens-Glisy 16.8.43
JP429	175 Hit trees on take-off, Westhampnett 18.2.44	JP445	174/183/245 Missing from attack on tanks near Trun 18.8.44
JP430	245/181/3 TEU/181 Shot down by flak near Pont d'Ouilly 2.8.44	JP446	Missing Bois-Rempré V-1 site. 18.8.44
JP431	183 Engine cut. Crash landed Week St Mary, Cornwall 7.11.43	JP447	Engine cut. Abandoned 20 miles S St Catherine's Point, Isle of Wight

Serial No	Delivered To and Significant History	Serial No	Delivered To and Significant History
	7.11.43	JP507	257 Dived into ground, West Harting, Hants 11.3.44
JP480	174/182/3 TEU/55 OTU		
JP481	245 Belly-landed at Lydd 25.8.43	JP508	198 Shot down by flak in attack on small craft near Kats 10.9.43
JP482	247/123 Wg/198 Shot down by flak off Cap Gris Nez 18.9.44	JP509	Dived into sea 8 miles SSE Ventnor, Isle of Wight 25.11.43
JP483	1 Engine cut, crash landed near Tergnier 2.3.44	JP510	257 Engine cut. Crash landed 20 miles S Fécamp 16.3.44
JP484	174 Engine cut, crash landed near Lydd 9.9.43	JP511	266/3/3 TEU/245/121 Wg/184/245/247 Crashed on landing Achmer 25.4.45. Not repaired
JP485	Shot down by flak off Le Havre 16.9.43	
JP486	198 Dived into ground attacking train between Ypres & Menin 20.7.43	JP512	266/AFDU/174/175/245
JP487	247 Collided with JP505 over new Romsey 15.8.43	JP513	181 Shot down by flak, Caen 25.10.43
JP488	Collided with JP461 and crashed near Ferndown, Dorset 8.5.44	JP514	3 Shot down by FW190s near Wevelgem 5.10.43
JP489	181 Abandoned in spin near Westhampnett 20.10.43	JP515	181/168
JP490	257 Collided with JP788 while taxying, Warmwell 16.10.43	JP516	198 Shot down by flak 2 miles W Breskens 28.8.43
JP491	257/193/257 Missing, presumed shot down by flak near Cap d'Antifer 29.1.44	JP532	486 Ditched 8 miles S Worthing, Sussex 30.12.43
		JP533	197 Shot down by flak near Ghent 11.8.43
JP492	266 Shot down by FW190 near Guipavas 15.8.43	JP534	3/609
JP493	181 Damaged by Me109, crash landed Merston 30.7.43	JP535	174/245/174/193/184 Forced landed with glycol leak near Soest 21.2.45
JP494	257/609 Hit by flak, crash landed near Bruges 30.7.43	JP536	175 Shot down by FW190, Quincampoix 11.9.43
JP495	486/184 Shot down by flak near Annay-sur-Odon 30.7.43	JP537	175/3 TEU Engine cut, crash landed near Witney, Oxon 7.9.44
JP496	175/3 TEU/56 OTU	JP538	182/127/247/137/247
JP497	193 Engine cut. Belly-landed Harrowbeer 26.10.43	JP539	181 Engine cut, crash landed near Shripney, Sussex 15.10.43
JP498	1 Missing on sweep near Amiens 29.1.44	JP540	182/55 OTU
JP499	193/3 TEU/174 Crash landed with glycol leak near Malmédy 27.12.44	JP541	174 Missing, presumed shot down by flak near Sassy 10.8.44
JP500	193/174 Hit by flak and abandoned near Condé	JP542	183 Shot down by flak, Cherbourg 24.10.43
JP501	486 Destroyed when Halifax HX181 hit hangar, Tangmere 20.11.43	JP543	609 Abandoned after engine failure over Channel 26.9.43
JP502	197 Ran out of fuel on approach, Tangmere 24.9.43	JP544	247 Bomb fell off on take-off, aircraft dived into ground Ford, Sussex 10.11.43
JP503	195/164/198 Crashed on sweep near Lisieux 7.6.44	
JP504	197/137 Hit by flak and crashed, Schleiden 26.12.44	JP545	247 Hit by flak and crashed in sea off Gravelines 31.7.43
JP505	247 Collided with JP487 over New Romsey and crashed on approach	JP546	197/257 Crashed on landing, Needs Oar Point 12.4.44
		JP347	174 Forced landed in sweep near Montreuil 5.10.43
JP506	245/181	JP548	174 Engine cut, crash landed near Marigny 14.2.44

Serial No	Delivered To and Significant History	Serial No	Delivered To and Significant History
JP549	195 Crashed on sweep 1 mile N Bergen-op-Zoom 4.8.43		4.9.43
JP550	174 Abandoned after engine cut 8 miles off Le Touquet 19.8.43	JP588	197 Missing on night intruder to Poix 10.11.43
JP551	181/56 OTU Caught fire running up, Milfield 24.1.45 DBR	JP589	182/174/245
JP552	182 Shot down by FW190 near Amiens 19.8.43	JP590	281 Shot down by flak, Caen 25.10.43
		JP591	198 Shot down by flak attacking shipping Oosterschelde 2.9.43
JP576	174 Damaged landing at Eastchurch 24.1.44	JP592	1 Shot down by flak near Cherbourg 25.11.43
JP577	175 Shot down by flak near Amiens-Glisy 16.8.43	JP593	245 Abandoned after engine cut 15 miles W Le Touquet 30.12.43
JP578	181/55 OTU Tyre burst on take-off Aston Down 11.4.45. DBR	JP594	3 Ditched on ASR patrol 13.9.43
JP579	181/198 Undershot landing at Wünstorf 24.6.45	JP595	56 Engine cut. Abandoned 4 miles off Cap Gris Nez 9.9.43
JP580	181	JP596	198/174/175/245
JP581	247 Crashed on sweep near Ablis 5.10.43. Possibly shot down by Me109	JP597	181/174/175/245
		JP597	181 Ditched off Shoreham, Sussex 13.11.43. NFD
JP582	609/263/183/56 OTU/183	JP598	AAEE/181
JP583	245/263/183/56 OTU/183 Shot down by flak, Poteau 24.12.44	JP599	182
		JP600	174 Collided with JR373 over Béthune 7.1.44
JP584	175/243/184/182	JP601	183/1/3 TEU/59 OTU
JP585	3 Hit by flak, crash landed near Sluis, 5.9.43	JP602	174/245/174 Engine cut, crash landed on Chickerell Down, Dorset 16.11.44
JP586	3 Belly landed Manston 18.8.43		
JP587	3 195 Spun into ground Coltishall	JP603	181 Spun into ground, Chevening,

BELOW: Roland Beamont's combat record panel at the RAF Museum. (Bruce Robertson)

Serial No	Delivered To and Significant History
	Kent 30.9.43
JP604	181 Shot down by flak near Caen 6.6.44
JP605	182 Collided with JP723 over Berck-sur-Mer 20.12.43
JP606	56/245/174/55 OTU
JP607	195/164/3 TEU/55 OTU
JP608	174/56 OTU
JP609	182 Abandoned after engine fire near Crowborough, Sussex 17.10.43
JP610	182/3 TEU/55 OTU
JP611	198/1 Engine cut, crash landed near Acklington 25.3.44
JP612	182/3 TEU/55 OTU
JP613	198 Hit by flak and ditched 2 miles W Knocke 28.8.43
JP614	174/175
JP648	195/164/257/3 TEU/55 OTU
JP649	246 Crashed on sweep near Châteaudun 14.2.44
JP650	245/181 Crash landed on sweep near Courvaudon 1.8.44
JP651	56/175/181 Hit by flak and abandoned near Vendes 5.8.44
JP562	198 Collided with JP727 and crashed in Channel 31.12.43
JP653	247 Engine cut, ditched off Dymchurch, Kent 24.9.43
JP654	175/182 Destroyed in air raid Eindhoven 1.1.45
JP655	198 Crashed after engine trouble on sweep near Caen 8.6.44
JP656	175/184 Hit by flak, Mezidon, and failed to return 7.6.44
JP657	56 Tyre burst on take-off, belly landed Bradwell Bay 15.9.43
JP658	174 Flew into ground in low visibility 1 mile E Brighton 3.2.44
JP659	609 Missing near Falaise 15.8.44
JP660	198/245 Engine cut, crash landed on Isle of Sheppey, Kent 28.4.44
JP661	147/245
JP662	609 Missing on sweep off Walcheren 29.1.44
JP663	183/137 Caught fire in air on sweep and forced landed 2 miles S Zaltbommel 11.10.44
JP664	84 GSU Flew into ground in cloud, Piddletrenthide, Dorset 18.8.44
JP665	197 Shot down by flak 8 miles SW Caumont 1.11.43
JP666	198/175 Engine cut, crash landed at

Serial No	Delivered To and Significant History
	West Wellow, Hants 21.11.44
JP667	486/198/197
JP668	245 Missing presumed shot down by fighters near Hautot-sur-Mer 4.10.43
JP669	198/245/266/257/198 Shot down by flak near Goch 14.2.45
JP670	198 Engine cut, crashed near Manston 30.12.43
JP671	174 Crash landed on sweep near Gavray 29.7.44
JP672	247/181 Hit HT cables and crashed near Meschede 13.2.45
JP673	Napier
JP674	609 Shot down by P-47s near Doullens 21.12.43
JP675	247 Blew up after bomb fell off on landing Merston 11.11.43
JP676	486 Hit by flak and ditched off Barfleur 3.10.43
JP677	1/137/168 Crash landed on beach, Brighton, Sussex 26.11.44
JP678	609 Missing from attack on Sissonne airfield 11.9.43
JP679	1/FLS
JP680	197 Destroyed when hangar hit by Halifax HX181, Tangmere 20.11.43
JP681	56/183 Shot down by Me109s Le Neubourg 17.8.44
JP682	56/197/183 Missing on sweep near Geldern 24.2.45
JP683	486 Overshot landing at Lympne 9.10.43. DBR
JP684	3 Ditched 30 miles off Lowestoft, Suffolk 8.2.44
JP685	1/83 GSU Crashed on landing Westhampnett 28.1.45
JP686	195/164/1 FPP Engine cut. Crash landed on ferry flight near Langley, Bucks 24.4.45
JP687	1/164/198
JP688	486/247 Missing from attack on transport near Loon-op-Zand 24.10.44
JP689	486 Crashed in forced landing 25 miles NE Chartres 10.2.44
JP723	198 Shot down by flak near Bray Dunes, Dunkirk 20.9.43
JP724	3 Collided with belly-landed Mosquito on landing Manston 17.9.43
JP725	182/175/182

Serial No	Delivered To and Significant History	Serial No	Delivered To and Significant History
JP726	247/CFE/FLS		Farm, Norfolk 5.1.44
JP727	198 Collided with JP652 and crashed in Channel 31.12.43	JP784	193 Engine cut, crash landed Powerstock, Dorset 29.1.44
JP728	56 Engine cut on take-off, Martlesham Heath 7.11.43	JP785	247/83 GSU Abandoned after engine cut over Channel 8.8.44
JP729	247 Engine cut. Crash landed New Romney, Sussex 4.10.43	JP786	182 Hit by MN821 while parked, Coulombs 6.7.44
JP730	247 Engine cut, abandoned 3 miles N Sark 28.2.44	JP787	197 Destroyed when Halifax HX181 hit hangar, Tangmere 20.11.43
JP731	175 Spun into ground during dogfight with Spitfire, Brooklands, Kent 6.10.43	JP788	257 Collided with JP490 while taxying, Warmwell 16.10.43
JP732	Missing near Pleneuf 31.10.43	JP789	486/183 Shot down by Me109s near Le Neuborg 17.8.44
JP733	3 Shot down by flak during attack on refinery, Evergem 5.10.43	JP790	257/183/56 OTU
JP734	3/3 TEU/55 OTU	JP791	198 Hit by flak, abandoned near Klundert 4.10.43
JP735	198 Shot down by flak, Dixmude 20.9.43	JP792	609/182/247 Missing from attack on tanks near Gavray 7.8.44
JP736	175/182/247/137 Damaged by flak, crash landed Brunen 26.3.45	JP793	174 Missing in snow storm 20 miles SSE Beachy Head 18.2.44
JP737	181 Hit by flak, abandoned near Paris 13.11.43	JP794	247/182
JP738	1/198/257	JP795	1 Engine caught fire during running up, Lympne 12.12.43
JP739	181 Hit sea during air-to-ground firing practice and crash-landed near Merston 26.2.44	JP796	198/184
JP740	175 Dived into English Channel 26.10.43. NFD	JP797	197 Shot down by flak off Le Havre 22.10.43
JP741	3	JP798	245 Hit trees on take-off, Westhampnett 24.3.44
JP742	257 Ditched off Casquettes, Channel Islands 31.12.43	JP799	257 Forced landed during sweep near Cap d'Antifer 29.1.44
JP743	197/609/183	JP800	181 Crashed near Eindhoven 22.9.44. NFD
JP744	3/55 OTU	JP801	245 Hit by flak, Beauvoir and crash landed near Hawkinge 23.12.43
JP745	609 Hit by flak, ditched near Dieppe 20.9.43		
JP746	Napier/193	JP802	245/193/183
JP747	198 Shot down by flak near Poix 7.2.44	JP836	174 Abandoned after engine failure over Channel 6.3.44
JP748	609 Engine cut. Crash landed Dungeness 3.12.43	JP837	198 Hit by flak and abandoned near Schowen 27.9.43
JP749	56/56 OTU	JP838	175/197/247/181 Missing on sweep near Kiel 3.5.45
JP750	609 Shot down by flak near Poix 4.10.43	JP839	486 Spun into ground 1 mile SW Croxton, Cambs 5.4.44
JP751	198/1	JP840	198 Hit by flak and abandoned over Schowen 27.9.43
JP752	Mkrs/266/198/181/182 Hit by flak, crash landed near Dindgden 30.3.45	JP841	1 Engine cut on approach, Lympne 30.1.44
JP753	175	JP842	198/193/198/247 Dived into ground during attack on troops near Arnhem 21.9.44
JP754	56 Hit by flak and abandoned 5 miles N Scheveningen 3.1.43		
JP755	3 Shot down by flak, Overflakkee 4.10.43	JP843	197/609 Shot down by flak, Poussey-
JP756	3 Engine cut, crash landed Manor		

Serial No	Delivered To and Significant History
	Campagne 27.7.44
JP844	197 Ran out of fuel and crashed near Newport, Isle of Wight 5.11.43
JP845	486 Engine cut. Crash landed 12 miles SW Abbeville 21.12.43
JP846	266 Shot down by ship's flak off Aber-Vrac'h, Brittany 6.2.44
JP847	3/3 TEU Spun into ground, West Hannay, Berks 24.7.44
JP848	182
JP849	195/164/193/192/123 Wg/198
JP850	247/182/609/247 Engine cut, crash landed 2 miles E Odiham 5.1.44
JP851	609/197/609/59 OTU Crashed in forced landing, Goswick Sands, Northumberland 10.1.44
JP852	245 Shot down by flak, Londonières 10.1.44
JP853	486 Destroyed when Halifax HX181 hit hangar, Tangmere 20.11.44
JP854	247
JP855	195/164/3 TEU/55 OTU
JP856	266/183 Forced landed 5 miles S Antwerp 10.10.44
JP857	3 Engine cut, crash landed after take-off, Bradwell Bay 19.3.44
JP858	197/609 Engine cut, crash landed near Deventer 19.3.45
JP859	247/3 TEU/55 OTU
JP860	182/3 TEU/55 OTU
JP861	193/3 TEU/55 OTU
JP897	183 Ran into JP382 on landing, Predannack 4.11.43
JP898	257/245 Crash landed during attack on tanks, Ticheville 17.8.44
JP899	198/197
JP900	198 Shot down by flak near Utrecht 28.11.44
JP901	486/198
JP902	Bomb exploded when jettisoned over sea. Aircraft caught fire and crashed 10 miles N Cap de la Hague 4.2.44
JP903	Napier
JP904	193/3 TEU Engine cut. Crash landed 1 mile E Ashburton, Glos
JP905	245 Abandoned after engine cut over Pevensey, Sussex 21.10.43
JP906	266 Hit by return fire from Ju88 near Lorient and failed to return 1.12.43
JP907	609
JP908	193/3 TEU/55 OTU

Serial No	Delivered To and Significant History
JP909	609/257/164/183 Swung on take-off and hit vehicles, Martragny 31.7.44
JP910	247/3 TEU/55 OTU
JP911	3 Shot down by flak near Ghent 5.10.43
JP912	182 Missing on sweep near Londonières 15.12.43
JP913	182/55 OTU
JP914	486 Missing from night intruder sortie to Coxyde 10.11.43
JP915	56 Hit by flak and forced landed near Fôret d'Hesdin 3.1.44
JP916	157/181/3 TEU/55 OTU Hit tree in forced landing 2 miles E Aston Down 14.1.45
JP917	609/181/247/181
JP918	193/245/174/175 Hit flak, crash landed near Malmédy 25.12.44
JP919	193/3 TEU/168 Hit by flak near Malmedy. Failed to return 25.12.44
JP920	181/168/182
JP921	3 Hit by flak, crash landed near Volkel 29.2.44
JP922	193/181/182 Shot down by flak 3 miles N Moers 23.2.45
JP923	181/183/56 OTU
JP924	609 Shot down by fighters near Valenciennes 1.12.43
JP925	266 Shot down by flak, Morlaix airfield 15.2.44
JP926	3 Shot down by flak, Cap Gris Nez 10.11.44
JP927	247 Engine cut. Ditched 2 miles S Selsey, Sussex 3.2.44
JP928	197
JP930	181 Crashed while attacking train 5 miles E Formerie 12.11.43
JP931	175 Shot down by flak near Hardelot 30.5.44
JP932	183 Hit by flak, crashed 5 miles SW St Mathieu 15.11.43
JP933	257/263 Missing on sweep over Schelde estuary 10.9.44
JP934	266/247/182 Hit by bomb, Coulombs 8.7.44
JP935	195 Shot down by flak off French coast 10.1.44
JP936	Hit HT cables while attacking train, Amden 7.3.45
JP937	186/440/247 Engine cut, crash landed Niewchirken, Belgium 9.11.44
JP938	266/257

Serial No	Delivered To and Significant History	Serial No	Delivered To and Significant History
JP939	193/84 GSU Engine cut on overshoot, Thruxton 28.7.44		repaired
JP940	Napier Crashed on trials 16.3.45	JR136	183/175 Engine cut. Crash landed Hursley, Hants 19.5.44
JP941	266 Shot down by flak, Morlaix airfield 15.2.44	JR138	257/197
JP961	1 Forced landed near Eclimeux during attack on V-1 site 22.12.43	JR139	195/164/257 Shot down by flak near Bougincourt, 9.4.44
JP962	266 Engine cut, crash landed near Harrowbeer 21.2.44	JR140	55 OTU
JP963	609/198 Tyre burst on take-off, Martragny 31.7.44	JR141	Napier/183/164 Shot down by flak near Kleve 13.2.45
JP964	193/266/183/164	JR142	175
JP965	181 Missing on sweep to Paris 13.11.43	JR143	245 Shot down by flak near Etampes 16.3.44
JP966	195/609 Missing near Falaise 14.8.44	JR144	1 Engine cut, ditched Dover 21.12.43
JP967	197 Flew into ground in cloud 6 miles N Chichester, Sussex 18.12.43	JR145	183/198
JP968	181 Spun into ground during attack on V-1 site 25.1.44	JR146	486 Engine lost power on overshoot, crashed 3 miles S Downham Market 13.4.44
JP969	266/183 Tyre burst on take-off, crash landed Gilze-Rijen 1.3.45. Not repaired	JR147	1/609 Missing on sweep near Rouen 17.11.43
JP970	197 Destroyed when Halifax HX181 hit hangar, Tangmere 20.11.43	JR148	186/438/183 Shot down by Me109s near Evreux 17.8.44
JP971	245 Damaged by return fire from Ju88 near Evreux and failed to return 8.1.44	JR149	195/164/181/56 OTU
		JR150	197 Shot down by flak on sweep near Ligescourt 3.1.44
JP972	245 Shot down by flak during attack on V-1 site, Croisette 20.3.44	JR151	257 Shot down by flak near Barfleur 11.3.44
JP973	183 Missing from attack on Guipavas airfield 29.1.44	JR152	486/257/55 OTU
		JR183	183/56 OTU
JP974	266/609	JR184	183 Hit by flak and crash landed 5 miles W Camaret 7.11.43
JP975	257/609 Missing from sweep near Orbeck 19.8.44	JR185	197
JP976	609/181/56 OTU	JR186	486/3 TEU/55 OTU
JR125	609/181/56 OTU	JR187	183 Crashed on landing, Predannack 30.11.43
JR126	1	JR188	3 Ditched 30 miles W Overflakkee after engine cut 3.2.44
JR127	182/1ADF Stalled recovering from dive and crashed near Aston Down 14.7.44	JR189	184/255 Crashed on take-off, Achmer 19.4.45
JR128	183/181 Shot down by flak near Livarot 18.8.44	JR190	175 Missing from attack on V-1 site near Dieppe 6.1.44
JR129	263/247	JR191	56/609 Missing on sweep near Rouen 17.11.63
JR130	183/193	JR192	Hldg Sqdn/609/ATTDU
JR131	183/193 Engine cut, belly-landed on approach, Tain 1.2.44	JR193	182/3 TEU/55 OTU
		JR194	174/245/175/184 Engine cut on take-off. Forced landed near Kastrup 20.8.45
JR132	186/438/55 OTU		
JR133	174 Damaged by FW190, forced landed near Amiens 18.2.44	JR195	174/56 OTU
JR134	181/164	JR196	247 Abandoned after engine fire 10 miles S St Valéry 14.1.44
JR135	266/438/245 Damaged by flak near Villers-Bocage 6.8.44. Not	KR197	56/198 Hit by flak near Cherbourg

Serial No	Delivered To and Significant History
	and abandoned 22.6.44
JR198	609/174/184
JR199	186/183/4 Del Flt. Hit tree on emergency approach to Tangmere, Norton, Sussex 14.3.44
JR200	186 Ran into Spitfire AD329 after landing Ayr 25.11.43
JR201	197/268/84 GSU Engine cut. Crash landed on ferry flight, Kent 18.10.44
JR202	197.247 Caught fire and forced landed near Eindhoven 29.10.44. DBR
JR203	263 Dived into ground near Wimbourne, Dorset 24.12.43
JR204	183/168
JR205	183/182
JR206	83 GSU Hit hedge, low flying and crashed near Chilham, Kent 23.5.44
JR207	400/137 Crashed in forced landing 2 miles SW Geilenkirchen 19.11.44
JR208	183/247
JR209	183/181/55 OTU
JR210	Mkrs/55 OTU
JR211	193 Abandoned with glycol leak 30 miles S Lands End 21.12.43
JR212	181/55 OTU Flew into Severn while recovering from RP dive 12.3.45
JR213	183 Spun into ground off turn, Chywood Farm, Cornwall 1.1.44
JR214	197/357
JR215	263 Shot down by flak Etampes/Mondésir 13.2.44
JR216	56 Hit by flak and crashed 2 miles S Schevenigen 13.11.43
JR217	486/257/486
JR218	186 Collided with JR313 and crashed near Beith, Renfrewshire 29.12.43
JR219	257 Hit by MN947 while parked, Manston 6.9.44
JR220	182/56 OTU
JR221	266 Engine cut. Crash landed half mile W Tavistock, Devon 21.12.43
JR222	1195/164/3 TEU/198 Tyre burst on take-off. Belly landed Nijmegen 7.4.45
JR223	195/164/175 Missing from sweep over Seine near Rouen 22.8.44
JR237	1 Missing from attack on V-1 site, Lampent 22.12.43
JR238	245 Developed glycol leak over Normandy. Did not return 4.1.44
JR239	263 Flew into high ground in cloud 2 miles S Shaftesbury, Dorset 26.12.43
JR240	193/56/OTU
JR241	174/198
JR242	198 Shot down by flak near Poix 7.2.44
JR243	197/164
JR244	181 Engine cut; abandoned 20 miles S The Needles, Isle of Wight 7.6.44
JR245	175/198 Shot down by flak near Zaltbommel 11.12.44
JR246	181/175/245 Engine cut. Crash landed Halvebronn 28.3.45
JR247	197/137/247/175/245
JR248	186/197/198 Missing on sweep near Hoevelaken 8.12.44
JR249	186/438/247
JR250	186/138/84 GSU DBR in accident 27.6.45. NFD
JR251	263 Missing, presumed shot down by flak off Cap de la Hague
JR252	174
JR253	263/198 Shot down by flak near Cormeilles 22.8.44
JR254	198/FLS/266/609
JR255	247/182
JR256	486/198 Shot down by flak Ste Marguerite-de-Viette 9.8.44
JR257	175 Caught fire and dived into ground 3 miles N Emsworth, Hants 7.5.44
JR258	247 Hit by flak and dived into sea 10 miles N Cabourg 21.2.44
JR259	195/164/CFE
JR260	183 Abandoned 18 miles S St Catherines Point, Isle of Wight 11.2.44
JR261	174/182/137
JR262	56/183 NFT
JR263	56/183
JR264	186/439 Missing, presumed ditched off Beachy Head 10.4.44
JR265	247/181 Crashed on take-off Kastrup 4.9.45
JR266	182/3 TEU/55 OTU
JR289	266/245 Shot down by flak 3 miles N Fleury-Harcourt 7.6.44
JR290	247 Missing from attack on enemy positions near May-sur-Orne 25.7.44
JR291	198/3 TEU/55 OTU
JR292	55 OTU
KR293	182 Crashed in forced landing Ile de

Serial No	Delivered To and Significant History	Serial No	Delivered To and Significant History
	Marcourt 28.4.44	JR258	247 Hit by flak and dived into sea 10 miles N Cabourg 21.2.44
JR214	197/257		
JR215	263 Shot down by flak Etampes/Modésir 13.2.45	JR259	195/164/CFE
JR216	56 Hit by flak and crashed 2 miles S Scheveningen 13.11.45	JR260	183 Abandoned 18 miles S St Catherines Point, Isle of Wight 11.2.44
JR217	486/257/486	JR261	174/182/137
JR218	186 Collided with JR313 and crashed near Beith, Renfrewshire 29.12.43	JR262	56/183 NFT
		JR263	56/183
JR219	257 Hit by MN947 while parked, Manston 6.9.44	JR264	186/439 Missing, presumed ditched off Beachy Head 10.4.44
JR220	182/56 OTU	JR265	247/181 Crashed on take-off, Kastrup 4.9.45
JR221	266 Engine cut. Crash landed half mile W Tavistock, Devon 21.12 43	JR266	182/3 TEU/55 OTU
JR222	195/164/3 TEU/198 Tyre burst on take-off. Belly landed Nijmegen 7.4.45	JR289	266/245 Shot down by flak 3 miles N Fleury-Harcourt 7.6.44
JR223	195/164/175 Missing from sweep over Seine near Rouen 22.8.44	JR290	247 Missing from attack on enemy positions near May-sur-Orne 25.7.44
JR237	1 Missing from attack on V-1 site Lampent 22.12.43	JR291	198/3 TEU/55 OTU
		JR292	55 OTU
JR238	245 Developed glycol leak over Normandy. Did not return 4.1.44	JR293	Crashed in forced landing Ilede Marcourt 28.4.44
JR239	263 Flew into high ground in cloud 2 miles S Shaftesbury, Dorset 26.11.43	JR294	181/182/263/609 Shot down by flak near Marienbaum 22.2.45
JR240	193/56 OTU	JR295	257 Engine cut, crash landed 10 miles E Le Touquet 2.3.44
JR241	174/198		
JR242	198 Shot down by flak near Poix 7.2.44	JR296	197/183 Shot down by flak near Marienbaum 22.2.45
JR243	197/164	JR297	181/55 OTU
JR244	181 Engine cut. Abandoned 20 miles S The Needles, Isle of Wight 7.6.44	JR298	186/438/198 Engine lost power. Belly landed Wünstorf 11.9.45
JR245	175/198 Shot down by flak near Zaltbommel 11.12.44	JR299	186/439
		JR300	609/247/182 Missing on sweep near Fontaney Roguancourt 25.7.44
JR246	181/175/245 Engine cut. Crash landed Helvebronn 28.3.45	JR301	266/3 TEU Engine cut. Crash landed near Kewstoke, Somerset 29.8.44
JR247	197/137/247/175/245		
JR248	186/197/198 Missing on sweep near Hoevelaken 8.12.44	JR302	263 Abandoned 8 miles NW Guernsey, Channel Islands 22.2.44
JR249	186/438/247	JR303	263/266 Shot down by Me109s near Lisieux 19.7.44
JR250	186/183/84 GSU DBR in accident 27.6.45. NFD	JR304	263 Ditched 8 miles NW Guernsey 22.2.44
JR251	263 Missing, presumed shot down by flak off Cap de la Hague 6.2.44	JR305	263/137
		JR306	609/266/198 Hit by flak and abandoned near Potigny 10.8.44
JR252	174		
JR253	263/198 Shot down by flak near Cormeilles 22.8.44	JR307	A & AEE Broke up recovering from dive 3 miles N Crichel Down, Dorset 26.3.44
JR254	198/FLS/266/609		
JR255	247/182		
JR256	486/198 Shot down by flak Ste Margueritte-de-Viette, 9.8.44	JR308	168/175
		JR309	263 Damaged by flak and abandoned near Rambouillet 13.2.44
JR257	175 Caught fire and dived into ground 3 miles N Emsworth, Hants	JR310	174/184 Flew into high ground in

Serial No	Delivered To and Significant History	Serial No	Delivered To and Significant History
	formation, Shorncliff Barracks, Kent 3.12.44	JR363	609/164 Forced landed near Neumünster 19.3.45. DBF
JR311	245/175 Lost tail recovering from dive, crashed Le Havre 24.5.44	JR364	609/3 TEU/55 OTU
JR312	609/263/266	JR365	263/257 Shot down by flak near Bergen-op-Zoom 8.10.44
JR313	186 Collided with JR218 and crashed near Beith, Renfrewshire 29.12.43	JR366	197 Shot down by flak near Ederveen 5.10.44
JR314	3/3 TEU/247	JR367	197/83 GSU Engine cut. Crash landed near Louvain 19.10.44
JR315	186/438/198	JR368	263/193/257/193/146 Wg/266
JR316	198 Crashed after engine trouble near Dreumel 20.12.43	JR369	183 Ditched 36 miles N Ile de Batz, Brittany 21.1.44
JR317	181/247/181/45 OTU	JR370	182 Shot down by flak, Beaumont airfield 21.2.44
JR318	186/3 ETU/55 OTU Engine cut. Forced landed 2 miles E Whitfield, Glos. 13.2.45. DBF	JR371	198/184/59 OTU
		JR372	182/609/182/247
JR319	175 Hit by flak over Villaroche airfield and crash landed 16.3.44	JR373	174 Collided with JP600 over Bethune 7.1.44
JR320	197/257/263	JR374	609 Dived into Channel 4.1.44. NFD
JR231	198/CFE	JR375	609 Engine cut. Crash landed near Helmond 14.1.44
JR322	486/198/137/174 DBR in accident 3.10.45	JR376	609/193/175 Missing bad weather near Steinhudersee 27.2.45
JR323	245 Shot down by flak near Cherbourg 6.2.44	JR377	195/164/174 Hit by flak and abandoned near Lessay 7.8.44
JR324	186/439 Crashed on landing, Funtington 4.4.44	JR378	609/FLS
JR325	186/183	JR379	609/197/609/439
JR326	3TEU/55 TEU	JR380	1/184
JR327	263/137/175	JR381	181 Hit by flak, ditched 10 miles off Cherbourg 23.5.44
JR328	1/137/182 Destroyed in air raid, Eindhoven 1.1.45	JR382	263/175/263/55 OTU/263
JR329	197/486 Shot down by flak south of Paris 14.1.44	JR383	183 Shot down by flak near Cherbourg 14.1.44
JR330	263/257 Crashed on overshoot, St Croix 9.7.44	JR384	266/198 Crashed in forced landing Llangennith Ranges, Glam. 14.9.44. Overtaken by tide
JR331	486/FLS/CFE	JR385	185/56 OTU Engine cut. Crash landed 3 miles W Longformacus, Berwick 13.2.45
JR332	609/168 Shot down by FW190s near Steinfurt 29.12.44		
JR333	Mkrs and A & AEE	JR386	609 Hit by flak and abandoned 15 miles NW Formerie 30.5.44
JR334	3/3 TEU/181 Hit by flak, crash landed in Normandy 28.6.44	JR387	266 Shot down by flak, Morlaix airfield 15.2.44
JR335	186 Spun into sea off Cromarty 1.2.44	JR388	175 Lost glycol and abandoned near Falaise 14.8.44
JR336	Napier/438		
JR337	184/181 Engine cut on take-off, Helmond 26.3.45	JR389	2263/609/55 OTU
		JR390	183/164/Little Staughton. Spun into ground during aerobatics, Little Staughton 19.10.45
JR338	197/257/198 Girder fell on aircraft from roof of damaged hangar, Gilze-Rijen 7.12.44. DBR		
JR360	56/198/175	JR391	247/56 OTU
JR361	198 Shot down by flak near St Omer 20.1.44	JR392	183
JR362	439/263 Hit by flak, abandoned near Deventer 19.3.45	JR426	20 MU Crashed in forced landing 2

Serial No	Delivered To and Significant History	Serial No	Delivered To and Significant History
	miles SW Stonehouse, Glos. 7.1.44	JR499	198/184/245 Damaged by flak near Falaise and belly landed Camilly 10.8.44. DBR
JR427	183/182/56 OTU		
JR428	FLS/164		
JR429	609/245 Hit flak and crash landed 4 miles SE Trun 19.8.44	JR500	137/439 Stalled at low altitude and hit ground, Eindhoven 3.11.44
JR430	185/164/193 Engine cut. Crash landed near Detling 2.3.44	JR501	198/184/175
JR431	186/440/183	JR502	175 Missing near St Lô 9.7.44
JR432	263/174/175/245/121 Wg	JR503	56
JR433	1/55 OTU/137 Shot down by fighters 10 miles SW Bruges 21.3.44	JR504	137/56 Engine cut. Ditched 5 miles off Dover 8.5.44
JR434	263/18 APC/FLS Dived into ground near Selsey, Sussex 22.4.45	JR505	137/198
JR435	198 Shot down by flak, Juvincourt 13.1.44	JR506	186/439/440/439
		JR507	257/164 Shot down by flak near Utrecht 11.12.44
JR436	193 Shot down by FW190s 2 miles NE Guernsey 7.1.44	JR508	175
JR437	137/197	JR509	FLS
JR438	137/181 Shot down by flak near Lengerich 24.2.45	JR510	184/174 Tyre burst on take-off. Belly landed Warmwell 30.8.45
JR439	186/440 Flew into high ground, Little Water of Fleet Viaduct, Kircudbright 18.3.44	JR511	198/137/245 Shot down by flak off Colynsplaat 30.3.45
JR440	263/609 Undercarriage jammed, belly landed Melsbroek 5.7.45	JR512	198/183/198 Shot down by flak near Carentan 14.6.44
JR441	263/55 OTU	JR513	182/181/182/247
JR442	56 Abandoned 5 miles S Dungeness 9.2.44	JR514	182/164
		JR515	164 Shot down by flak, Bruges radar station 28.5.44
JR443	609/137/55 OTU		
JR444	186/439/168/439/168/137 Shot down by flak near Jampe 12.4.45	JR516	137/3 TEU Caught fire in air and dived into ground Tibberton, Glos. 5.8.44
JR445	198/183 Crashed on overshoot 2 miles W Martragny 31.7.44	JR517	182/173 Crashed in forced landing SE Greven 6.4.45
JR446	198/183 Hit by flak, crash landed near Caen 26.7.44	JR518	198 Crashed on sweep near Mechelin 29.1.44
JR447	198/181/198 Hit trees while low flying over France. Overshot landing at Lydd 9.3.44	JR519	FLS
		JR520	137/164
		JR521	247/439 Crashed in forced landing near St Germain d'Ectot 8.8.44
JR448	A & AEE Crashed on smoke-laying trials 1 mile SW Grately, Hants 24.3.44	JR522	1/3 TEU/198/123 Wg/55 OTU
JR449	124 Wg/184	JR523	56/198 Missing from sweep near Compiègne 3.1.44
JR492	183		
JR493	245/184 Collided with MN318 during RP attack 2 miles NW Wiesbaum 27.12.44	JR524	247/184/193 Shot down by flak near Caen 12.6.44
		JR525	184/245/174/173
JR494	184 Engine cut, abandoned over Channel 7.5.44	JR256	174 DBR in accident 23.9.44. NFD
		JR257	198/175/198 Shot down by flak, Jobourg 24.5.44
JR495	174/175/184		
JR496	Napier	JR528	182/198 Shot down by flak near Weeze 24.2.45
JR497	137/56/438 Hit by flak and abandoned near Papenbeek 28.9.44	JR529	197 Caught fire in air and crashed into ground 3 miles NNE Buchy 24.1.44
JR498	263/244	JR530	137/56/440

Serial No	Delivered To and Significant History	Serial No	Delivered To and Significant History
JR531	263/84 GSU Engine cut on take-off, belly-landed. Dunsfold 18.5.45		26.9.44
JR532	137/263	MM974	137 Engine cut. Crashed in forced landing near Ardouval, Seine Maritime 12.2.44
JR533	137/183	MM975	247/440/55 OTU
JR534	181/175 Crashed on landing, Holmsley South 29.5.44	MM976	183/168
		MM977	FLS
800 IB delivered between January and August 1944		MM978	137/3 TEU/609
MM951	247 Shot down by flak attacking vehicles near Lette 8.12.44	MM979	247/182/247 Hit by flak near Zutphen. Did not return. 30.3.45
MM952	174/164	MM980	56/137 Shot down by flak off Scheveningen 5.5.44
MM953	183/266 Crashed into sea while trying to ditch 40 miles S Portland 19.5.44	MM981	266 Missing after engine failure near Dieppe 9.5.44
MM954	174	MM982	609/3 TEU/CFE
MM955	257/164/197	MM983	609
MM956	184/174/184	MM984	TFU/Napier
MM957	438 Crashed in forced landing after engine failure near Béthune 8.5.44	MM985	198/56 OTU
MM958	609/197/3 TEU Engine cut. Belly landed 1 mile N Cirencester, Glos. 3.9.44	MM986	609
		MM987	198/245/175
		MM988	55 OTU
MM959	438/55 OTU	MM989	486/263/439/438 Stalled and spun into ground in circuit, 14.4.45
MM960	257/RAE/AFDU/RAE/Napier		
MM961	186/440/247/181 Hit by flak and abandoned 2 miles E Vimoutiers 19.8.44	MM990	426/263
		MM991	257/56 OTU
MM962	174 Lost fuel while jettisoning LR tanks. Forced landed 3 miles NW Percy, Calvados 14.2.44	MM992	56/193
		MM993	245
		MM994	137/609/198 Sent for repair 12.4.45. NFT
MM963	183/247	MM995	182/55 OTU
MM964	183 Shot down by flak Kerlin Bastard 31.1.44	MN113	193/164/56 OTU Overshot landing, ground looped and undercarriage leg collapsed, Milfield 20.9.45
MM965	263		
MM966	137/3 TEU/175/184/137 Tyre burst on take-off, belly landed Lübeck 1.8.45	MN114	FLS Engine cut, hit trees on approach Milfield 17.8.44. DBR
		MN115	440 Hit by flak. Abandoned 2 miles S Christchurch 12.6.44
MM967	174 Engine cut, belly landed Hinton Admiral, Hants 24.4.44	MN116	609/3 TEU/55 OTU
MM968	182/174 Hit by flak and abandoned 8 miles W Vauville, Calvados	MN117	56/137 Hit bulldozer on take-off Manston 24.4.44. DBF
MM969	137/56 Missing on weather reconnaissance near Dieppe 3.5.44	MN118	257/183/3 TEU/247
		MN119	56/198 Shot down by flak near Vimoutier 19.8.44
MM970	137/183 Shot down by flak, Guipvas airfield 29.1.44	MN120	198/183 Spun into ground out of cloud, Joiners Farm, Kent 27.3.44
MM971	257/84GSU Engine cut on ferry flight. Crashed near Charfield, Glos. 24.5.44. DBF	MN121	245 Crashed forced landing after fuel flow problems 40 miles SW Caen 7.6.44
MM972	137 Engine cut on navex. Belly landed St Mary's in the Marsh, near Dymchurch, Kent 25.3.44	MN122	FLS/609/168
		MN123	3.56 Missing on night training flight over North Sea 5.3.44
MM973	247 Shot down by flak near Schijndel		

Serial No	Delivered To and Significant History	Serial No	Delivered To and Significant History
MN124	1/3 TEU/438/439 Hit by flak near Borken and abandoned E Rhede 21.11.44		2.5.45. DBR
		MN148	56/266/440/175
MN125	486/197 Shot down by flak Villers-Bocage 7.6.44	MN149	184 Engine cut on take-off. Belly landed, hit mound. Eastchurch 22.3.44
MN126	56/137 Shot down by flak near Vimoutiers 18.8.44	MN150	56/266/438/609 Crashed after control lost on weather recce in cloud near Gorinchem 9.12.44
MN127	3 TEU Dived into ground during low-level aerobatics Monslow Hall near Stoneleigh, Warks. 5.7.44		
		MN151	FLS/198/609/198
		MN152	56/137/3 TEU/55 OTU
MN128	198/181/182	MN153	198/174 Abandoned after glycol leak, St Antonis near Volkel 28.10.44
MN129	263 Crashed during low-level aerobatics, Warmwell 12.3.44	MN154	56/440/438/440 Missing, presumed shot down by flak near Orbec 19.8.44
MN130	164/438/164/183 Shot down by flak off Dunkirk 26.9.44	MN155	609 Shot down by flak near Rouen 13.5.44
MN131	609/184/609/184 Missing from sweep near Trun Orne 18.8.44	MN156	56/137 Collided with MN596 on anti-flying bomb patrol and crashed Denton Court, Kent 27.7.44
MN132	198 Missing from sweep near Caen 18.6.44		
MN133	266 Shot down by Me109s N Lisieux 19.7.44	MN169	56/137 Shot down by flak, Kassel 28.9.44
MN134	137	MN170	486/263 Damaged by Me410 and abandoned near Morlaix 31.3.44
MN135	Overshot flapless landing, Lasham, 25.5.45. DBR	MN171	3/440 Shot down by flak near Juvigny 23.6.44
MN136	486/263/429/184 Flew into high ground in formation, Shorncliffe Barracks, Kent 3.12.44	MN172	164/183/56 OTU
		MN173	Napier/56 OTU
		MN174	184/198/609
MN137	198 Engine cut during night training. Belly landed and hit hedge, West Malling 6.3.44. DBR	MN175	266/198 Shot down by flak, Duclair, Seine Maritime 15.6.44
		MN176	197/609
		MN177	164/55 OTU
MN138	197/175 Shot down by flak near Bernay 14.8.44	MN178	486/263/609 Shot down by flak near Weeze 25.2.45
MN139	486/263	MN179	56/609/181/197/181 Hit by flak, crash landed Coulombs 19.7.44
MN140	486/197/609 Spun off turn into ground, North Seaton, Northumberland 23.3.44	MN180	56/137 Engine cut in circuit due to fuel shortage. Forced landed Ruan Manor, Predannack, Cornwall 29.4.44
MN141	174/175/245/175/184		
MN142	FLS/609 Shot down by flak near Rouen 26.8.44	MN181	266 Missing after engine cut near Beaumont 9.4.44
MN143	FLS/198/Wg Ldr 123 Wg Engine cut on sweep. Abandoned 25 miles S Beach Head 23.5.44	MN182	56/245
		MN183	Shot down by flak near Crécy 8.2.44
		MN184	56/266 Shot down by flak near Falaise
MN144	183/349 Shot down by flak near Dulmen 2.3.45	MN185	175/55 OTU
MN145	56/137 Missing from sweep off Belgian coast 1.4.44	MN186	609/197/186/181 Shot down by flak near Caen 25.7.44
MN146	193/55 OTU Overshot landing, crash landed, Chedworth 18.3.45	MN187	486/263
		MN188	3 Shot down by Me109s near Poix 6.3.44
MN147	184/55 OTU Overshot landing, undercarriage collapsed Aston Down	MN189	440/186/440

Serial No	Delivered To and Significant History
MN190	174/137/245 NFT
MN191	56/137 Shot down by flak near Randern
MN192	198 Shot down by flak near Dieppe
MN193	257/245/137
MN194	175/439/175
MN195	198
MN196	440/263 Tyre burst on take-off, hit bulldozer and bombs exploded. Deurne 11.11.44
MN197	183
MN198	56/137
MN199	181
MN200	181 Shot down by flak, Normandy 16.6.44
MN201	184/257
MN202	175/266
MN203	197/164/175/245
MN204	182 Shot down by FW190s near Venlo 28.10.44
MN205	184/609 Shot down by flak, Dunkirk 11.11.44
MN206	56/266/183/266 Believed shot down by flak. Crashed near Winterswijk 25.12.44
MN207	1/3 TEU Engine cut. Dived into ground on approach to Cliffe Pypard, West Cliffe, Wilts. 25.8.44
MN208	198/1197
MN209	3/197 Shot down by Me109s near Lisieux 13.7.44
MN210	439 Shot down by flak 1 mile off St Peter Port, Guernsey 5.6.44
MN211	609 Shot down by flak near Douai 29.2.44
MN212	183/247/181
MN213	439 Caught fire on ground, Ayr 17.2.44
MN229	198/CFE
MN230	266/609/84 GSU Swung in heavy landing and undercarriage leg collapsed, Lasham 17.4.45
MN231	609/3 TEU Engine cut on take-off, belly-landed Aston Down 16.11.44. DBF
MN232	193/Mkrs/245/184 Belly-landed Volkel 16.4.45
MN233	184 Shot down by flak near Gisors 25.5.44
MN234	198/137 Missing from sweep near St Vith 27.12.44
MN235	To USA 24.3.44 as FE-491. Returned

Serial No	Delivered To and Significant History
	and preserved
MN236	257/1320 Flt/3 TEU/55 OTU Engine cut on approach, hit Nissen hut, Aston Down 25.3.45
MN237	Hit by flak near Tiel and forced landed 4.12.44
MN238	3/198/55 OTU
MN239	3/609 Shot down by flak near Viessoix, Calvados 31.7.44
MN240	183/56 OTU
MN241	198/181 Shot down by flak near Erp, Eriège 22.9.44
MN242	1/3 TEU/55 OTU
MN243	266
MN244	Napier/123 Wg/263
MN245	486/263/609
MN246	198/183 Engine cut, belly landed, hit dyke and overturned, Ham Marshes, near Faversham, Kent 31.3.44
MN247	198/183 Shot down by flak near Nijmegen 21.3.44
MN248	198/609/182 Shot down by flak near Oostrum 18.10.44
MN249	263 Ditched on sweep 8 miles NW Guernsey 22.2.44
MN250	263 Hit by flak, Morlaix. Belly-landed Harrowbeer 27.4.44
MN251	175/440
MN252	184 Missing off Walcheren 21.5.44
MN253	174/198/174/198/174/247
MN254	Mkrs/TRE/FIU/257/3 TEU/55 OTU
MN255	184 Shot down by FW190 near Vimoutiers 17.8.44
MN256	193
MN257	3/440 Hit by flak and abandoned near Caen 7.6.44
MN258	266/440/193 Hit HT cables and crash landed, Potigny, Calvados 12.6.44
MN259	266 Hit tree during sweep, ditched in Channel 2.3.44
MN260	247/263/183
MN261	466/263/198/263
MN262	266/183/137 Hit by flak St Vith 31.12.44
MN263	1329 Flt/FIU/FIDS/ASWDU/CCDU
MN264	193/263
MN265	3/183/439/268/168 Engine cut, crash landed near Paderborn 2.2.45
MN266	3 TEU/55 OTU
MN267	168/174/245

Serial No	Delivered To and Significant History	Serial No	Delivered To and Significant History
MN268	468/263/609 Engine cut on patrol, belly landed and overturned, near Estaires 29.10.44		failure, belly landed near Oldenburg 12.9.45
MN269	197 Bomb exploded in flight. Dived into ground Thury Harcourt 17.6.44	MN307	A & AEE/440 Shot down by flak near Caen 7.6.44
MN282	4486/263	MN308	A & AEE/439/175 Hit by flak and abandoned 5 miles S Goch 14.2.45
MN283	183/193/438	MN309	A & AEE/440
MN284	164 Abandoned after engine cut near Nijmegen 10.12.44	MN310	A & AEE/439/184/439 Shot down by flak, St Pierre La Vieille, Calvados 12.8.44
MN285	1/3 TEU/55 OTU		
MN286	1/3 TEU Engine cut on take-off, belly-landed, Aston Down 4.8.44. DBR	MN311	A & AEE/440/181 Overshot emergency landing on ferry light, Christchurch 25.7.45. DBR
MN287	257/164	MN312	137 Hit by flak, crashed off Ostend 21.5.44
MN288	184/182 Shot down by flak 3 miles NE Vimoutiers 19.8.44	MN313	3/440 Shot down by flak near Ussy, Calvados 8.8.44
MN289	197/181/137/174		
MN290	Napier/AAEE/Mkrs/Middle East Tropical trials aircraft. NFT	MN314	198/245/198 Shot down by flak near Caen 18.6.44
MN291	257/198 Shot down by flak near Hoeverlaken 8.12.44	MN315	Mkrs/Gatwick/Benson/Mkrs/CFE
		MN316	439/438
MN292	486/263 Engine cut, belly-landed and overturned, Launceston, Cornwall 15.6.44	MN317	247/181 Overshot landing and hit bank, Diest 24.12.44
MN293	257/164/198/193/198 Hit by flak. Crash landed Cuverville, Calvados 25.7.44	MN318	440/184 Collided with JR493 during RP attack 2 miles NW Wiesbaum 27.12.44
MN294	Crashed on sweep NW of Schwarzenbeck 25.4.45	MN319	A & AEE/245 Hit by flak and blew up near Horst 18.10.44
MN295	486/263 Damaged by flak, abandoned 2 miles SE Zaltbommel 24.10.44	MN320	266/197
		MN321	438 Shot down by flak 3 miles N Henonville 3.8.44
MN296	1320 Flt/263 Shot down by flak off St Malo 26.6.44	MN322	609/198/609 Hit by flak and abandoned in Normandy beach-head 3.8.44
MN297	266 Abandoned over sea 40 miles N of Caen 8.6.44	MN323	609/263
MN298	3/438 Shot down by Me109s near Vendes, Calvados 16.6.44	MN324	197/55 OTU
		MN235	A & AEE/245/438/263/438 Engine lost power on overshoot. Crash landed Flensburg 29.5.45
MN299	247/245/184/175		
MN300	486/263 Hit by flak, abandoned 35 miles off Bolt Head 23.6.44	MN339	609 Missing on sweep near Couches, Sambre-et-Loire 29.6.44
MN301	174/184	MN340	247/182
MN302	245 Engine cut in circuit. Crash landed and overturned, Holmsley South 8.5.44	MN341	197 Crashed after being hit by debris near Vimoutiers 17.8.44
		MN342	440 Stalled off turn and spun into ground, West Bransgore, Hants 27.5.44
MN303	182 Hit by MN821 while parked, Coulombs 6.7.44		
MN304	257/164/197/84 Gp CS/198/174	MN343	266/197 Engine cut, belly-landed Hildesheim 12.5.45
MN305	57/164/413 RSU Engine cut on take-off, belly landed, Thorney Island 10.6.44. DBR	MN344	184/193/198 Hit by flak, crash landed Helmond 8.2.45
MN306	183/137/174 Engine cut after fuel	MN345	438/439 Abandoned after glycol leak

Serial No	Delivered To and Significant History
	near Deventer 6.11.44
MN346	438 Hit by flak and abandoned off Normandy 12.6.44
MN347	438 Shot down by flak near Orbec 18.8.44
MN348	440/439 Shot down by flak near Buldern 3.12.44
MN349	164/257
MN350	193 Engine cut returning from sweep. Belly-landed Broadstairs 7.5.44. DBF
MN351	137/56 OTU
MN352	439/440 Hit by flak and abandoned near Geldrop 29.10.44
MN353	175/266 Engine cut. Belly landed in circuit Hildesheim 8.7.45
MN354	257/193/198 Shot down by P-51s during RP attack on shipping in Rhine near Neuss 2.3.45
MN355	245 Damaged by flak, abandoned 7 miles NNW Cherbourg 2.6.44
MN356	439/247 Damaged by flak near Osnabrück 29.12.44
MN357	Mkrs/137/439
MN358	266/247/175 Shot down by flak NE Venlo
MN359	183/184 Hit by flak, crash landed 3 miles SE Haldern 24.3.45
MN360	184/609/183/609 Hit tree while changing tanks. Abandoned near Handel 8.2.45
MN361	266 440/168 Engine cut, dived into ground near Domfront 28.7.44
MN362	245/439/174/175 Crashed on landing, Goch 7.4.45
MN363	247/181/56 OTU
MN364	193/266/439
MN365	247/257/183 Engine cut. Belly landed on approach Nijmegen 3.4.45
MN366	440/168
MN367	257 Shot down by flak, Picquigny, Somme 24.5.44
MN368	198/164/193/439/164 Engine cut. Dived into sea 15 miles off Cabourg 6.7.44
MN369	440 Blew up entering dive near Rocquancourt, Calvados 26.7.44
MN370	439
MN371	174/175/245
MN372	257 Shot down by flak 8 miles S Caen 12.6.44

Serial No	Delivered To and Significant History
MN373	247/182 Shot down by flak 2 miles E Cully 11.7.44
MN374	193/137
MN375	438/439 Ran out of fuel, abandoned near Luxembourg
MN376	245/1175 Hit by flak, abandoned near Nijmegen 6.10.44
MN377	245 Shot down by flak 5 miles NNE Falaise 7.6.44
MN378	440
MN379	439 Hit by flak, crash landed 15 miles E Volkel 2.10.44
MN380	245/438/440 Swung on landing and overshot on return from sweep, Eindhoven 2.3.45
MN381	257
MN396	257/164
MN397	193/183/56 OTU
MN398	609.55 OTU
MN399	Mkrs/247 Shot down by FW190s near Styeinhuddermeer 31.12.44
MN400	266 Hit by flak and crash landed in beach-head 7.8.44
MN401	439 Missing on sweep near Vimoutiers 19.8.44
MN402	438/164
MN403	440 Hit by flak and abandoned near Caen 26.7.44
MN404	263/266/164
MN405	257 Shot down by Me109s near Cormeilles 13.7.44
MN406	WgLdr 124 Wg Abandoned after engine cut on armed recce 40 miles E North Foreland, Kent 9.5.44
MN407	263/440
MN408	257/193/164/123Wg
MN409	609/198/182
MN410	198 Shot down by flak, Joburg, Manche 24.5.44
MN411	438/56 OTU
MN412	197/266/56 OTU
MN413	438/440/1184
MN414	609 Shot down by flak near Fleury 13.5.44
MN415	198 Shot down by flak 2 miles SE Falaise 10.6.44
MN416	257 Engine lost power. Crash landed 3 miles SW Caen 17.6.44
MN417	439 Hit by flak and abandoned Carpiquet 15.6.44
MN418	AFDU/CFE
MN419	164/183

Serial No	Delivered To and Significant History	Serial No	Delivered To and Significant History
MN420	440/257 Engine cut, belly-landed on approach and overturned, Mill 22.2.45		Vimoutiers 18.8.44
		MN464	439 Damaged by flak and spun into ground on approach, Lantheuil 8.7.44
MN421	245/247/137 Ran into MN664 on landing Eindhoven 23.9.44	MN465	183 Engine cut. Ditched 11 miles S Selsey Bill, Sussex 2.5.44
MN422	257/182 Engine cut after take-off; hit tree and crash landed 3 miles SSE Helmond 23.2.45	MN466	A & AEE
		MN467	263/198 Engine cut, hit ground on approach, Gilze-Rijen 16.2.45
MN423	197 Missing on sweep near St Lô 7.6.44	MN468	137 Engine caught fire, belly landed on approach, Manston 6.7.44. DBF
MN424	438/439	MN469	137 Shot down by flak 1 mile off Ostend 24.5.44
MN425	198/184/175/184		
MN426	438 Hit tree and spun into ground near Trun 15.8.44	MN470	174/175/245 Hit by flak near Wesel 25.3.407
MN427	183	MN471	175/174/175/247 Engine cut on sweep, belly landed 15 miles SE Münster
MN428	440 Shot down by flak near Condé 6.6.44		
MN429	137	MN472	182 Missing from sweep to Breda 11.9.44
MN430	247/182		
MN431	440 Hit balloon cable and crashed, Eastleigh, Hants 44.5.44. DBF	MN473	438/193
		MN474	137 Shot down by flak 2 miles E Aire 23.5.44
MN432	183 Shot down by Me109s near Caen 6.6.44	MN475	440/438/440 Shot down by flak near Wassenburg 18.11.44
MN433	AFDU/CFE/FLS Engine cut. Belly landed West Wittering, Sussex 18.5.45	MN476	263 Shot down by flak near Hoogstraten 13.10.44
MN434	245/609 Collided with RB250 and crashed near Grave 13.4.45	MN477	263 Shot down by flak near Pont Audemer, Eure 25.8.44
MN435	1/439/440/263		
MN436	198 Spun into sea during RP training off Llanbedr 28.4.44	MN478	183 Shot down by flak off Cap d'Antifer 23.5.44
MN449	263 Missing from sweep near St Lô	MN479	183/55 OTU
MN450	56 OTU	MN480	245 Dived into sea during RP training, Leysdown Ranges, Kent 27.4.44
MN451	247/182		
MN452	257/183 Missing from sweep near Meppel 24.1.45	MN481	175 Abandoned after engine cut 1 mile off Normandy coast 15.6.44
MN453	198/440/137/440 Shot down by flak near Schleiden 24.12.44	MN482	438/439
		MN483	266 Engine cut, crash landed near Rouen 9.5.44
MN454	183/164 Shot down by FW190s near Caen 6.6.44	MN484	197/55 OTU
MN455	56/137	MN485	184
MN456	175 Hit by flak and abandoned 15 miles off Cherbourg 5.6.44	MN486	184/168 Shot down by fighters near Eindhoven 1.1.45
MN457	440	MN487	263/198 Missing on sweep near Goch 16.2.45
MN458	197 Shot down by flak off Pointe de la Percée 24.5.44	MN488	197/84 GSU Engine cut, overshot Aston Down, hit wall and overturned Chalford, Glos. 20.6.44. DBF
MN459	245 Spun into ground, Mesnil-Tove 17.6.44		
MN460	137/5 TEU/55 OTU	MN489	440 Hit by flak Arromanches and abandoned 5 miles off French coast.
MN461	183 Missing from sweep near Rouen 7.6.44		
MN462	193/438	MN490	245 Hit by flak and abandoned near Falaise 15.6.44
MN463	197 Missing on sweep near		

Serial No	Delivered To and Significant History
MN491	197/164/609
MN492	257 Windscreen oiled up. Belly landed on beach and overtaken by tide Llangennith, Glam. 23.8.44
MN493	266 Hit by debris from ammunition ship off Hook of Holland and crash landed 2.10.44
MN494	609 Shot down by flak, Tilly-la-Campagne 27.7.44
MN495	609 Missing from sweep near Caen 13.6.44
MN496	609 Hit by flak and abandoned 20 miles WNW Fécamp, Seine Maritime 11.5.44
MN513	1/3 TEU/55 OTU
MN514	245
MN515	263 Shot down by flak near St Malo 7.6.44
MN516	439 Crash landed on return from sweep after engine fire 4 miles SE Horsham, Sussex 24.5.44
MN517	609/438
MN518	143 Wg/266
MN519	RAE
MN520	609/247
MN521	439/263/609

Serial No	Delivered To and Significant History
MN522	193 Hit by flak near Caen and crash landed in beach-head 10.6.44
MN523	164
MN524	263 Shot down by flak off St Malo 24.6.44
MN525	174 Shot down by flak St Pierre sur Dives, Calvados 26.7.44
MN526	198
MN527	198/263 Hit by flak and abandoned near Kerpert, Côtes du Nord 3.7.44
MN528	440
MN529	184/193 Blew up while attacking guns near Breskens, 12.10.44
MN530	245/174/184
MN531	182/137/266
MN532	245/56 OTU Flew into high ground in cloud on navex Stoney, Ayrshire 27.3.45
MN533	137
MN534	174/198/174/175 Hit by flak and abandoned, Dulmen 24.2.45
MN535	193 Hit by flak and crash landed near Vire 7.8.44
MN536	175/245 Hit by flak and crash landed near Verden 21.2.45
MN537	198/168
MN538	438 Hit by flak, abandoned over Channel 12.6.44
MN539	266/56 OTU

BELOW: A Typhoon IB taking off. (Philip Jarrett)

Serial No	Delivered To and Significant History	Serial No	Delivered To and Significant History
MN540	245/182 Hit by flak, crash landed St Vitch 31.12.44		Apeldoorn 26.9.44
MN541	257/56 OTU	MN583	440/174/440/609
MN542	247/WgLdr 124 Wg Hit by flak, St Nicholas, abandoned 3 miles N Dieppe 22.5.44	MN584	137
		MN585	198/247 Stalled on landing and undercarriage collapsed, Helmond 5.4.45. DBF
MN543	183	MN586	137 Hit by flak and abandoned near Dinslaken 5.12.44
MN544	609 Shot down by flak Cap d'Antifer 11.5.44		
MN545	263 Hit by flak, crashed 10 miles off Cap Fréhel, Côtes du Nord	MN587	266/197
		MN588	164 Missing on sweep near Rouen 25.8.44
MN546	198/56 OTU Engine cut, belly landed Ayton, Berwickshire 7.5.45	MN589	DH/438/439 Shot down by FW190 near Helmond 1.1.45
MN547	Forced landed after glycol leak 8 miles S Sneek 11.11.44	MN590	184 Shot down by flak, Westerschelde 10.9.44
MN548	440 Shot down by flak near Caen 7.6.44	MN591	247/182
		MN592	181/182
MN549	197/175/197/245/609	MN593	164
MN550	184/257/183/164	MN594	175/245
MN551	Mkrs and A & AEE	MN595	440/183 Shot down by Me109s near Evreux 18.8.44
MN552	245 Hit by flak and abandoned 30 miles off Cherbourg 5.6.44		
MN553	439 Shot down by flak, Le Pont de Vers, Calvados 12.8.44	MN596	137 Collided with MN156 on anti-flying bomb patrol and crashed Denton Court, Kent 27.7.44
MN554	183/266	MN597	247 Engine cut, crash landed and overturned after take-off, Amblie 18.7.44
MN555	440/439/438 Engine cut, belly landed 5 miles S Rheden 18.10.44. DBF		
		MN598	247/609/WgLdr 123 Wg/182
MN556	137 Bounced on landing, swung and overturned, Manston 9.7.44	MN599	247/182 Missing near Huizen 29.9.44
		MN600	266 Crashed in forced landing 10 miles NE Falaise 9.8.44
MN569	439/168/440/439 Shot down by flak near Rips 1.1.45		
MN570	198/247/174 Engine cut after take-off, belly landed Volkel 8.2.45	MN601	245/253
		MN602	193 Shot down by flak near Argentan 15.8.44
MN571	175/245	MN603	440/439/440/59 OTU
MN572	439/263/164/123 Wg	MN604	164
MN573	183/193/198	MN605	164 Missing from ASR search off Cabourg 6.7.44
MN574	439 Shot down by flak near Mesnil-Frementel 18.7.44		
		MN606	245/247 Overshot landing and hit embankment, Diest 8.3.454
MN575	247/182/137/174		
MN576	183 Hit by debris, crash landed near Bernay 24.6.44	MN607	181/168/438 Destroyed in air raid, Eindhoven 1.1.45
MN577	174/193/609/174 Shot down by flak near Sentilly 14.8.44	MN608	174 Crash landed near Albert 31.8.44
		MN623	184 Shot down by flak near Trun 18.8.44
MN578	266/56 OTU		
MN579	438 Hit by flak and abandoned near Roiville, Orne, 18.8.44	MN624	184/266 Dived into ground near Thury-Harcourt 25.7.44
MN580	439/245/439/245/184	MN625	245
MN581	439/440/439 Engine cut. Crashed in forced landing 9 miles N Nordhorn 2.4.45	MN626	483/440
		MN627	137 Crash landed 2 miles SW Nijmegen, presumed hit by flak 30.9.44
MN582	175 Shot down by Me109s near		

Serial No	Delivered To and Significant History	Serial No	Delivered To and Significant History
MN628	184/175		Steinfurt 29.12.44
MN629	197 Hit by flak, crash landed in beach-head 24.6.44	MN640	181 Shot down by flak near Amersfoort 13.10.44
MN630	609 Hit by JR379 on runway after landing Martragny 12.8.44	MN641	193/440 Shot down by flak near Hamminkeln 7.10.44
MN631	164	MN642	184 Shot down by flak near Mezidon, Calvados 7.6.44
MN632	137/59 OTU		
MN633	438/174/184/174/245 Crash landed near Velzen 17.4.45	MN643	257/197/257/56 OTU
MN634	197 Shot down by FW190s near Gronau 24.12.44	MN644	440 Hit by flak and abandoned near Frementel 18.7.44
MN635	440/59/OTU	MN645	3 TEU/55 OTU
MN636	184/440/184	MN646	164
MN637	440 Hit by flak attacking radar station near Cherbourg and abandoned 23.5.44	MN647	247 Crashed in forced landing after engine cut near Xanten 29.11.44
		MN648	181 DBR by enemy artillery Coulombs 22.6.44
MN638	183 Shot down by flak near Falaise 9.8.44	MN649	198 Hit by flak, crashed 1 mile S Montebourg, Manche 14.6.44
MN639	181/168 Shot down by flak SW	MN650	193

BELOW: A Typhoon with conspicuous nose and under-wing recognition marking. (Philip Jarrett)

Serial No	Delivered To and Significant History	Serial No	Delivered To and Significant History
MN651	266/193 Swung on landing and tipped up, St Croix-sur-Mer 8.8.44. DBR	MN693	181/182 Swung on landing and tipped up, Twente 11.4.45
MN652	257 Abandoned after engine cut near Goirle 11.12.44	MN694	198/182 Missing sweep near Clecy, Calvados 9.8.44
MN653	Napier	MN695	DH
MN654	DH/181	MN696	198/181/609/257 Iced up in cloud and crashed SW Utrecht 20.1.45
MN655	DH		
MN656	184/193 Engine cut, belly-landed 4 miles W Bayeux 16.6.44	MN697	609 Hit by flak, abandoned near Caen 6.6.44
MN657	183 Hit by flak and abandoned 10 miles S St Catherines Point, Isle of Wight 3.7.44	MN698	164/183/164/609/183/609/183/257
		MN699	183/182 Shot down by flak near Weerl 2.11.44
MN658	440/198/609 Flew into high ground in bad weather 2 miles E Schedehausen 8.8.45. DBF	MN700	193 Shot down by flak near Falaise 11.6.44
		MN701	609
MN659	184/440/439/440/438/440/438	MN702	183/198 Shot down by flak off Zuid Beveland 3.11.44
MN660	137 Shot down by flak near Hunterburg 31.12.44	MN703	440 Swung on take-off and hit MN633. Bombs exploded, Lanmtheuil 16.7.44
MN661	263 Hit by flak. Crash landed Grantez, Jersey 14.6.44		
MN662	193/35 OTU	MN704	247/83GSU Stalled on approach after engine cut in circuit, Dunsfold 9.2.45
MN663	439 Hit by flak, abandoned over Channel 23.6.44		
MN664	182 Hit by MN421 after landing Eindhoven 23.9.44	MN705	193 Missing, presumed shot down by fighters near Enschede 24.12.44
MN665	439/440 Shot down by FW190 near Eindhoven 24.12.44	MN706	197/609/263 Hit by flak, crashed off Harderwijk 17.4.45
MN666	FLS	MN707	440/438 Shot down by flak over Orne 18.7.44
MN667	184 Shot down by flak near Mézidon, Calvados 7.6.44		
		MN708	RAE
MN680	266 Shot down by FW190s near Livbarot, Calvados 17.8.44	MN709	440 Engine cut, crash landed Carpiquet and blew up 26.7.44
MN681	182/247/183 Engine cut, belly landed Rheine 13.5.45	MN710	247 Hit MN704 on take-off in dust, Coulombs 18.6.44
MN682	257/245/184 CSU failed. Abandoned near Schleiden 27.12.44	MN711	164 Shot down by flak near Rouen 25.8.44
MN683	174/266	MN712	266
MN684	440/197/193	MN713	257 Engine cut. Abandoned 2 miles S St Lô 16.7.44
MN685	246/56 OTU		
MN686	Mkrs	MN714	181/182 Engine cut. Belly landed and overturned 5 miles SE Evreux
MN687	438 Shot down by flak, Le Mesnil Villement, Calvados 12.8.44		
MN688	197/181/247 Hit tree low flying and crashed 5 miles WNW Bad Segeburg 16.6.45	MN715	438/440 Hit by flak, abandoned near Maltot, Calvados 17.7.44
		MN716	439/438
MN689	183/263	MN717	175 Hit by flak and abandoned over Ruhr 27.9.44
MN690	181 Hit by flak and abandoned near Vielsalm 31.12.44	MN718	184 Hit by flak and abandoned near Mortrain 7.8.44
MN691	440/439 Engine caught fire on start up, Flensburg 31.7.45	MN719	198 Hit by flak and crash landed near Vermoutiers 20.8.44
MN692	184/440/439	MN720	440 Shot down by flak near Flers

Serial No	Delivered To and Significant History	Serial No	Delivered To and Significant History
	13.8.44	MN752	197 Collided with MN981 in cloud, crashed near Amersfoort 21.11.44
MN735	182 Engine cut, belly-landed Newport, Isle of Wight 8.6.44	MN753	174 Hit by flak, abandoned S Ghent 10.9.44
MN736	257/245	MN754	257/WgLdr 146 Wg Shot down by flak 3 miles W Caen 16.6.44
MN737	609/198/18 APC		
MN738	263/266	MN755	257/197/440
MN739	266 Caught fire when starting up, Hildesheim 26.6.54. DBR	MN756	181/440/181
		MN757	257/184/181
MN740	245	MN758	438/168/438
MN741	266 Shot down by flak while attacking MT near Caen 12.6.44	MN759	197/257
		MN760	193 Presumed ditched in low cloud returning from sweep 1 mile S The Needles, Isle of Wight
MN742	183 Hit by flak, abandoned 10 miles SW Caen 14.6.44		
MN743	193 Shot down by flak near Caen 18.7.44	MN761	193 Hit by flak, abandoned 15 miles SW Isle of Wight 5.6.44
MN744	193/182	MN762	182 Shot down by flak near Troarm, Calvados 18.7.44
MN745	184		
MN746	438/245/438 Shot down by flak near Caen 27.6.44	MN763	193 Drifted off runway and overturned in V-2 crater, Deurne 28.11.44
MN747	257/183		
MN748	245 Missing from attack on gun positions at La Forge à Camro 13.7.44	MN764	440 Overshot landing and hit obstruction, Illiers l'Evêque 3.9.44. DBR
MN749	184/247/245/184 Crashed on sweep near Bocholt 21.2.45	MN765	439 Shot down by flak near Speelberg 5.10.44
MN750	197 Engine cut. Belly-landed and hit tree, Langley, Fawley, Hants. 27.6.44. DBF	MN766	257 Hit by debris and abandoned near Livard 6.7.44
MN751	266 Shot down by Me109s near Lisieux 19.7.44	MN767	193 Hit by flak and crash landed near

BELOW: Typical scene at dispersals on a forward airstrip: a Typhoon being bombed up with thousand-pounders. (Philip Jarrett)

Serial No	Delivered To and Significant History	Serial No	Delivered To and Significant History
	Merxem 28.10.44		Bretteville, Manche 17.6.44
MN768	182/183/182 Destroyed in air raid, Eindhoven 1.1.45	MN810	183/174 Caught fire starting up, Volkel 6.3.45. DBR
MN769	263 Collided with R8923 in formation and crashed near Oostburg 14.10.44	MN811	257/263
MN770	245 Shot down by flak near Gavray, Manche 7.8.44	MN812	247 Hit by flak near Evrecy; failed to return 15.7.44
MN771	182 Hit by flak near Troarn, crash landed near Deauville-en-Auge, Calvados 18.7.44	MN813	198 Hit by flak and abandoned over beach-head 13.8.44
		MN814	181 Spun into ground out of cloud on air test near Ringwood, Hants 25.6.44
MN772	245	MN815	198 Missing on sweep near St Aubain-sur-Algot, Calvados 20.6.44
MN773	266/175 Hit by flak and abandoned near Varenrode 4.4.45		
MN774	257	MN816	438 Destroyed in air raid Eindhoven 1.1.45
MN775	198/181 Hit by flak and crash landed near Enschede 31.3.45	MN817	440 Developed glycol leak and crash landed near Venlo 9.9.44
MN776	439 Engine cut on approach; belly landed Camilly 27.6.44	MN818	609 Shot down by FW190 near Laval 27.6.44
MN777	440/384/440	MN819	245/181 Engine cut, crash landed near Nordhorn 1.4.45
MN778	193/55 OTU		
MN779	184	MN820	257 Hit by flak and crash landed near Argentan 22.6.44
MN791	438/439 Shot down by FW190 near Coesfeld 29.12.44	MN821	182/181 Hit by flak. Crash landed at Coulombs and hit parked Typhoon 6.7.44
MN792	193/174/137		
MN793	440 Missing from bombing attack near Grainville-sur-Odon 30.7.44	MN822	184/137
		MN823	247/182 Damaged in air raid, Eindhoven 1.1.45. Not repaired
MN794	164 Missing near Kleve 14.2.45	MN851	184 Crashed during sweep near Neukirchen 19.10.44
MN795	247 Hit by MN821 while parked Coulombs 6.7.44	MN852	164 Forced landed in beach-head 22.6.44. DBR
MN796	Engine cut after take-off; belly-landed on approach Melsbroek 10.9.44	MN853	257/164 Hit by own AA and blew up near Lingen 10.4.45
MN797	193	MN854	197 Missing, presumed ditched in Channel on sweep 5.7.44
MN798	247/182 Shot down by flak near Halst 15.12.44	MN855	245/56 OTU
MN799	247/609	MN856	175
MN800	247	MN857	257 Engine cut. Ditched off Keyhaven, Hants 21.6.44
MN801	440/439/440 Shot down by flak 2 miles E Goch 19.11.44	MN858	193
MN802	198/183	MN859	197/55 OTU
MN803	198/137 Hit by flak and abandoned near Rouen 27.8.44	MN860	197/84 GSU Engine cut, belly-landed Warren Farm, Wokingham, Berks 16.5.45
MN804	198/59 OTU		
MN805	440 Missing from sweep near Geldern 6.10.44	MN861	AAEE
MN806	183 Shot down by flak Cap d'Antifer 12.7.44	MN862	164 Missing from sweep near Aardenburg 7.10.44
MN807	266 Crashed in forced landing 4 miles SSE Leerdam 19.11.44	MN863	245/137 Damaged by flak and crash landed 2 miles N Kleve 4.4.45
MN808	182/247 Hit by flak near Esquay, Calvados. Failed to return 15.7.44		
MN809	247 Hit by flak and abandoned near		

Serial No	Delivered To and Significant History
MN864	184 Force landed near Habloville, Orne 13.8.44. NFD
MN865	263 Shot down by flak off Lanmeur, Finisterre 7.7.44
MN866	197/266 Hit by flak and abandoned near Rotterdam 6.10.44
MN867	197/247 Engine cut. Crash landed near Ménil-Hermei, Orne 15.8.44
MN868	609/183/257 Engine cut. Belly landed and overturned near Hensden 13.10.44
MN869	439 Destroyed in air raid, Eindhoven 1.1.45
MN870	439/438/440/439 Shot down by flak 4 miles W Deventer 28.10.44
MN871	183/59 OTU
MN872	197
MN873	184/198
MN874	184/175
MN875	439 Shot down by flak 4 miles SSW Enschede 31.3.45
MN876	83 GSU Missing, presumed ditched on air test off Dungeness, Kent 11.6.44
MN877	198 Missing on sweep near Vimoutiers 19.8.45
MN878	263 Shot down by flak near Bernay 16.8.44
MN879	257 Damaged by explosion of own bomb. Abandoned near Caen 16.7.44
MN880	1987 Hit water and overshot runway on take-off. Overturned Merville 2.10.44
MN881	197 Collided with MN752 in cloud and crashed near Amersfoort 21.11.44
MN882	198/197
MN883	263 Damaged by flak and crash landed Theillement, Eure 25.8.44
MN884	257/266/198
MN885	164
MN886	183/193 Collided with MN982 on landing, Mill 16.4.45
MN887	193 Shot down by flak near Argenton 10.8.44
MN888	181 Missing on sweep near Dummersee 8.12.44
MN889	181/184 Flew into high ground in formation, Shorncliff Barracks, Kent 3.12.44
MN890	164/257/164/123 Wg
MN891	182 Shot down by flak near Bretteville-le-Rabet Calvados 25.7.44
MN872	182/124 Wg
MN893	197/182/124 Wg
MN894	440/439 Shot down by flak near Mayen 24.12.44
MN895	193/263/193 Crashed on landing, Mill 16.4.45. DBR
MN896	197/164 Hit by debris and forced landed near Neumünster 25.4.45
MN912	193 Shot down by flak near Voorthuizen 25.11.44
MN913	812 Hit by flak near Vimoutiers, failed to return 19.8.44
MN914	439/168/184
MN915	245 Missing on sweep near Trun 18.8.44
MN917	175/181/174 Ran out of fuel, belly landed Straelen, near Venlo 24.3.45
MN918	3 TEU/55 OTU
MN919	184/257 Shot down by flak 10 miles E Caen 26.7.44
MN920	181 Crashed on sweep near Vimoutiers 19.8.44. NFD
MN921	263/197 Shot down by flak near Hensden 13.10.44
MN922	181/137/174
MN923	183
MN924	Abandoned on weather check in bad weather near Louvain 15.2.45
MN925	197/193
MN926	193
MN927	257 Engine cut on take-off. Crash landed and overturned St Croix 7.8.44
MN928	247 Shot down by flak near Flers 12.8.44
MN929	440 Shot down by flak near Vimoutiers 18.8.44
MN930	257/55 OTU
MN931	257 Shot down by flak near Utrecht 24.12.44
MN932	257/266
MN933	245 Caught fire and abandoned near Quesnay 11.8.44
MN934	266/184/245
MN935	266/609
MN936	193/168/439 Hit by flak on sweep near Dingden and failed to return 24.3.45
MN937	193/257
MN938	3 TEU/55 OTU Engine cut. Hit ditch and overturned in forced landing 2 miles W Malmesbury, Wilts. 17.1.45.

Serial No	Delivered To and Significant History	Serial No	Delivered To and Significant History
	DBF	MN983	175 Shot down by flak, Terneuzen 11.9.44
MN939	263/193		
MN940	DBR in air raid Eindhoven 1.1.45	MN984	440 DBR in air raid Eindhoven 1.1.45
		MN985	198/174/184
MN941	123 Wg/183 Shot down by flak near Udem 22.2.45	MN986	245/175 Destroyed by artillery fire Deurne 23.9.44
MN942	257/Tangmere/197/146 Wg	MN987	245/193/245/193
MN943	RAE	MN988	184/175/245 Hit by flak, crash landed near Minden 16.4.45
MN944	164/59 OTU Engine cut. Belly-landed 1 mile N Warkworth, Northumberland 18.5.45	MN989	439/266/175/266
		MN990	175 Hit by flak and crash landed in beach-head 18.8.44
MN946	198/197		
MN947	266/257 Tyre burst on take-off, swung and hit JR219, Manston 6.9.44. DBF	MN991	263/56 OTU/609
		MN992	263/175
		MN993	245/266/168/CFE
MN948	184 Engine cut, belly-landed Camilly 2.8.44	MN994	181/198
		MN995	137 Abandoned on sweep near Roermond 29.10.44. NFD
MN949	266/247		
MN950	197/137	MN996	197
MN951	198	MN997	197/184 Taxied into RB457, Volkel 10.3.45
MN952	174/164		
MN953	245/175/245	MN998	247 Tail broke off during dive bombing attack. Spun into ground 3 miles SE Boxtel 28.9.44
MN954	609 Hit by flank and abandoned near Rotterdam 28.9.44		
MN955	137 Shot down by FW190s near Goch 24.9.44	MN999	439/440/168/181 Spun into ground off high speed stall 8 miles NE Schleswig 13.9.45
MN956	174/184/56 OTU		
MN968	247/193 Engine cut. Abandoned near Havekost 25.5.45	MP113	197 Engine cut. Belly-landed 3 miles SE Vlkel 3.3.45
MN969	439	MP114	3 TEU/55 OTU Hit by JR443 while awaiting take-off, Aston Down
MN970	182 Shot down by flak near Rheydt 29.11.44		
		MP115	198
MN971	440/198	MP116	198 Tyre burst on take-off, swung and overturned Merville 10.9.44. DBR
MN972	175/184 Engine cut. Abandoned 4 miles N Rees 25.2.45		
		MP117	257/263/439
MN973	247 Shot down by flak near Kevalaer 24.9.44	MP118	55 OTU Engine cut, belly-landed Charndon, Oxon 28.2.45
MN974	AFDU/CFE/FLS Lost power on take-off. Undercarriage raised to stop. Tangmere 13.6.45	MP119	197
		MP120	247 Hit by flak. Crash landed 6 miles NW Wesel 24.3.45
MN975	56 OTU Engine cut at low altitude. Crashed in field, Cornhill, Northumberland 20.7.45. DBF	MP121	257 Hit by flak near Oosterschelde and failed to return 5.9.44
		MP122	440 Shot down by flak near Condé-sur-Noireau, Calvados 12.8.44
MN976	168/263		
MN977	197/174 Crash landed on sweep 6 miles N Osnabrück 24.2.45. NFD	MP123	197
		MP124	124 Wg/440 Shot down by flak near Staphorst 11.11.44
MN978	609/164/609		
MN979	247	MP125	137 Shot down by flak, Kassel 28.9.44
MN980	137/181	MP126	247 Shot down by flak near Bocholt 5.12.44
MN981	174		
MN982	193	MP127	55 OTU Collided with RB486 in dive, crashed 2 miles W Wollaston, Mon

Serial No	Delivered To and Significant History	Serial No	Delivered To and Significant History
	7.4.45		14.4.45
MP128	438 Hit by flak, spun into ground near Montford 22.1.45	MP155	245
MP129	181/440 Blew up attacking railway in Germany 11.11.44. Presumed bomb exploded prematurely	MP156	247/124 Wg Hit by flak and abandoned near St Vith 26.12.44
		MP157	197 Shot down by flak near Korteven 18.10.44
MP130	197/440	MP158	266 Sent for repair 26.10.44. NFT
MP131	438 Hit by flak, abandoned 4 miles SSE Arnhem 18.11.44	MP172	182 Hit by flak, crash landed 10 miles E Helmond, 25.3.45
MP132	198/193/263 Hit by flak, blew up near Deventer 26.12.44	MP173	439/440
		MP174	164 Engine cut. Belly-landed near Wavre 8.11.44
MP133	137/174/184	MP175	3 TEU/55 OTU
MP134	439 Shot down by flak, Uetterach 22.1.45	MP176	175 Ran out of fuel on approach and belly-landed Volkel 8.12.44
MP135	438 Shot down by flak attacking railway near Coesfeld 7.10.44	MP177	439/438 Destroyed in air raid, Eindhoven 1.1.45
MP136	439 Blew up in air near s'Gravenhage 22.10.44	MP178	438 Shot down by flak near Bullange 24.12.44
MP137	245 Hit by flak during attack on tanks, crashed near Les autels, Calvados 17.8.44	MP179	197/266
		MP180	266 Shot down by FW190s near Dortmund 25.12.44
MP138	440/438/440/438 Hit sea recovering from dive during dive bombing practice off Portland, Dorset 23.3.45	MP181	438 Shot down by Me109s near Diepholz 4.4.45
		MP182	439/184
MP139	438/440 DBR in air raid Eindhoven 1.1.45	MP183	440 Hit by flak, abandoned 2 miles WNW Papenbeek 28.11.44
MP140	440/266	MP184	174/184/174/175
MP141	Napier. Engine cut on air test and undercarriage jammed. Belly-landed Heston 19.9.45	MP185	193 NFT
		MP186	438 Shot down by flak near Dahlem 24.12.44
MP142	Napier/266	MP187	56 OTU Spun into ground during dogfight with Spitfire, Kettleburn, Northumberland 8.3.45
MP143	197 Hit by flak, abandoned near Breda 21.10.44		
MP144	247 Shot down by flak near Vermoutiers 18.8.44	MP188	197
MP145	439 Hit by flak, abandoned NW St Vith 27.12.44	MP189	181/247 Forced landed in fog near Duren 23.12.44
MP146	184 Crashed while attacking train, Donspen 28.11.44	MP190	193/197 Shot down by flak near Neustadt 3.5.45
MP147	183/182 Tyre dropped off on take-off. Belly landed Warmwell 11.8.45. DBR	MP191	181 Collided with another Typhoon and crashed near St Vith 27.12.44
MP148	193/197	MP192	439/438 Hit by flak and abandoned near Weumme 16.4.45
MP149	440 Hit by flak, abandoned near Malmedy 25.12.44	MP193	193 Hit by flak, crash landed near Zutphen 18.3.45
MP150	164/56 OTU	MP194	197
MP151	439 Shot down by flak near Haldern 22.2.45	MP195	1193/137/174
MP152	439 Hit by flak and abandoned near Vlissingen 9.9.44	MP196	193/197 Shot down by FW190s near Gronau 24.12.44
MP153	263 Shot down by flak near Quillebeuf-sur-Seine, Eure 24.8.44	MP197	245/121 Wg
MP154	137 Shot down by flak near Verden	MP198	197 Shot down by flak near Boulogne 13.9.44

Serial No	Delivered To and Significant History	Serial No	Delivered To and Significant History
MP199	168/182	PD467	263 Shot down by flak, Wetten 14.2.45
MP200	440/182 Overshot landing and hit obstruction, Warmwell 10.8.45. DBR	PD468	257/197/193/257/197 Engine cut on navex, crash landed near Hanover 26.7.45
MP201	247 Hit by RB209 while taxying, Eindhoven 2.1.45	PD469	440 Shot down by flak near Nijverdal 20.10.44
MP202	83 GSU Lost tail recovering from dive 1 mile NE Bognor Regis, Sussex 11.9.44	PD470	609 Hit by flak and abandoned near Ede 5.12.44
MP203	181 Shot down by flak near Otersen 12.4.45	PD471	197 Shot down by flak near Aalborg 31.12.44
		PD472	266/263
145 IB delivered between July and September 1944		PD473	193/226 Shot down by flak, Lonnecker 1.4.45
PD446	438 Damaged by flak, crashed on approach, Eindhoven 20.1.45	PD474	193
PD447	197 Missing from attack on German HQ Kalkar 10.2.45	PD475	438 Engine cut in circuit, belly landed, Eindhoven 6.11.44
PD448	439 Shot down by flak near Vermoutiers 19.8.44	PD476	438 Hit by flak while attacking V-1 site, abandoned near Piershil 21.2.45
PD449	609/198/609 Engine cut in circuit, overshot landing, undercarriage raised to stop. Gilze-Rijen 10.3.45	PD477	182 Hit by flak, crash landed near Oostnun 12.10.44
PD450	182 Engine cut on take-off, undercarriage raised to stop. Helmond 14.1.45	PD478	440/438/439 Shot down by flak near Haltern 15.12.44
PD451	439 Tyre burst on landing, overshot runway and overturned, Eindhoven 22.3.45	PD479	440/438 Shot down by Me109s near Nijmegen 29.9.44
PD452	438/440	PD480	263 Overshot landing and swung, Ahlhorn 2.6.45. DBR
PD454	257 Engine cut, hit tree in forced landing near Eindhoven 5.1.45	PD492	438/439 Shot down by P-47s 4 miles SE Düren 24.12.44
PD455	193	PD493	440 Shot down by flak near Legden 2.2.45
PD456	193/198	PD494	175 Hit by flak, abandoned 2 miles E Megan 24.10.44
PD457	164 Missing near Rouen 25.8.44		
PD458	439 Shot down by flak near Goch 27.9.44	PD495	247 Engine cut 10 miles E Borken, crash landed 24.1.45
PD459	438/439 Hit by flak, crashed on approach, Eindhoven 26.12.44	PD496	198/175/184 Engine cut, belly-landed Chessilfeld, Dorset 18.5.45
PD460	197 Shot down by flak near Dunkirk 28.10.44	PD497	440 Spun into ground attacking train near Bocholt 3.2.45
PD461	440/439	PD498	266
PD462	440 Shot down by FW190s near Malmedy 24.12.44	PD499	198/350
		PD500	183/193
PD463	193/440	PD501	197/266 Tyre burst on take-off, swung and overturned, Mill 26.3.45
PD464	263/257 Shot down by flak near Utrecht 24.1.45	PD502	263
PD465	439 Flew into ground during attack 3 miles N Oosterhout 24.9.44	PD503	438 Destroyed in air raid Eindhoven 1.1.45
		PD504	197/266
PD466	164/609/198/257/198 Engine cut during shipping strike. Belly-landed Eimke 3.5.45	PD505	609 Engine caught fire on sweep. Belly-landed Merville 14.9.44. DBF
		PD506	263 Hit by flak and forced landed near Zwolle 7.11.44
		PD507	197

PD508	198 Engine cut, abandoned near Beers 13.4.45
PD509	193 Ran out of fuel, belly-landed Deurne 24.1.45
PD510	440
PD511	164 Hit by flak, abandoned near Kalkar 21.2.45
PD512	263/182/247
PD513	266 Hit by flak, abandoned near Goch 18.10.44
PD514	263/266
PD515	164 Abandoned NE Roosendaal 13.9.44. NFD
PD516	183 Flicked over and crashed recovering from RP attack NNE Ede 19.11.44
PD518	257/193
PD519	609 Tyre burst on take-off, swung and overturned, Gilze-Rijen 18.3.45. DBF
PD520	55 OTU
PD521	266/257/266
PD522	263/266
PD523	440 Hit by flak, crashed near Horst
PD524	263/198

PD525	193/257
PD526	257 Caught fire during attack on railway near Zwolle and spiralled into ground 19.11.44
PD527	266
PD528	263/266 Crash landed during sweep to Groningen 11.4.45
PD529	183/WgLdr 123 Wg/263
PD530	263
PD531	197
PD532	175
PD533	56 OTU
PD534	197
PD535	164/193/198
PD536	137/181
PD548	193
PD549	181/55 OTU
PD550	193 Skidded on landing and undercarriage collapsed, Mill 14.2.45
PD551	137 Caught fire in air and crashed near Rethy, Antwerp 20.9.44
PD552	182 Shot down by flak 5 miles N Eindhoven 29.11.44
PD553	266/182/266
PD554	439
PD556	438 Destroyed in air raid Eindhoven 1.1.45
PD557	439

BELOW: A Typhoon IB in 1942. (Philip Jarrett)

Serial No	Delivered To and Significant History	Serial No	Delivered To and Significant History
PD558	55 OTU	PD610	439/59 OTU
PD559	175	PD611	137/174 Swung on landing, undercarriage leg collapsed. Warmwell 26.8.45
PD560	174		
PD561	181 Shot down by flak near Wietzen 6.2.45	PD612	247 Shot down by flak near Münster 31.12.44
PD562	182		
PD564	439 Engine cut on air test. Belly landed near Helmond 10.2.45. DBF	PD613	168/175/245 Engine lost power, overshot landing, hit railway. Schneverdingen 28.5.45. DBF
PD565	55 OTU		
PD566	263 Hit by flak near Heinsberg, crash landed near Geilenkirchen 18.11.44	PD614	263 Damaged in action 25.2.45
		PD615	RAE
PD567	55 OTU	PD616	197/413 RSU Damaged by blast from V-1, Deurne 11.2.45
PD568	55 OTU		
PD569	438	PD617	193
PD570	137	PD618	247/198 Engine cut, belly landed near Neustadt returning from shipping strike 3.5.45
PD571	197		
PD572	609 Shot down by flak, Nieuwolde 23.4.45		
		PD619	137
PD573	247	PD620	197
PD574	137/174	PD621	440 DBR in air raid Eindhoven 1.1.45
PD575	56 OTU	PD622	263
PD576	263/266	PD623	609/197
PD589	440		
PD590	59 OTU		*255 IB delivered between September 1944 and January 1945*
PD592	439/438/440 Hit by flak near Münster, crash landed near Enschede 24.2.45		
		RB192	440 Destroyed in air raid, Eindhoven 1.1.45
PD593	609 Hit by flak and abandoned near Friesoythe 12.4.45	RB193	182/137 Shot down by flak, Lingen 1.4.45
PD594	257/263	RB194	137 Damaged by flak, crash landed near Solingen 29.12.44
PD595	440 DBR in air raid Eindhoven 1.1.45		
PD597	440/193 Hit by flak, abandoned near Wezel 24.3.45	RB195	439/182
		RB196	182 Shot down by flak near St Vith 31.12.44
PD598	257 Iced up in cloud and crashed near Utrecht 20.1.45		
		RB197	193/266
PD599	182	RB198	439/438
PD600	193	RB199	197/168/197
PD601	440 Shot down by flak Montfoort 21.1.45	RB200	174/184 Shot down by flak near Bocholt 14.1.45
PD602	257/193	RB201	440 Shot down by flak near Gronau 29.12.44
PD603	247 Shot down by flak attacking German HQ near Apeldoorn 4.11.44		
		RB202	440/439/440/168/182
PD604	263/151 RU Damaged on ground 11.2.46	RB203	438/440
		RB204	439 Damaged by flak, crash landed near Bertmerborg 14.1.45
PD605	123 Wg/198 Caught fire starting up, Kluis 10.4.45. DBR		
		RB205	440 Destroyed in air raid Eindhoven 1.1.45
PD606	257		
PD607	439 Hit by flak and abandoned 10 miles NE Roermond 19.11.44	RB206	493/438
		RB207	438
PD608	439	RB208	137/181/124 Wg Damaged by flak, crash landed near Wesel 24.3.45
PD609	137 Engine cut, overshot and belly landed in field near Evère 5.12.44		
		RB209	168 Swung on take-off for air

Serial No	Delivered To and Significant History	Serial No	Delivered To and Significant History
	test and hit MP201 Eindhoven 2.1.45		Dorset 11.8.45. RP motor believed to have exploded
RB210	56 OTU Flew into ground in low cloud, North Charlton, Northumberland 13.1.45	RB257	439
RB211	197	RB258	183
RB212	197	RB259	193
RB213	Damaged 27.12.44. Not repaired	RB260	266 Stalled on landing and cartwheeled Deurne 20.1.45. DBR
RB214	245/175 Spun into ground near Hamm on sweep 19.3.45	RB261	193/146 Wg
RB215	263 Damaged by flak, crash landed Niebull 26.4.45	RB262	439
RB216	175	RB263	18 APC
RB217	438 Shot down by Me109s near Diepholz 4.4.45	RB264	164 Damaged by flak abandoned near Wilhelmshaven 26.4.45
RB218	193 Shot down by flak near Zuilichem 1.1.45	RB265	18 APC/1 APS Ground-looped to avoid overshooting runway and undercarriage leg collapsed. Fairwood Common 15.12.45
RB219	266		
RB220	197/193/151 RU Caught fire starting up, Wevelghem 8.9.45. DBR	RB266	14 APC
		RB2167	266 Engine cut, belly-landed near Eemshaven 9.4.45. DBR
RB221	182	RB268	55 OTU
RB222	183	RB269	174/245 Ran off runway on landing in heavy rain and tipped up, Twente 15.8.45
RB223	198		
RB224	266		
RB225	247 Damaged by flak, abandoned near Helmond 25.3.45	RB270	168 Shot down by flak near Dorenthe 3.2.45
RB226	438 Shot down by flak near Geldern 14.2.45	RB271	193/413 RSU Engine cut, crash landed and overturned, Deurne 28.1.45
RB227	257/193/146 Wg		
RB228	197 Engine cut on sweep. Belly landed near Leer 12.4.45	RB273	257/193
		RB274	Hit HT cables during low-level attack and crashed 3 miles E Arnhem 10.4.45
RB229	197		
RB230	197		
RB231	263	RB275	438
RB232	263	RB276	182 Engine cut, hit trees in forced landing 7 miles N Hasselt 1.2.45
RB233	439/168/181 Damaged by flak. Abandoned near Schwarzenbeck 20.4.4		
		RB277	263
RB235	197	RB278	181/137/247
RB248	266	RB279	193 Damaged by flak, abandoned near Kampen 13.4.45
RB249	182		
RB250	609 Collided with MN434, crashed near Grave 13.4.45	RB280	183 Damaged by flak, abandoned N Boxmeer 8.2.45
RB251	197 Hit by debris and abandoned Broeksketel 12.4.45	RB281	439
		RB282	174 Abandoned 10 miles E Ahaus 23.2.45
RB252	137 Missing near Roermond 3.3.45		
RB253	266 Damaged by flak, abandoned near Xanten 28.2.45	RB283	56 OTU
		RB284	257
RB254	182/137	RB285	438 Shot down by flak near Appelhulsen 2.3.45
RB255	197		
RB256	182 Blew up recovering from RP dive, crashed off Chesil Beach,	RB286	439/438
		RB287	168/175 Crashed near Wuppertal

Serial No	Delivered To and Significant History	Serial No	Delivered To and Significant History
	31.3.45	RB336	182/197/609
RB288	CFE	RB337	263/439/263/181
RB289	Damaged by flak, crash landed near Mechelen 25.3.45	RB338	440 Shot down by flak near Wesel 28.2.45
RB303	137/174	RB339	56 OTU
RB304	175	RB340	245
RB305	263/197	RB341	181 Swung on landing, undercarriage collapsed, Eindhoven 25.3.45
RB306	Mkrs/247 Bounced on landing, swung and undercarriage collapsed, near Mechelen 25.3.45	RB342	440/438 Missing in cloud near Luneberg 23.4.45
		RB343	56 OTU Engine cut after take-off. Dived into ground in circuit Milfield 1.2.45
RB307	55 OTU		
RB308	197/WgLdr 124 Wg Crash landed during air test near Ypres after running out of fuel 26.12.44	RB344	182/247 Damaged by flak and abandoned near Helmond 25.3.45
RB309	257/263	RB345	RAE
RB310	440/83 GDC Engine cut on take-off. Crash landed Dunsfold 21.9.45	RB346	193 Shot down by flak near Appeldoorn 14.4.45
		RB347	174/175
RB311	609 Shot down by flak near Kleve 14.2.45	RB361	168 Missing sweep near Haltern 22.1.45
RB312	14 APC	RB362	174 Lost power, crash landed near Emmerich 24.2.45
RB313	1 FP Engine cut, belly-landed 6 miles SE Ghent 7.1.45	RB263	Mkrs/262/84 GDC Swerved while taxying, hit cylinder and tipped up, Breighton 29.11.45
RB314	174/247 Damaged by flak, Borken 25.3.45		
RB315	440	RB364	181 Damaged by flak and abandoned near Soest 11.2.45
RB316	197		
RB317	439 Damaged by flak, crash landed near Laffeld 20.1.45	RB365	440/Napier
		RB366	182 Collided with SW407 in heavy rain on landing Husum 30.6.45. DBR
RB318	182/137/174		
RB319	257 Missing in cloud on sweep SE Utrecht 20.1.45	RB367	266/198
		RB368	174
RB230	174/247/181	RB369	438/440/439
RB231	197 Hit by flak, crash landed 2 miles SW Cullemborg 31.12.44	RB370	266
		RB371	55 OTU
RB322	182	RB372	56 OTU
RB323	438 Shot down by flak, Bovenau 25.4.45	RB373	257/193 Shot down by flak near Almelo 1.4.45
RB234	439	RB375	174/175
RB325	440 Shot down by flak, Dremmen 23.1.45	RB376	168/137 Damaged by flak, abandoned near Brunen 24.3.45
RB236	439	RB377	439/440
RB239	RAE	RB378	247 Hit by flak, crash landed 4 miles NW Kleve 24.3.45
RB330	263		
RB331	174 Shot down by P-47s near Haltern 14.1.45	RB379	263/680 To Russia 20.7.45
		RB380	174/245
RB332	164	RB381	193 Damaged by own bomb burst during attack on Raalte bridge. Failed to return 9.3.45
RB333	438 Blew up in dive attacking rail target near Geldern 23.1.45		
RB334	174	RB382	174/184 NFT
RB335	263 Shot down by flak near Utrecht 24.12.44	RB383	257/263

Serial No	Delivered To and Significant History	Serial No	Delivered To and Significant History
RB384	257/263	RB439	56 OTU
RB385	174 Engine cut, belly-landed Volkel and hit crater 8.2.45	RB440	175 Hit by flak, abandoned near Ijsselberg 26.3.45
RB386	257/197	RB441	440/439
RB387	438/439 Undercarriage leg collapsed on landing, Warmwell 17.4.45	RB442	55 OTU
		RB443	174/181
RB388	440	RB444	438/83 GSU Hit by Tempest SN258 while parked Dunsfold 27.7.45
RB389	438/440/438/439	
RB390	84 GSU	RB445	440
RB391	439/438	RB446	438 Engine cut. Crash landed after take-off, Flensberg 14.5.45
RB392	181 Missing on sweep near Soest 13.2.45	
		RB447	Napier
RB393	438	RB448	183
RB394	181	RB449	55 OTU/439
RB395	181	RB450	182/247/Napier
RB396	174 Hit by flak, crash landed near Denekamp 1.4.45	RB451	266
		RB452	245/175
RB397	174/438 Hit by PD592 while parked Eindhoven 21.1.45. DBR	RB453	183 Engine cut, belly-landed Wünstorf 27.5.45
RB398	1263 Tyre burst on take-off, overturned. Drope 17.4.45. DBR	RB454	137 Hit by flak, abandoned near Brunen 26.3.45
RB399	440	RB455	164
RB400	168/174/184	RB456	439
RB401	55 OTU/440	RB457	168/184/174
RB402	438/439	RB458	247
RB403	168	RB549	247
RB404	193 Caught fire starting up, Deurne 31.1.45. DBR	RB474	197
		RB475	440
RB405	247/440/247/137/174	RB476	182/175
RB406	245/197/175	RB477	56 OTU/439
RB407	55 OTU	RB478	266/198
RB408	174/184	RB479	263 Hit by flak, Deventer, abandoned over Allied lines 8.4.45
RB423	266 Shot down by flak near Leer 23.4.45	
		RB480	247 Hit by flak Herford, crash landed near Appelhülsen 19.3.45
RB424	183/197/183	
RB425	440	RB481	55 OTU
RB426	440	RB482	193 Hit by debris, abandoned near Scharrel 18.4.45
RB427	168/440	
RB428	56 OTU	RB483	247
RB429	438 Hit trees attacking vehicles near Gnissau, crashed 26.4.45	RB484	164
		RB485	440 Undercarriage jammed on ferry flight. Belly-landed Nordholz 8.7.45
RB430	174/175	
RB431	609/123 Wg	RB486	55 OTU
RB432	181	RB487	174 Crashed in bad weather 6 miles W Rheims 3.4.45
RB433	404/438	
RB434	263	RB488	55 OTU
RB435	440/439 Shot down by flak 4 miles S Lengerich 30.3.45	RB489	609
		RB491	55 OTU
RB436	55 OTU	RB492	168/175 Undercarriage leg distorted in flight. Belly-landed Hustedt 4.5.45
RB437	183	
RB438	238/263 Hit by flak and abandoned near Naarden 7.4.45	RB493	181
		RB494	440

Serial No	Delivered To and Significant History	Serial No	Delivered To and Significant History
RB495	168/439/440	SW409	245/175
RB496	175/174	SW410	164
RB497	182/609	SW411	609
RB498	609	SW412	182 Shot down by flak near Wedel 19.4.45
RB499	439		
RB500	193	SW413	184
RB501	8g GSU Engine cut. Belly landed in Knowle Park, Cranleigh, Surrey 4.2.45	SW414	183
		SW415	182 Shot down by flak near Osnabrück 28.2.45
RB502	56 OTU	SW416	174
RB503	257/263	SW417	245/175
RB504	137/247 Undercarriage jammed. Belly landed West Malling 13.9.45	SW418	182 Hit by flak, crash landed Eindhoven 28.3.45
RB505	182 Hit by flak. Crash landed Wettringen 30.3.45	SW419	263
		SW420	439
RB506	438/440	SW421	184/181
RB507	56 OTU	SW422	247
RB508	168/438	SW423	440/439
RB509	181	SW424	197
RB510	439	SW425	247 Hit by flak and crash landed in Germany 1.4.45
RB511	175		
RB512	55 OTU	SW426	137 Crashed in sea 3 miles S Langeland 3.6.45
		SW427	182 Tyre burst on landing, overturned, Helmond 10.4.45
	300 IB delivered between January and November 1945		
SW386	181 Broke up in air recovering from dive, Kastrup 18.7.45	SW428	439/440
		SW443	439 Shot down by flak, Eringen 3.5.45
SW387	137/175	SW444	184
SW388	55 OTU	SW445	247 Damaged by flak near Cloppenburg 5.4.45
SW389	193		
SW390	181	SW446	439/438
SW391	182 Shot down by flak near Rethem 12.4.45	SW447	609 Forced landed after engine lost power over Germany 9.3.45
SW392	609		
SW393	438 Crashed in forced landing Schelde, Denmark 1.6.45	SW448	175/246
		SW449	266
SW394	55 OTU	SW450	175 Crashed forced landing in Germany 11.5.45
SW395	83 GSU		
SW396	5 OTU	SW451	438
SW397	174/245	SW452	440/438/440
SW398	438	SW453	438
SW399	175	SW454	183 Crash landed Fehmarn 4.5.45
SW400	438/439		
SW401	440/438/440	SW455	183
SW402	137/182/137/174	SW456	245 Caught fire in air and crash landed 24.3.45
SW403	181/137/174		
SW404	438	SW457	247
SW405	440	SW458	266/193
SW406	266/197	SW459	183
SW407	175/182	SW460	245
SW408	247 Shot down by flak near Lingen 1.4.45	SW461	247/56 OTU
		SW462	440/439
		SW463	183

Serial No	Delivered To and Significant History	Serial No	Delivered To and Significant History
SW464	174/175		Plantlunne 26.4.45
SW465	266 Engine cut, crash landed E Goch 24.3.45	SW521	84 GSU
		SW522	182
SW466	183	SW523	164
SW467	181	SW524	439
SW469	609	SW525	439 Crash landed 6 miles SE Hartzeburg 23.4.45
SW470	123 Wg/350/123 Wg		
SW471	438	SW526	247 Hit by flak, forced landed in Germany 5.4.45
SW472	198 Shot down by flak near Bremen 23.4.45		
		SW527	193
SW473	137/174	SW528	263
SW474	56 OTU	SW529	175
SW475	175 Crashed during attack on tanks 13.4.45	SW530	WgLdr 124 Wg Shot down by flak SW Neustadt 2.5.45
SW476	183 Missing near Zutphen	SW531	59 OTU
SW473	137/174	SW532	245
SW474	56 OTU	SW533	247
SW475	175 Crashed during attack on tanks 13.4.45	SW534	439/438
		SW535	A & AEE
SW476	183 Missing near Zutphen 1.4.45	SW536	181
SW477	266/85 Gp CS/193	SW537	245
SW478	198	SW551	137/174
SW493	193	SW552	181 Shot down by flak near Furstenau 5.4.45
SW494	181/440/181		
SW495	174 Forced landed on sweep near Nienberg 30.3.45	SW553	175/245
		SW554	247/181/247/1237/174
SW496	198	SW555	Mkrs/Napier
SW497	609 Crashed in forced landing near Meppen 8.5.45	SW556	198
		SW557	59 OTU
SW498	439/438/439	SW558	193/266/193
SW499	609/193	SW559	59 OTU
SW500	84 GSU	SW560	245
SW502	182	SW561	137 Belly-landing at Vaerlose 30.6.45
SW503	183		
SW504	247/181 Hit building on overshoot, Kastrup 24.8.45	SW562	59 OTU/56 OTU
		SW563	59 OTU
SW505	247/609	SW564	175
SW505	175 Undercarriage collapsed while taxying and long-range tanks caught fire, Volkel 8.4.45	SW565	197
		SW566	59 OTU/SF Acklington
		SW567	59 OTU
SW508	247	SW568	59 OTU
SW509	183	SW569	59 OTU
SW510	137 Crashed forced landing 1 mile NW Havighorst, Germany 11.8.45	SW570	59 OTU
		SW571	59 OTU/56 OTU
SW512	184	SW572	59 OTU
SW513	247	SW573	59 OTU/56 OTU Crashed after control lost in cloud, Lowick, Northumberland 30.10.45
SW515	184		
SW517	197		
SW518	RAE/A & AEE and TDU		
SW519	DH Crashed on propeller trials near Brockenhurst, Hants 30.5.45	SW574	59 OTU
		SW575	59 OTU
SW520	198 Overshot landing at B103,	SW576	59 OTU
		SW577	59 OTU

Serial No	Delivered To and Significant History	Serial No	Delivered To and Significant History
SW578	59 OTU	SW623	56 OTU
SW579	59 OTU	SW624	56 OTU
SW580	59 OTU	SW625	56 OTU
SW581	538	SW626	55 OTU
SW582	245/175	SW627	55 OTU
SW583	266/197	SW628	59 OTU/56 OTU
SW584	263 Engine cut. Forced landed near Twente 2.6.45. DBR	SW629	59 OTU/56 OTU
		SW630	263
SW585	440	SW631	59 OTU/56 OTU
SW586	266	SW632	59 OTU/56 OTU Hit ground during air-to-air firing, Goswick, Northumberland 22.11.45
SW587	164		
SW588	263		
SW589	193	SW633	59 OTU/56 OTU
SW590	266/263	SW633	59 OTU/56 OTU
SW591	59 OTU	SW634	59 OTU/56 OTU
SW592	59 OTU/56 OTU	SW635	59 OTU/56 OTU
SW593	59 OTU/56 OTU Hit by SW638 while parked, Milfield 23.8.45	SW636	59 OTU/56 OTU
		SW638	59 OTU/56 OTU Swung on landing and hit SW593, Milfield 23.8.45
SW594	55 OTU		
SW595	59 OTU/56 OTU	SW640	266/197
SW596	59 OTU/56 OTU	SW641	440
SW620	59 OTU/56 OTU	SW642–SW709 were all either struck off charge or sold for scrap.	
SW621	56 OTU		
SW622	56 OTU		

Index